Recognizing Indigenous Languages

OXFORD STUDIES IN THE ANTHROPOLOGY OF LANGUAGE

Series editor: Alessandro Duranti, University of California at Los Angeles

This series is devoted to works from a wide array of scholarly traditions that treat linguistic practices *as* forms of social action.

Editorial Board
Patricia Baquedano-López, University of California, Berkeley
Donald Brenneis, University of California at Santa Cruz
Paul B. Garrett, Temple University
Janet McIntosh, Brandeis University
Justin Richland, The University of Chicago

Thank You for Dying for Our Country: Commemorative Texts and Performances in Jerusalem
Chaim Noy

Singular and Plural: Ideologies of Linguistic Authority in 21st Century Catalonia
Kathryn A. Woolard

Linguistic Rivalries: Tamil Migrants and Anglo-Franco Conflicts
Sonia Neela Das

The Monologic Imagination
Edited by Matt Tomlinson and Julian Millie

Looking like a Language, Sounding like a Race: Raciolinguistic Ideologies and the Learning of Latinidad
Jonathan Rosa

Talking like Children: Language and the Production of Age in the Marshall Islands
Elise Berman

The Struggle for a Multilingual Future: Youth and Education in Sri Lanka
Christina P. Davis

The Last Language on Earth: Linguistic Utopianism in the Philippines
Piers Kelly

Rethinking Politeness with Henri Bergson
Edited by Alessandro Duranti

Other Indonesians: Nationalism in an Unnative Language
Joseph Errington

Recognizing Indigenous Languages

Double Binds of State Policy and Teaching Kichwa in Ecuador

Nicholas Limerick

OXFORD
UNIVERSITY PRESS

Oxford University Press is a department of the University of Oxford. It furthers
the University's objective of excellence in research, scholarship, and education
by publishing worldwide. Oxford is a registered trade mark of Oxford University
Press in the UK and certain other countries.

Published in the United States of America by Oxford University Press
198 Madison Avenue, New York, NY 10016, United States of America.

© Oxford University Press 2023

All rights reserved. No part of this publication may be reproduced, stored in
a retrieval system, or transmitted, in any form or by any means, without the
prior permission in writing of Oxford University Press, or as expressly permitted
by law, by license, or under terms agreed with the appropriate reproduction
rights organization. Inquiries concerning reproduction outside the scope of the
above should be sent to the Rights Department, Oxford University Press, at the
address above.

You must not circulate this work in any other form
and you must impose this same condition on any acquirer.

Library of Congress Cataloging-in-Publication Data
Names: Limerick, Nicholas, author.
Title: Recognizing indigenous languages : double binds of state policy and
teaching Kichwa in Ecuador / Nicholas Limerick.
Description: New York, NY: Oxford University Press, [2023] |
Series: Oxford studies in the anthropology of language |
Includes bibliographical references and index.
Identifiers: LCCN 2023011404 (print) | LCCN 2023011405 (ebook) |
ISBN 9780197559185 (paperback) | ISBN 9780197559178 (hardback) |
ISBN 9780197559208 (epub)
Subjects: LCSH: Education, Bilingual—Ecuador. | Language policy—Ecuador.
| Multicultural education—Ecuador. | Quechua language—Study and
teaching—Ecuador. | Quechua language—Dialects—Ecuador. | Indians of
South America—Ecuador—Ethnic identity.
Classification: LCC LC3735.E2 L56 2023 (print) | LCC LC3735.E2 (ebook) |
DDC 370.117/509866—dc23/eng/20230602
LC record available at https://lccn.loc.gov/2023011404
LC ebook record available at https://lccn.loc.gov/2023011405

DOI: 10.1093/oso/9780197559178.001.0001

Paperback printed by Marquis Book Printing, Canada
Hardback printed by Bridgeport National Bindery, Inc., United States of America

For friends who started and who currently work on intercultural bilingual education in Ecuador

Contents

Acknowledgments ix
Notes on Transcription xiii

PART I: INTRODUCTION

Introduction: Registers of Kichwa, Intercultural Ecuador, and Ethnographic Research across State Institutions 3

1. Introducing Double Binds of State Institutions and Linguistic Recognition 29

PART II: HISTORICAL AND SOCIOLOGICAL TRAJECTORIES

2. The Intercultural Era: Histories of Kichwa, Literacies, and Schooling in National Politics and Policy 47

3. Unified Kichwa?: Unions, Divisions, and Overlap in the Making of a Standardized Register 78

4. Employment as Professionals: Promise and Predicament 108

PART III: DAILY ACTIVITIES AS STATE AGENTS

5. Translating the Law to Kichwa: Intertextuality, Authorship, and Intelligibility from Textbooks to Legal Texts 129

6. Speaking for a State: How and Whom to Greet? 155

7. Modeling Intercultural Citizenship through Language Instruction 174

   Conclusions 196

Notes 219
References 227
Index 251

Acknowledgments

This work has benefited from a vast of array of people's ideas and comments. A heartfelt thanks is due to many. The collaboration, support, and feedback of others has significantly bettered this book. I so regret that I am unable to properly thank all who have contributed, some in the United States for their anonymous comments as reviewers and others in Ecuador because of the political concerns of removing anonymity.

This book would not exist without friends who have worked in intercultural bilingual education in Ecuador. I send a huge *yupaychani* or *pague por todo*. In the National Directorate of Intercultural Bilingual Education, countless employees invited me to meetings and workshops, generously spoke with me inside and outside of interviews despite all that they were juggling, and shared their lives outside of office spaces with me. Daily office employment was never dull, especially with all the jokes. In the two schools where I researched, one where I continue to work routinely today, the directors, teachers, and students were such a pleasure to spend time with and provided incisive perspectives on the school system. Clearly, this book is an amalgamation of the words of those employed throughout the school system. Many Kichwa intellectuals who have been a part of the school system in one way or another also generously agreed to interviews, including Alberto Conejo, Ariruma Kowii, and Luis Montaluisa.

I am also so grateful to all who have advised me on this manuscript, read parts of it, or shared ideas or comments with me. This book began as a dissertation while I was a student at the University of Pennsylvania. Asif Agha has long provided formative ideas for my work and been a kind intellectual guide. Nancy Hornberger has been a model for the ethnographic study of Quechua language ideologies and bilingual education, and her intellect, advice, and long-standing relationships to the Andes were integral to this research, even introducing me to some employees in bilingual education coordinating offices. Stanton Wortham has been a generous and sage source of guidance from ideas, to writing, to navigating academic life. Philippe Bourgois's keen ethnographic eye has long been inspirational. Greg Urban's encouragement to more closely situate this work within other cases of South America made this book a better one.

Others beyond my dissertation committee at Penn provided crucial feedback or guidance. Rob Moore generously read of parts of what become this book and provided insightful comments and encouragement. Deborah Thomas, as graduate coordinator, provided gentle but essential guidance on several of the themes here. Virginia Zavala, whom I first met at Penn, has been beyond gracious in her support and even guided me to one of my favorite schools in Ecuador. This book has also benefited from the advice of generous mentors when I was an undergraduate student who taught me how to do ethnography and excited me about topics around language and power: David Nugent, Susan Tamasi, Benny Hary, and Debra Spitulnik Vidali.

Other friends from graduate school were major sources of support throughout course work, research, and beyond, especially Basak Can, Britt Dahlberg, Christa Cesario, Derek Newberry, Genevieve Leung, Jamie Schissel, Holly Link, Hoa Nguyen, Krystal Smalls, Rachel Throop, and Rebecca Pardo. During the two years of dissertation research on which this book is primarily based, I was so fortunate to be around others carrying out ethnographic research. Conversations with several US-based researchers in Quito helped make sense of things that I was seeing, including Anna Wilking, Jamie Shenton, Jeff Shenton, Julie Gamble, Nick Welcome, Taylor Nelms, and Thea Riofrancos. Scholars in Ecuador were also instrumental for my carrying out this research. I am grateful for conversations, support, and even visa help from Marleen Haboud, José Sinchi Yánez del Pozo, Michael Uzendoski, X. Andrade, and Enrique Contreras. FLACSO Ecuador sponsored my visa for one of the years during which this research was conducted.

Friends, colleagues, writing-group members, and mentors have read parts of this book and provided thoughtful feedback. In addition to graduate faculty advisers, Anna Wilking, Bradley Levinson, Christa Cesario, Elsie Rockwell, Miranda Weinberg, Petra Shank, Rosanna Dent, and Stephen Peters have all provided thoughtful commentary on chapters of the book. The students of my Spring 2020 Political Anthropology class provided an ideal mix of enthusiasm and insightful critique of several chapters. Grey Gundaker has been a fountain of wisdom and support, and her guidance and ideas have greatly shaped the course of and the pages of this book, including in her close reading of several chapters. Jackie Urla generously provided superb feedback, insight, and analysis on the entire manuscript. Anonymous reviewers—both from Oxford University Press and the articles that I have published about this research—gave thorough and thoughtful comments on this resulting book or articles, without which this book would be quite different.

Sandro Duranti's gentle and incisive guidance has also greatly improved the ideas and writing. I am so thankful that he, Meredith Keffer, and the Oxford

University Press team took this writing project on and for their professionalism, including Stefano Imbert, Ganga B, and Timothy DeWerff. Alicia Banks meticulously double-checked this book's dates, references, and quotes both in English and in Spanish. I am also grateful to the artist Borrego who graciously made the cover art.

At Teachers College, colleagues have given me the space and support to produce this research and writing. I am grateful to my department colleagues, Hervé Varenne, Amina Tawasil, Grey Gundaker, Carol Benson, Garnett Russell, Gita Steiner-Khamsi, Hope Leichter, Oren Pizmony-Levy, and Regina Cortina. Beyond the department, many others have provided advice and support that allowed me to finish writing this book, especially Lalitha Vasudevan and Kevin Dougherty. Several members of the administrative team, especially Dianne Marcucci-Sadnytzky, Bridget Bartolini, and Rachael Morales Simon, have taken many tasks off my plate that enabled me to work on this book while also being much valued interlocutors during writing breaks.

Several funding institutions have supported the research or writing of this book. I am immensely grateful to the National Science Foundation, Wenner-Gren Foundation, National Academy of Education/Spencer Foundation, the Ruth Landes Memorial Fund of the Reed Foundation, the University of Pennsylvania, Teachers College, Columbia University, and Columbia's Institute for Latin American Studies for their financial support.

I am also appreciative of those in Ecuador who have transcribed recordings for this project, including Antonio, Atik, Juliana, Gaby, Lisa, and Luis. They also provided helpful analyses. Other friends in Quito have been a constant stream of support over the years, and their ideas and perspectives manifest here as well, especially Alexa, Antonio, Esthelita, Fernanda, Fernando, Gaby, Julio, Irma, Lu, and Maru.

I reserve a special thanks for my dear partner, Gabriela, who never stops teaching me about radical political thought and practice and who has confirmed or challenged my analyses of transcripts throughout this book. My family in the United States—my mom, dad, and brother—have provided endless care, patience, and support, for which I am perpetually grateful.

Some chapters of this book are updated versions of previous publications. I am appreciative of a handful of journals' forward-thinking copyright policies. An earlier version of Chapter 6 was published in *Signs & Society*, and an earlier version of Chapter 7 was published in the *Journal of Linguistic Anthropology*. Some of the information about Kichwa alphabets that appears in Chapter 3 was published in *Comparative Education Review* and *Compare*.

Notes on Transcription

There are Spanish and Kichwa transcripts throughout this book. There are more Spanish transcripts than Kichwa ones, which is one indication of how most who work in intercultural bilingual education speak Spanish more regularly.

This book describes the plurality of registers and ways of communicating in Kichwa. The scale of difference across ways of speaking Spanish is vast too, of course. The Spanish texts here demonstrate that range. On the one hand, there are policy documents and academic texts in Spanish that are more standardized. On the other hand, transcripts are especially varied. My interlocutors spoke Spanish in so many different ways. Readers of Spanish, especially those from outside of Ecuador, will find many transcripts to be nonstandard. Spanish in Quito is often viewed as nonstandard by speakers from other countries, and many of my interlocutors speak Spanish with much influence from Kichwa. I list transcribed speech here as closely as possible to how it was spoken. I made minimal changes for clarity, lightly editing some transcripts so that they are more understandable to those who speak Spanish and also to avoid caricature that might manifest in the printing of speech that is especially ambiguous or nonstandardized.

Kichwa transcripts are transcribed with the most recent Unified Kichwa alphabet. Most written work now uses that alphabet, so I adhere to those norms. I also transcribe Kichwa throughout the book to faithfully represent how my interlocutors spoke, as close as possible, without seeking to transcribe phonological differences unless they are relevant for the analysis.

I number only the transcripts that I analyze in greater depth, as a means to more seamlessly integrate speech into the narrative of the text. Brackets in the transcript mean that I have added small clarifications to better reader understanding. Ellipses in the transcript mean that I have removed parts of what someone said that are redundant or less relevant for the context or analysis.

PART I
INTRODUCTION

Introduction

Registers of Kichwa, Intercultural Ecuador, and Ethnographic Research across State Institutions

The lobby inside the fourteen-story Ministry of Education in Quito, Ecuador, appears like many administrative offices. Chairs line the entrance. Security guards check the badges of those awaiting elevators. Bustling personnel wear mostly the same uniforms, such as dress shirts and trousers. One directory lists offices and their educational topics of focus, all in Spanish. Yet, there are also glimpses of differences. For example, there is a second directory translated to another language that has been rarely seen and heard in government buildings: Kichwa, known as Quechua outside of Ecuador, the most-spoken Indigenous language family in the Americas. A closer look at employees also reveals that a few have their hair pulled back into single long braids or are wearing skirts—colorful pleated ones or long black ones—associated with Indigenous *pueblos* (peoples). Ascending the building by elevator, if the doors open to the coordinating offices of intercultural bilingual education—the name of Ecuador's national public school system for Indigenous students—the norms shift a bit more. Employees and teachers mostly wear colorful embroidery or ponchos. Though the office has the same concrete walls as the rest of the building, many of them are papered over with posters promoting Ecuador's approximately fourteen Indigenous languages.[1]

These signs of difference, such as previously uncommon routines or languages in offices, indicate advancement within state institutions for those who have historically been marginalized by them. They signify how the long struggle of social movements demanding justice has, to some degree, changed institutions like workplaces and schools. The past three decades have seen policy improvements with respect to Indigenous communities throughout Central and South America and beyond. There have been sweeping rights and recognition.[2] For example, constitutions have named Indigenous languages as "official," which has led to results like state-sponsored translations. Such is the case in Ecuador, where the 2008 Constitution named Kichwa and Shuar (another Indigenous language), in addition to Spanish, "*idiomas oficiales de relación intercultural*" (official languages of intercultural relation), leading to signage like the directory in the Ministry. Furthermore, for more than thirty years, members of Indigenous *pueblos* and nationalities have directed *educación intercultural bilingüe* (intercultural bilingual education, routinely referred to as EIB, its initials in Spanish) to promote Indigenous languages and reinforce their use through rising generations of speakers. In 1988, activists, including many Kichwa speakers, pressured President Rodrigo Borja to establish this second school system over which they would preside. These more recent tendencies stand in sharp contrast to how colonial governing regimes long presided over genocide and the forced migration and labor of Native peoples. Later, modern state policy in the region tended at best toward assimilation by promoting *mestizaje*, "mixing," in efforts to make Indigenous peoples more like dominant society.[3]

Such changes evoke new questions, such as: how are state institutions and Indigenous languages remade in this era of greater inclusivity? And, what is it like to serve as a state agent in the very offices and institutions that previously sought to assimilate Indigenous peoples and denied them state recognition? This book examines governance, cultural politics, and communication in bilingual education. Based on more than two years of ethnographic research in Ecuador with state actors and mediators including policymakers, administrators, linguists, curriculum designers, translators, and teachers, it considers how Indigenous languages are adapted for use in national politics

Figure I.1 The entrance to the Ministry of Education building. Photo by author.

and state institutions and the constraints on what the languages and their speakers become in the process.

A major achievement is that bilingual education directors have complemented official recognition with the promotion of Indigenous languages, with the authoring of curriculum and pedagogy for more than 2,500 schools in their own school system that exists in addition to the primary one, and by planning for the school system.[4] Those who direct the system make decisions about hiring colleagues and administering a budget of state funds. Activists throughout the Americas have sought bilingual education for many reasons, including to remake the institutions of assimilation like schools and to gain institutional authority for their knowledges and languages.[5] Ecuador is perhaps the only nation-state in which Indigenous political organizations have had primary control over the administration of a national bilingual school system, even if such control was reduced in 2009 under President Rafael Correa's administration (further explained in Chapter 2). The existence of bilingual education demonstrates how Ecuador is exemplary for political organizing. Ecuador's bilingual school system preceded similar efforts in other countries, like Bolivia and Peru, and was more sweeping in reform.

However, directors work in the Ministry of Education with colleagues and bosses who mostly self-identify as *mestizos*, the common name for those whose relatives descend from a combination of "white" Spanish ancestors and those who predated the arrival of the Spanish colonizers. Official numbers report Ecuador's Indigenous populations at 7 percent, though the share is likely higher, perhaps as much as 25 percent.[6] For decades in Ecuador, state offices and schools had largely been run by those who identify as *mestizo*, a small indication of how such institutions are racialized.[7] As scholars like Mexican and Ecuadorian philosopher Bolívar Echeverría (2019) note, "whiteness" is not just about skin color. Rather, it also reflects ways of interacting with and seeing the world, such as demonstrating and adapting to ways of life more influenced by state institutions.

The reform of oppressive institutions and the shifting of long-established norms is, thus, not necessarily transformative and may result in other challenges. Institutional expectations and regulations can thwart social movements or redirect priorities away from what members seek.[8] Scholars have long emphasized the challenges to making schools promising sites of Indigenous language instruction (Hornberger & De Korne 2018; Sumida Huamán 2020), and those challenges are magnified in national state planning offices. For example, the directories situate Kichwa alongside Spanish, now seemingly equal. However, few who speak Kichwa would be able to

6 Recognizing Indigenous Languages

Figure I.2 The Kichwa directory. Readers of Kichwa will note that, in addition to being written in Unified Kichwa, the sign has errors and typos. These kinds of mistakes were common in printed materials in which non-Kichwa speakers ultimately carried out the final stages of design for written materials. Photo by author.

understand much of the directory. Bilingual education employees in the Ministry of Education had to invent Kichwa words to refer to bureaucratic processes and offices, such as "human resources." Many such word combinations are literally translated from Spanish and unknown to most Kichwa speakers, leaving visitors who read Kichwa perplexed. Even the translation for the intercultural bilingual education office name is ambiguous (*Kawsaypura Yachay Pushakkamay*, "between-life knowledge directorate"). If Kichwa speakers see signage that they do not understand, they may become frustrated with the school system and those who direct it. Furthermore, the depiction of Kichwa on a sign is not the same as routine use and instruction, which are harder to accomplish.

I argue that the state's recognition of Indigenous languages and bilingual education is double-edged. Such recognition constitutes a citizenship project that is both trailblazing and limiting. It is trailblazing because advocates-turned-state agents now disseminate policies, speeches, and curricula in the Indigenous-language family Kichwa and some Kichwa speakers see the benefits of state power, educational credentials, and linguistic recognition. If teachers or parents seek to meet about schooling, they can even go to the Ministry of Education offices and do so in Kichwa with representatives of the state who self-identify as Indigenous. Yet, it is limiting because even as directors experience significant strides toward equality, the everyday work of directing a national school system and speaking as a state agent in and about Kichwa presents constraints that thwart the very goals of autonomous schooling and getting people to speak and write Kichwa.

This book shows how a politics of state recognition has necessitated that bilingual education directors make their communication analogous to the norms, expectations, and language use of outsiders, in this case largely *mestizos*, who do not speak historically oppressed languages.[9] Similar to the experiences of Indigenous state agents elsewhere, the school system's

Figure I.3 Bilingual education directors attend the National Assembly for meetings about translating the Constitution to Indigenous languages. This file is licensed under the Creative Commons Attribution-Share Alike 2.0 Generic license.

coordinators endure ongoing oversight including of speaking Kichwa. Furthermore, the requirements of working as national state agents often contrast with the ways of understanding and acting in the world among constituents, family members, and friends, such as translating signage to a form of Kichwa that most relatives would not use. Indigenous state agents inevitably upset someone based on how and by whom their actions are perceived. The case of bilingual education planners demonstrates that shifting the management of state institutions into the hands of those historically marginalized by them produces *double binds*, a concept used by scholars like Gregory Bateson (1987 [1972]) and Silvia Rivera Cusicanqui (2018) and on which I elaborate in the next chapter.

Even the term *Indigenous* (*indígena* in Spanish) indicates both widespread success and challenge. *Indigenous* began as an arcane legal category and became a common self-referent around the globe.[10] Ecuadorian state policy recognizes some citizens as *Indigenous*, and many self-identify in this way, too. *Indigenous* implies the legal recognition of those with a shared experiences of oppression by state institutions, a history of inhabiting territories before European or other forms of colonization, a connection to land and the generations of family members and friends who have lived with the land, and similar ways of understanding the world, such as those more rooted in balanced and harmonious coexistence.[11] Those who direct the school system, and others in Ecuador, use the term to describe themselves, and I use it in this book.

However, *Indigenous* also elides difference. In Ecuador alone, there is much diversity among who is considered Indigenous. Speakers of Kichwa, more specifically, are often called "Kichwas" in Spanish or *runakuna* in Kichwa. They constitute the largest Indigenous nationality in Ecuador and have mainly been those in charge of the school system. But the term *nacionalidades* (nationalities), another common self-descriptor, refers to fourteen Indigenous groups who may speak different languages and live in contrastive geographical regions like the Andean mountains, the Amazonian lowlands, or the Pacific coast. Solely within Ecuador there is much diversity and, certainly, there is more on a global scale. The use of *pueblos* (peoples) further specifies difference, since there are more *pueblos* than nationalities and the designation is closely linked to territory, such as the Otavalo or Cayambi *pueblos* both located in the Northern Ecuadorian Highlands that simultaneously belong to the Kichwa nationality. Referring to many solely as "Indigenous" inevitably disregards differences, including these.

Anthropologist Charles Hale (2006, 105) writes that, though studies of resistance movements tend to romanticize actors' efforts, the overlooked tensions and contradictions—such as around self-referents—provide insights for understanding multiple pathways for effecting change. I extend this observation to unpack the ways of communicating—including different ways of speaking and writing Kichwa—and how those are bound up in what it means to be Kichwa and how state institutions affect expectations and linguistic norms. This case sheds light on how seeking change through state institutions tends to involve a tension, where Indigenous state agents find a challenge in "wag[ing] struggles for rights and redress using the language, the legal and political tools, and even the funding of their oppressors" (Hale 2006, 111). Following the observations of Audre Lorde, Chela Sandoval, and others, Hale notes that such efforts are not predictable or totalizing and, instead, involve subversion and maneuvering.

Though this subject is underexamined in research about Indigenous movements, I extend these insights to show how part of the success of Ecuador's activists resulted from what linguistic anthropologists would call metalinguistic and metasemiotic labor, which, in this case, is the ongoing work to make languages and other cultural emblems relatable to those who are unfamiliar with them and, further, to fit them with the needs and expectations of state employment.[12] As social theorists have long shown, such labor manifests strategic essentialism. In other words, for political advances like collective resistance efforts, actors tactically offer one overarching identity (such as "Indigenous") that depends on flattening differences across those who form a part of that identification.[13] But, moreover, this work involves commensuration to make speakers and speech more like the norms of state institutions and comparatively dominant populations.[14] This approach ultimately raises questions about colonial reproduction in linguistic recognition, such as whether Kichwa becomes more like Spanish.

Though research sometimes tends toward romanticization of efforts to halt language shift, I emphasize the double-edged nature of linguistic movements that rely upon state institutions.[15] State documents, for example, were once wielded to seize land from those who could not read and write bureaucratic varieties of colonial languages. Now, such documents are written in bureaucratic and standardized forms of *Indigenous* languages which, nonetheless, exclude many rural or working-class Kichwa speakers, indicating how remedies lie beyond an increase in Kichwa use and benefits like the authority provided by state institutions. The case shows challenges in *language reclamation*, efforts to support historically oppressed forms of knowledge and communication and confront marginalization (Leonard 2017; McCarty, Nicholas, & Wigglesworth 2019). Another challenge occurs with *language revitalization* and its more specific focus on acquisition and increased use of comparatively marginalized languages like Kichwa. Language reclamation and revitalization efforts often focus on schools, in which educational authorities formerly administered corporal punishment to children for speaking Indigenous languages (Brayboy & Bang 2019; Sumida Huamán & Brayboy 2017). Now, these same institutions are repurposed to teach Indigenous languages.[16] One challenge has been that teachers may disagree with Kichwa as used in school curriculum by noting differences from their own ways of speaking. Parents and grandparents may also not understand the variety adopted for school instruction. I use both *language reclamation* and *language revitalization* in this book. Another term I use here is *linguistic recognition*, as *recognition* draws from academic research that studies efforts to make emblems (like languages) of populations of diverse societies visible to state institutions; to codify rights in state documents like Constitutions by referencing those emblems; and to seek visibility and awareness from others (further discussed below). Reclamation efforts routinely focus on linguistic recognition. In Ecuador, bilingual education employees tended to stress recovery (*recuperar*), emphasizing the importance of Indigenous knowledges and the teaching of Indigenous languages while acknowledging a significant shift to Spanish, and I sometimes use this term, too.

This book partially echoes a burgeoning literature that critiques current state policy throughout the world by arguing that employment as state agents requires political neutrality and pressure not to reject the requests of bosses, especially requests that place them at odds with the members of society whom they represent and serve. Authors have demonstrated how marginalization continues despite advances to positions of authority.[17] For example, Hale (2004, 16) influentially argues elsewhere that multicultural reforms—such as when state documents recognize Indigenous languages and award rights to historically oppressed peoples—"empower some while marginalizing the majority" and leave racialized hierarchies unchanged. Hale emphasizes that, while they have gained increased acceptance, Indigenous state agents now must offer proposals instead of protest. Those who dissent are further marginalized, such as in being demoted, fired, or ignored. This Ecuadorian case also shows how assuming a role in state planning presents the predicament of not angering bosses if one is to continue in the position, especially in the uppermost leadership roles.

This research in Ecuador, however, shows how domination, and even regulation, provide an incomplete picture of the challenges that bilingual education directors face as national state agents. Upper- and mid-level Indigenous policymakers have significant decision-making influence over schooling and language planning. Constraints within this context of advancement are not exactly examples of direct linguistic domination since Kichwa's ascent ruptured Spanish's dominance as imposed in official policy. Spanish is no longer recognized as the sole legitimate language.[18] Thus, a major advance is also limiting: the effects of state recognition include an expanded audience of listeners and new uses for Kichwa, which have transformed how Kichwa is spoken, written, read, and heard.

The study of Kichwa and bilingual education in Ecuador provides at least three lessons for Indigenous language reclamation in an era of increased emphasis on state institutions. First, large-scale language shift in Ecuador continues apace despite remarkable advances in policy and planning. Many members of Indigenous *pueblos* and nationalities speak Spanish with its pervasive use in schools and workplaces, and Kichwa is spoken less by young people (Andrade & Howard 2021; Haboud 2004, 74). As with examples of language shift elsewhere, this scenario results in part from years of repression from the very institutions that now recognize and prominently feature the language family. Alberto Conejo, a well-known Kichwa linguist and bilingual education director, put it this way: "*Por un lado, [hay] el hecho de que [el kichwa] es oficial, eso está explicitado en la Constitución. . . . Pero, por otro lado, es innegable también su perdición porque los hijos, las hijas de las futuras generaciones cada vez hablan menos pero crecen y ya de jóvenes se dan cuenta que es importante.*"[19] (On the one hand, [there's] the fact that [Kichwa] is official. That's made explicit in the Constitution. But, on the other hand, its loss is also undeniable because the sons and daughters of future generations speak less each day, but they grow up and realize as young people that it's important.) He demonstrates the vast difficulties in translating official recognition to an increase in Kichwa's use. By the time young people see Kichwa as important, he said, they are adults and find it harder to learn Kichwa. Recognition and schooling are insufficient for overcoming Kichwa's marginalization.

In addition to studying the politics of language shift, this book makes a second and underexamined point about Indigenous language reclamation: while simultaneously honoring Indigenous languages, recognition politics encourages language shift from one *variety of Kichwa* to another. Language standardization efforts have foregrounded and facilitated official recognition. *Kichwa unificado* (Unified Kichwa) is the common name for standardized Kichwa. While language politics has elevated Indigenous languages to the national stage, *national* usually means that some singular forms are foregrounded over innumerable local, varied ways of speaking and writing. Regional varieties of Indigenous languages like Kichwa have immense morphological, syntactic, and phonetic variation,[20] which is one reason Unified Kichwa is hard for many to understand. Many Kichwa speakers see Unified Kichwa as a somewhat different language and have supported local ways of speaking that they understand as more indicative of who they are (Ennis 2020; Montaluisa-Chasiquiza 2019). Recognition has increased the domains and genres of the language family's use.[21] However, many Kichwa speakers struggle to understand standardized Kichwa, and even fewer can speak it. There are approximately 600,000 to 2 million speakers in Ecuador and 6 million total speakers throughout South America of Quechua varieties (Andrade & Howard 2021; Haboud 2010), so there are challenges to representation across this number of speakers. Quechua was the main language family of the vast Incan empire. Following the conventions of linguistic anthropology, I use the term *register* to describe different forms of Kichwa, such as regional varieties or standardized Kichwa. *Register* connects repertoires such as words and other ways of communicating to ideologies—ideas about how people communicate and who they are based on those ideas (Agha 2005; Urla et al. 2017). Many speakers identify these speech forms with certain kinds of people, for example, those from a particular region or people with educational degrees who work in offices. They may come to associate Unified Kichwa with the speech of state-authorized persons, contributing to this register's rejection. Like linguistic anthropologists Susan Gal and Judith Irvine (2019), I use the term *register* interchangeably with *variety*.

The use of Unified Kichwa, moreover, implies a third challenge: many Kichwa forms now used in state-authorized texts are literal translations from the grammatical forms, meanings, and uses of standardized Ecuadorian Spanish. This point expands research on schooling and bureaucratic workplaces that shows how state institutions tend to come with a "template" that influences the resulting projects (Levinson 2005, 254; Scott 1998; Shange 2019), in this case Indigenous languages themselves. The state-centered ways of speaking and writing that emerge—standardized, legal, and bureaucratic situations of language use and their terms unknown to everyday speakers—are concerning not solely for such colonial dimensions, but also because they have divided Ecuador's Indigenous movements. Planning efforts that standardize and change linguistic practices run the risk of provoking anger and even discouraging Kichwa use, examples in which disagreements can end disastrously for Indigenous language movements (Kroskrity 2009). How planners, teachers, and students speak Kichwa for state politics exemplifies the larger dilemma of what "inclusion" looks and

Figure I.4 A workshop for teachers in the school system. Photo by author.

sounds like and whether state institutions can be repurposed for a more fully emancipatory politics.

Ethnographic Approaches to Intercultural Bilingual Education in the Andes

This book is based mainly on two full years of ethnographic research in Ecuador, from 2011 to 2013, and is also influenced by ongoing trips, conversations, and involvement since then. I am from the United States and have spent more than eight years total in Ecuador, mainly in the capital of Quito. Before starting graduate school and this research, I had met professionals involved in Kichwa education when I spent a year as a high school teacher in Ecuador. During that time, I began to learn Kichwa and later began this research proficient in Unified Kichwa and Northern Highland Kichwa, in addition to Spanish, and I routinely spoke Kichwa in the Ministry of Education and in schools. The display of those abilities, which were surprising to many people in the school system, helped demonstrate my commitment to recovering Kichwa. At the beginning of the research, some employees in the school system became more excited about my presence when they heard that I spoke Kichwa, which they saw as promoting the school system's goals and as significant, given their experiences with many people's struggles to learn. I have also assisted in those goals over the years in various roles of support for Kichwa instruction and use, such as coauthoring with educators a Kichwa textbook for nondominant speakers after the conclusion of this research.

While becoming proficient in Kichwa required much dedication, I also benefited from a commonality in language revitalization efforts in which outsiders, especially white ones like myself, are praised for speaking Indigenous languages, while the children of people who grew up speaking the language are often subjected to more stringent expectations. I also struggled with some other registers, such as with Amazonian interlocutors, and worried that I was offering another example of Unified Kichwa as a more important register to learn over others. I routinely blended in words from Spanish when not speaking with linguists, but my Kichwa use was shaped by how and where I learned to communicate.

Through this research, I have sought to better understand sites in which state-sanctioned Kichwa ideologies and uses converged, how those ideologies contrasted with other perspectives less central to national bilingual education planning and politics, and how state-sanctioned Kichwa affects the participants in a social movement for bilingual education. During the 2011–2013 research period, I divided time between three main sets of interlocutors: the Dirección Nacional de Educación Intercultural Bilingüe (National Directorate of Intercultural Bilingual Education, referred to here as DINEIB or "National Directorate"), where bilingual education is coordinated within the Ministry of Education and where I was assigned a desk; and two intercultural bilingual schools in Quito. I conducted participant observation and interviews, making audio recordings of events like meetings and classroom interactions. I also routinely traveled with employees to workshops and conferences. In prior summers (such as in 2010), I carried out participant observation in regional directorate offices or schools most days of the week. For several months, I lived with a former employee of the National Directorate offices and his family, including a daughter who attended one of the schools that I studied. They have taught me much about Kichwa-speaking life outside of classrooms and office spaces. Readers will also note that this book analyzes documents and archives, such as policies and textbooks in Ecuador and documentation of bilingual education in other countries, to better understand how bilingual education emerged and changed and what assumptions from elsewhere manifest in the school system. I also examine academic texts that analyze Kichwa linguistically to better understand what linguistic features of the language family are foregrounded in the use of Unified Kichwa, and the philosophies tied to them, as well as what is effaced.

This project, thus, has focused on linguistic forms, ideologies, and uses across spaces of policymaking, schooling, markets, and homes to paint a fuller picture of Kichwa-language politics.[22] This goal takes into account a primary challenge in the anthropology of education: by focusing largely on schools and those within them—teachers and students—one may end up with a limited view of how those events are interconnected with others happening outside the school's walls.[23] In contrast, a strength of ethnographies of Indigenous movements is that they go "beyond the discursive and institutional boundaries of the aid project or the classroom" (Gustafson 2009, 20). Previous studies of schooling or language revitalization also tend to have less access to spaces of policymaking and national politics. In spending more than half my time with national directors, including in Ministry of Education offices, I learned much about their work lives and the opportunities and challenges they confront. My findings have methodological implications for anthropological studies with state agents, too, since those studies are almost entirely based upon information gleaned from interviews. While this line of research has shed light on the challenges of multiculturalism, interviews are limiting for making sense of the various ways that double binds play out.

I also started the research in the national offices based on the request of a longtime employee. He wanted an outsider to document information about the stricter control over the National Directorate under Ecuador's president Rafael Correa. That documentation occurs throughout this book, especially in Chapters 2 and 6. In 2009, Correa's Ministry of Education officials moved the National Directorate offices within the walls of the Ministry of Education. The vice minister established a regulatory office (a "Subsecretariat") that would have the final say over those who had historically directed the school system. The highest-level state agent of that office (*el subsecretario*/the subsecretary) has been a member of an Indigenous nationality, though someone relatively supportive of presidential policies. The change fit within the administration's disturbing pattern of curtailing and dividing the influence of Indigenous organizations (further examined in Chapter 2).[24]

My interlocutors also held several contrastive perspectives about what Indigenous schooling initiatives should look like and who should run them. Strategic essentialism masks an array of viewpoints and even acrimonious disagreements among members of Indigenous movements (Canessa 2014; Colloredo-Mansfield 2009). Within national state institutions, I found these tensions to be magnified. There was long-standing, deeply rooted discord among those who worked in the National Directorate (and others involved in the school system) around several topics, including the role of Unified Kichwa and that of the state in directing bilingual education. In fact, directors more allied with Correa's administration were some of the most enthusiastic about inviting me to events and meetings. They felt that others should see the advances that they were making, and Correa had also vastly increased the school system's budget.

A story with so many sides requires a careful telling. I have done my best to balance the contrasting perspectives of those who work in the school system, whom I also consider friends, experts, and teachers. Furthermore, although Ecuador was undergoing schooling reform, most of the questions and predicaments described in this book rarely seemed to change; yet, daily operations and political loyalties would sometimes suspend projects and shift employment ranks, changes that most employees found frustrating. In part because of their fraught political situation, I use pseudonyms for many in this book. For the best-known intellectuals or directors, especially on topics about which they routinely speak or write publicly, I use their actual names to cite their contributions.

Lessons from Ethnographies of Schooling in the Andes

The immediate constraints of working within state offices are intensified for adult Kichwa speakers who have endured a lifetime of racist disdain. For example, one longtime employee who hailed from the Central Ecuadorian Andes, Luis, described to me the effects of constant linguistic censure for all ways of speaking Kichwa in years past:

Como nosotros somos productos del mismo sistema,	Since we're products of the same system,
un sistema que todo el tiempo estaba desvalorizando la lengua,	a system that was constantly devaluing the language,

aunque ahora tengamos mucha conciencia	even though now we are very conscious,
es algo que te queda en el cerebro y que—¡chuta!	it's something that stays with you in the brain and that—shoot!
Poder retomar es difícil después de que me hayan atropellado,	It's hard to be able to resume [Kichwa-speaking] after they've run me over,
después de que me hayan discriminado	after they've discriminated against me
justamente porque sabes la lengua.	exactly because of knowing the language.

Many who identify as Indigenous have experienced violent reprimand, and their experiences with hostility are often linked to speaking Indigenous languages and how those languages influence their speech or pronunciation in Spanish (Hornberger 1988; Pérez Silva & Zavala Cisneros 2010; Wroblewski 2021). This difficulty continues even today for planners in national state offices and can contribute to "devaluing" Indigenous languages.

Luis's concern about being "products of the same system" points to additional complications. On the one hand, scholars who examine educational attainment in the Andes have shown how preparing Indigenous professionals can shift power relations with the state and NGOs to benefit *pueblos* (Laurie, Andolina, & Radcliffe 2003; Hornberger 2014). In other words, schooling helps prepare Indigenous professionals who are proficient in the discourses of state institutions and NGOs, potentially leading to the altering of mainstream or neoliberal institutions from within. Researchers have described this change as "creative thinking outside the standard 'box' of development solutions" (Laurie, Andolina, & Radcliffe 2005, 472)—though the phrase indicates the history of racism and assimilation in the development sector that now makes Indigenous ideas "innovative" (Sumida Huaman 2017). Schools have also been sites of culturally relevant pedagogies (Laurie, Andolina, & Radcliffe 2005, 478), instruction that promotes Indigenous philosophies and contests official policy (Valdiviezo 2014), and even political organizing among teachers and the networks of graduates that they produce (García 2005, 140). Schooling has also been significant for providing credentials for members of *pueblos* and nationalities to assume authoritative roles in state institutions and middle-class jobs (García 2005, 144; Martínez Novo & de la Torre 2010, 16).

On the other hand, even though there have been major benefits from Indigenous schooling in the Andes in recent decades, my interlocutors described, somewhat differently, that schooling is double-edged: credentials may provide a pathway to economic advancement and institutional authority, yet they can also contribute to graduates being viewed by others as more comfortable in the "individual" ways of institutions. Graduates also less routinely speak Kichwa. These are challenges that Luis mentioned in being a part of the

Figure I.5 School system employees from Southern Highland Ecuador visiting a fair in Quito that was organized by the national coordinating offices. Photo by author.

same system—studying and receiving degrees, working in offices—and hesitating to speak Kichwa. Professionalization entails some division among the social movement's participants since directors now have advanced degrees and work salaried office jobs, which contrasts with most members of Indigenous movements. Bilingual education directors may now be seen as somewhat different—racialized and classed as more "Western" or "*mestizo*"—than their peers who form the support for Indigenous movements even as they work to promote Kichwa (see Chapter 4). This difficulty raises concerns about change within state institutions and how development initiatives can better support historically marginalized peoples without prioritizing the status quos of institutional employment.

Ethnographic accounts of Indigenous schooling in the Andes show that the teaching of Kichwa/Quechua varieties in classrooms has increased but remains conflicted. On the one hand, the existence of bilingual schooling at all demonstrates years of struggle, planning, and socialization. The ability to now teach Kichwa overcomes decades of societal disparagement and shame, as Luis mentioned. For example, parents and teachers less commonly view teaching or writing in Indigenous languages as stigmatized today. Their more common concerns have been that Indigenous languages are unnecessary or perhaps detrimental to academic achievement in more dominant languages like Spanish (Hornberger 1988; García 2005; Valdiviezo 2009). They may view Kichwa as less important than Spanish or English for use outside of the classroom.[25] That fewer parents wholly contest the teaching of Kichwa in classrooms speaks to the successes of the school system, state recognition, and how activists have convinced them, even as difficulties remain.

On the other hand, in addition to schools forcing students to learn Spanish, which has contributed to current perceptions that Spanish should be the language of such institutions, a recent challenge in Ecuador and elsewhere has centered on ideas about where Kichwa *is* used and where it *should be* used. Schooling contends with perspectives that contrast with the teaching of Indigenous languages in classrooms, such as that Indigenous languages are rooted in oral traditions linked to landscapes—not necessarily written in textbooks—and used to connect with family members and friends who have lived on those spaces over time (McCarty & Nicholas 2014; Sims 2005; Sumida Human & Valdiviezo 2020). This perceived contrast sometimes means that parents may think their children will learn those languages at home without intervention (Rindstedt & Aronsson 2002).

Increasingly, Indigenous families in the Andes have migrated to cities, and many children and even parents now speak Spanish as their most dominant language (Enrique López 2021; Kvietok Dueñas 2021). Urban speakers may see Indigenous languages as used largely to speak with rural, more proficient speakers instead of within cities (Kvietok Dueñas 2019; Zavala 2014). Comparable to how sociolinguist Virginia Zavala (2019, 63) describes bilingual education as an ongoing form of "mother tongue" education in Peru, curricular materials in Ecuador tend to presume that children grow up hearing Kichwa at home and can read and understand materials written entirely in Kichwa. However, most students are emergent bilinguals who understand some Kichwa but often struggle to speak, read, or write Kichwa. The inclusion of pedagogies for young people who are mostly "heritage" speakers, since they now commonly speak Spanish with their parents and friends, is a vastly different form of instruction for most teachers and is largely nonexistent.[26]

It is within this context that research in Ecuador—including the school system's own analysis—shows that although it is called bilingual education, many classrooms do not actually include instruction in Kichwa (King & Haboud 2007; Martínez Novo 2014b).[27] If taught, Kichwa (and other Indigenous languages) may include one class meeting per week, not unlike some foreign language classes in the United States. When Kichwa is taught, teachers tend to emphasize the performative effects of language use (Martínez Novo 2014b, 217; Chapter 7), such as memorized standardized greetings or singing songs in Kichwa. This book shows the significance of what register is used in instruction and how some registers relate back to national political projects or efforts to contest them. For example, there is conflict around different registers or dialects in schooling and policy initiatives.[28] Teaching strategies often model Kichwa as it is used in speeches by national planners, making classrooms the continuation or refutation of a particular kind of political project.

A national undertaking to present Kichwa as a standardized language of official recognition implicitly encouraged strategies that limited teaching Kichwa in classrooms. As I describe in Chapter 7, teaching Unified Kichwa greetings and songs allows students to present themselves as intercultural citizens to others, like *mestizo*-identifying and foreign-visitor onlookers. I did not observe many students who became proficient in Kichwa. However, in learning to use select Kichwa forms, students were better able to pass through spaces from which they may otherwise be excluded, or help schools gain much needed publicity or funds. By following Kichwa use across connected yet different domains, I show that Unified Kichwa in language teaching is not just about teaching "better" ways of speaking, common to grammar teachers throughout the world. It conveys a political project of *interculturalidad* (interculturality) that spans the institutions and networks through which official recognition is put into practice (see below).

Figure I.6 An anniversary event in the Ministry of Education to celebrate the school system. Photo by author.

Intercultural Advances and Challenges in State Politics and Language Standardization

Around the world, the official recognition of historically marginalized peoples and those who have migrated—such as by declarations of rights to governance, land, and cultural and linguistic difference—has provided increased visibility and a legal platform for claims-making for those most disparaged by state governance.[29] The respective fields of cultural and linguistic anthropology each offer relevant tools for analysis of recognition and multiculturalism, though they have primarily stressed contrastive topics and angles.[30] Within linguistic anthropology, scholars have shown how citizenship efforts often foreground languages as markers of identity[31] especially by bolstering a "one nation, one language" ideology that promotes an entire recognized population as speaking a single language.[32] Thus, bilingual education activists seek to expand which languages are state-sanctioned as they search for the official recognition of Indigenous languages and the support of bilingual instruction. They have seen how differences between school employees' use of official languages and how parents communicate can marginalize some students based on the medium of instruction, such as by ignoring or prohibiting their languages in institutional settings (García-Sánchez & Orellana 2019; Kosonen & Benson 2013; Sumida Huamán & Brayboy 2017). As state policies have increasingly recognized Indigenous languages, however, this ideology is often expanded where an additional language, an Indigenous one, represents all Indigenous citizens (Zavala 2019), which risks continued erasure of the linguistic diversity that exists among those speakers.

Cultural anthropologists and political philosophers have shown how recognition yields exactly these kinds of pitfalls, critiquing the difficulties that Indigenous activists face despite increasing acceptance and even questioning whether social movements should refuse to participate in multicultural initiatives at all (Coulthard 2014; Hale & Mullings 2019). One pitfall, for example, is a trade-off that foregrounds some traits (like constitutional identification of Indigenous languages) while avoiding more contentious claims like those for political and economic self-determination.[33] Another is that policies can bring about surprising and even detrimental alliances, such as financial elites who support inclusion to attract new consumers, all the while thwarting more radical economic efforts like redistribution (Fraser 2017; Hale 2011; Mbebe 2016). Still another is that the application of official recognition can yield standards of "tradition" and "authenticity" that are puzzling to the very people who are supposed to be recognized.[34]

This last pitfall applies to this case in how many reject Unified Kichwa and see it as unrepresentative of them. The case of Kichwa shows how one nation, one language ideologies can implicitly foreground a standardized linguistic register. In other words, the principles of modern linguistics guide and intersect with recognition politics, too. As sociolinguist Jan Blommaert (2008, 292) writes, such modernist beliefs hold that "the fantastic variation that characterises actual language in use can . . . be reduced to an invariable, codified set of rules, features, and elements in order to be the 'true' language that can qualify as an object of linguistic study." For example, standardization involves making and "naming" languages through elaborating codified norms seen in grammar books and dictionaries (Gal 2006, 165). As this book shows, a politics of recognition is only partially about designations in constitutions, legal documents, or linguistic texts.[35] Indigenous state agents, in particular, take such efforts a step further by embodying a politics of recognition in their daily talk and behavior geared toward building a more inclusive state, such as in how they speak Unified Kichwa for national audiences and put the intercultural state into practice.[36]

Yet, as the primary variety of state recognition, Unified Kichwa is a drastic change for most Kichwa speakers who fluidly borrow or transpose Spanish words and grammatical forms into everyday Kichwa speech. The register even sometimes excludes long-standing Indigenous ways of understanding the world that manifest in colloquial Kichwa lexicon and grammar. For instance, the case of the directory shows the prioritization of office-based, hard-to-understand Kichwa use. But there are many more examples of how this register's expressions supplant other ways of communicating, including through even basic greetings in the office. Teachers, parents, and some coordinators lament the absence of other, more heartfelt ways of greeting in Kichwa.

Interculturalidad (interculturality), the primary philosophy for cultural and linguistic recognition in Bolivia, Ecuador, Peru, and elsewhere in Central and South America, has also come with tensions around the significance of languages to recognition politics and who benefits from their recognition. While activists and policymakers have supported *interculturalidad* to promote equal dialogue and understanding across different peoples in the recognition and development of Indigenous schooling,[37] there is a growing skepticism of intercultural efforts among many Kichwa-speaking interlocutors employed in the school system. As Luis, my aforementioned interlocutor in the National Directorate office, put it, "*No es nuestro concepto. No hay una manera de decir interculturalidad en Kichwa*" (It's not our concept. There's no way to say *interculturalidad* in Kichwa).[38] Luis pointed to *interculturalidad* as foreign, and its status as a term from Spanish supported his view.

I show throughout this book how *equivalence*—such as the translation of grammar and ideas from standardized Spanish to Kichwa—constitutes a significant part of intercultural equality in state recognition (see also Chapter 1 for origins of the use of *intercultural*). At first glance and as most research would hold, an advantage of *interculturalidad* would be acknowledging and *preserving* cultural and linguistic difference. For example, Whitten and Whitten (2011, 119) describe *interculturalidad* as "the polar opposite" of *mestizaje*'s assimilatory policy because it reinforces and teaches about philosophical and racialized differences, albeit sometimes in a static way. *Interculturalidad*'s promotion of mutual support across interlocutors and respect for contrastive ways of speaking is built into the very foundations of the school system, including legal ones. By looking at the details of communication in Kichwa, Spanish, and the everyday efforts of promotion and coordination, this case questions how intercultural recognition preserves difference. Intercultural policies and talk carry out reproduction in subtler—but not less systematic—ways.[39] Though intercultural bilingual education has made policy and schooling more equal for a vast number of Kichwa speakers, intercultural politics simultaneously constrains speakers to translating standardized Ecuadorian Spanish and its attendant conceptualizations into Kichwa, rather than using Kichwa in its heterogeneous or local terms. In linking state-sponsored politics to Indigenous language use, intercultural policies have depended upon and promoted a version of Kichwa that parallels standardized Ecuadorian Spanish.

There is, thus, another pitfall—a colonialist one—in how state recognition can depend upon Indigenous languages and their speakers becoming more like more dominant languages and speakers. The making of Unified Kichwa has avoided the use of Spanish loanwords, which, paradoxically, has resulted in coined words and literal translations of grammatical forms and reference from Spanish called calques (Gómez-Rendón 2008). Unified Kichwa's neologisms and calques are foreign to most people who grew up speaking Kichwa. Therefore, in addition to paralleling Spanish, the forms must be acquired anew (Floyd 2004; King 2001; Wroblewski 2012). State-authorized uses of Kichwa, and how such uses make Kichwa commensurate with Spanish, are "double" or "hybrid." They include, as Mikhail Bakhtin put it, "two utterances, two speech manners, two 'languages', two . . . belief systems that take place within the limits of a single syntactic whole" (Bakhtin 1981, 304–5). In this case, Unified Kichwa consists of an "overlay register" (Mannheim 2018), which is based much on Spanish linguistic and social practices.

These overlapping meanings and forms (bivalency) blur the boundary between languages and, thus, illuminate underexamined parts of language standardization. Bivalency is common to language contact throughout the world, though it has more often been examined in loanwords and not as calques. In a more straightforward example, which does not necessarily include different "belief systems," linguistic anthropologist Kathryn Woolard (1998) shows the vast bivalency that exists for speakers of Catalán and Spanish. For instance, *autopista* ("highway") is virtually indistinguishable across the two languages. Many forms Woolard (1998, 9) cites are similar and sometimes differ only in stress on the final vowel. However, in the case of Kichwa and Spanish, directionality in translation has significant implications for state recognition as to whose word categories and grammar prevail and through what means. This case shows how intra-linguistic shift is intertwined with changing belief systems and the transformation of worlds alongside much calquing.

In other words, beyond reducing differences across languages, contemporary language planning poses another concern: the foregrounding of the concepts and grammar from more dominant languages (Webster 2014). Linguists and intellectuals have long used universalizing standards for comparison, which can remake other languages and registers through analogous forms from more dominant ones (Asad 1986; Leonard 2017; Pennycook & Makoni 2019). For instance, in the eighteenth century, European linguists assisted state agents by compiling word lists across as many languages as possible, including African ones, that presumed that words and their references from European languages could simply be applied to all world languages (Fabian 1991). Incommensurate words were left out. Colonial agents used such lists as they sought to impose order through adopting such words for language policies in African territories. Similarly, Franz Boas's critique in his introduction to the *Handbook of American Indian Languages* (1911) demonstrated how linguists in Europe were using Latin as the standard for writing the grammars of other languages. Such initiatives are often flagrantly pejorative, as anthropologist Miyako Inoue (2006, 82) writes about Japanese intellectuals' early translations of European texts in which they described Japanese as "lacking" a third person pronoun in comparison (also cited in Gal 2015, 234). Alton Becker (2000, 197) calls attention to how such labors are "one of the most subtle forms of colonialism, ancient or modern" in how they use more dominant forms and norms to undermine "not just the substance but the framework of someone's learning." He refers, specifically, to introducing a form-to-sound alphabet for Burmese to replace the historically used but quite different writing system. His point is an important lesson for standardization, often viewed as a first step for language revitalization, to avoid becoming a vessel for colonial dimensions of translation and planning.

As anthropologist Jacqueline Urla (2012, 42–45) shows for Basque in Spain, language-planning often draws from and reproduces dominant ideologies, which sometimes has benefits. She notes how planners developed a standardized alphabet, neologisms, and grammatical forms to make teaching Basque similar to teaching Spanish. They argued that printing materials in multiple dialects would be too expensive and difficult to use. These efforts were used in schools and later resulted in a younger generation of Basque speakers (Urla et al. 2017).[40] However, in another example, in Canada, Kaska textbooks teach Kaska grammatical forms based on those of English. Anthropologist Barbara Meek shows how, though the textbooks are teaching Kaska, English remains the textbooks' primary instructional language (Meek & Messing 2007). Furthermore, Kaska's grammar, which is morphologically complicated, is presented through the template of English's grammar. In Ecuador, Kichwa and Spanish are from radically different language families, and Unified Kichwa consists of similarly overwhelming translation from Spanish.[41,42] Such translations emerged long ago and have become predominant ways in which historically subordinated languages become more like dominant ones (Errington 2008) in the registers of recognition and schooling. They can erase differences in understanding the world, such as how Cheryl Crazy Bull and Emily White Hat (2019, 120) note that there is no easy equivalent for the word September in Lakota. *Wiyawapi Canwape Gi Wi* instead means "Moon when the tree leaves turn brown," offering a lengthier description that includes signifiers of life philosophies.

Everyday Andean Spanish, too, includes many forms borrowed from Kichwa. Yet, the very overlap of Kichwa-influenced words and their meanings in Spanish illustrates what can disappear in the large-scale aspirations of language planning. Peruvian Quechua speaker Justo Oxa (2004, 236) examines the narrowed meaning of *wawa*, a well-known borrowing from the Quechua and Aymara language families into Andean Spanish. *Wawa* has come to mean "child" in Spanish but has a somewhat different and much wider referent in Quechua/Kichwa:

Una palabra quechua que hasta hoy me da consuelo, cariño y optimismo es, waway,[43] *que volteado al castellano más o menos significa «hijo mío», pero no exactamente, ya que significa mucho más.*

A Quechua word that up until today gives me comfort, tenderness, and optimism is *waway*, that turned over [translated] to Spanish means "my child," but not exactly, since it means a lot more [in Quechua].

Todos quienes estamos aquí en este mundo somos wawa, *no solo los niños, también los adultos y los ancianos, y especialmente ellos que cuando envejecen se vuelven* wawas *a quienes hay que cuidar.*

Everyone here in this world, we are *wawa*, not only kids, also adults and old people, and especially those when they age return to being *wawas* who have to be cared for.

> *No solo los humanos son* wawas *y tienen* wawas; *los cerros, las plantas, los animales, el sol, la luna y todos los seres del mundo tienen* wawa. *Esta palabra es una profunda condensación de la sabiduría y cosmovisión andina.*
>
> Not only humans are *wawas* and have *wawas*; hills, plants, animals, the sun, the moon, all world beings have *wawa*. This word [in Spanish] is a profound condensing of Andean knowledge and worldview.

Oxa's example frustrates equivalency in what words refer to across languages, the kind of premise that exists in intercultural efforts. In this case, a borrowed Kichwa word is narrowed to resemble the Spanish reference of *niño* (child). *Wawa* is a Quechua/Kichwa and Aymara word used in Spanish. It may continue some positive connotations from Quechua ("comfort," "tenderness," "optimism") while offering a synonym for *niño*. Yet, there are differences in reference for the word in Kichwa, such as alternative understandings of the relationships between speakers and surrounding worlds (see also Uzendoski 2012). This condensing of Andean worldviews exemplifies the kinds of meanings that the "systematic linguistics" of language standardization "must always suppress" (Bakhtin 1981, 428).

Outline of the Book

This book is divided into three parts. The first part includes this Introduction and a chapter that further unpacks double binds and state recognition with ethnographic examples. Chapter 1 clarifies theoretical contributions, including that of double binds, anthropology of politics, and linguistic anthropology, and how they relate to the experiences of directors of the school system. It then turns to an ethnographic vignette with the members of the family with whom I lived. They are comparatively excluded from recognition and find Unified Kichwa comically different from their own ways of speaking. I then consider the trajectory of the word *intercultural* to show how it emerged in academic and educational contexts in the United States and Mexico decades before its use in educational policy in Central and South America. Many of the assumptions and challenges of those uses continue in intercultural policy today.

Part II paints a historical and sociological picture of Ecuador's bilingual education, including employees of the school system and Unified Kichwa. Chapter 2 describes the conditions in which organizers fought for the school system and how non-Indigenous-identifying state agents shaped the project. I examine three periods of linguistic and cultural recognition in Ecuador's recent history that tied state modernization and democratic transitions to the support of Indigenous literacy and schooling. In part because bilingual education was established through the parameters and organization of the national state, it developed analogously to mainstream schooling efforts.

Chapter 3 looks closely at standardized Kichwa forms, how they emerged, and how they are currently used. Though standardized varieties are often thought of as neutral and plain-spoken, here I show that Unified Kichwa, in addition to consisting of many Spanish calques, coincides more closely with registers of Northern and Central Highland Kichwa. The register thus prioritizes those speakers, as well as more urban-residing and middle-class members of the Kichwa nationality. Through a detailed examination of the talk of one director commonly identified as a "good speaker," the chapter considers how to effectively address Kichwa-speaking audiences by what I call "offsetting" or using forms from contrastive registers—some standardized, others not—during the same speech.

Chapter 4 presents the educational trajectories of some bilingual education employees, what it means to be considered a "professional," and some benefits and predicaments of higher education. Schooling has been key for the economic stability of many Indigenous citizens. Yet, schooling and professionalized employment have also contributed to a shift to Spanish and other more dominant racialized and classed ways of understanding the world, more generally. Such tensions are at the center of some of the controversies that continue in intercultural bilingual education. I foreground a double bind: many see professionalism as one of the only routes to stable employment for themselves and their children. Yet, community members, parents, and even bilingual education employees are frustrated with professionalism and see it as detrimental to Indigenous organizing and the worlds of *pueblos* and nationalities, more generally.

Part III consists of three chapters that examine activities during which state agents encounter double binds. Chapter 5 examines a workshop to translate the Organic Law of Intercultural Education to Kichwa. Naming a language as official may set forth the translation of legal documents to Indigenous languages. While such translations offer potential for reconfiguring the state through Indigenous worlds and language use, this chapter shows how most workshop participants were concerned with state norms for writing, such as either maintaining consistency across state documents through using the same Unified Kichwa forms, or making an intelligible translation for those who picked it up or downloaded it. Translators encountered double binds. For example, they saw the use of words that differed from those in other major state documents as flagging for readers that the authors were disregarding of previous Kichwa texts and as inconsiderate to future readers, even as they aspired to improve intelligibility. Furthermore, since many at the workshop were concerned with following grammatical norms and legal parameters, not breaking them, making Kichwa readable was virtually impossible, given that legal registers require years of schooling for proficiency and do not yet exist in Kichwa.

In Chapter 6, I consider how a politics of recognition influences the spoken Kichwa of Indigenous state agents. Directors routinely use standardized greetings in Kichwa for public speaking, thereby signaling Indigeneity, Indigenous languages, and the intercultural state. Yet, standardized greetings curtail Kichwa to the openings of events and translate the form and reference of Spanish office-talk into Kichwa. Such speech can anger other Kichwa-speaking listeners and restrict the movement to recognize Kichwa to standardized Kichwa and, in this case, highly curtailed speech acts. However, more extensive speech does not demonstrate the commensurate form of Kichwa familiar to non-Indigenous-identifying addressees and may trigger disapproval from Ministry higher-ups, thereby producing a double bind.

Chapter 7 examines how greetings and other forms of Unified Kichwa are used among teachers and students. I consider what greetings distinguish and how they make known certain identities in two ways. First, greetings co-occur with other markers, such as clothing and music, to project intercultural citizenship for non-Kichwa-speaking onlookers. Second, somewhat differently from bilingual education directors who conduct public speaking in state-sponsored events, students do not assume roles within state events that are cued as intercultural. Their use of Indigenous language greetings and songs, especially those that are literal translations of Spanish, are accepted, while other ways of speaking may be denigrated. Their use of Kichwa equivalent with Spanish helps guide others' reactions to the students by de-emphasizing some of their foremost markers of urban inequality. However, this indicates a double bind for language instruction. While teaching Kichwa greetings and songs fits within intercultural citizenship expectations and helps schools gain approval and funding, it does not develop full proficiency and Indigenous linguistic practices are remade as commensurate with those of *mestizo*-identifying listeners and intercultural citizenship initiatives. Teachers may further see extensive Kichwa-speaking as limiting social mobility and potentially closing off urban spaces to students.

In the Conclusion, I further examine how double binds work and consider possibilities for "loosening" them. I describe cases of Indigenous state agents, language standardization, and multilingual education in other nation-states and compare them with the case of Ecuador to offer insight for policymakers and others who find themselves in such roles. I also provide a brief epilogue on recent changes to bilingual education in Ecuador.

1
Introducing Double Binds of State Institutions and Linguistic Recognition

Introduction

Members of Indigenous *pueblos* and nationalities established intercultural bilingual education throughout the entire country as part of the larger state organizational structure but as a separate school system. This arrangement has presented an opportunity in how a legally recognized school system helps confront racism with institutional authority yet has raised questions of how to avoid the maintenance of a status quo in its similar organization to the other school system and its drawing from state funding and offices for its coordination (Montaluisa-Chasiquiza 2019, 329). This organization indicates a double bind, which is generally understood as a situation in which all possible actions may result in immense challenges. As I described in the Introduction, the difficulties and opportunities of directing the school system go beyond enduring or contesting forms of domination or regulation.

How do bilingual education coordinators experience double binds? I present theorizing for double binds here with the words of a bilingual education director in Ecuador, as well as with theory from linguistic anthropology and an anthropology of politics. State recognition and employment prioritize some Kichwa speakers over others, so I juxtapose analysis of double binds with an ethnographic example of the kinds of Kichwa speakers excluded from intercultural efforts and how they respond to Unified Kichwa. I conclude the chapter by showing how the term *intercultural* emerged in US academia and in Indigenist efforts in Mexico. Such beginnings—ones that stem from the US and *mestizo*-identifying worlds—demonstrate the lengthy trajectory of state policy as double-edged for Indigenous peoples.

Tensions are common in acts of recognition that attempt to reconcile Indigenous claims to nationhood and identity with state sovereignty (Dhillon 2017, 11; Coulthard 2014). Some double binds that Kichwa bilingual education directors encounter are similar for historically marginalized peoples elsewhere and follow the colloquial sense of the expression. For example, the

Seminole Tribe of Florida has required economic resources to gain sovereignty, and that revenue has come through state rights and recognition. Yet, others question the legitimacy of their sovereignty when they exercise the economic power that they gained from the state (Cattelino 2010). Bilingual education in Ecuador was never a separatist movement, and the case shows how double binds emerge in efforts to reclaim Indigenous languages within state institutions that previously disparaged them and their speakers.

I offer an example in the words of one bilingual education employee, Julio, who shows how double binds work and how Andean understandings of the world relate to them. One afternoon at the office, Julio described a double bind as we were discussing his employment. He worked in the National Directorate for two years, including the first six months that I was researching this project, before his contract was not renewed. He did not have tenure, unlike many in the office. He was a member of the Kichwa nationality and had grown up in Ecuadorian cities, especially Quito, which affected his Kichwa language proficiency. Julio had a harder time speaking Kichwa than did many in the office, though he understood most of what others said. He also supported President Rafael Correa—who was unpopular with numerous other employees—and critiqued the school system and routinely disparaged the Indigenous organization CONAIE. Julio was also a more marginal figure in the office because he was younger (in his thirties) by comparison to many employees who had worked in the office for decades. He was additionally, unusually, an architect who specialized in Indigenous forms of architecture and was working to better school infrastructure, while others were devoted to curriculum, translating, supervision of schools, accounting, or human resource management.

In our conversation, Julio focused on how coordinating the school system, including the use of multilingual communication, enacts interculturality. Rather than emphasizing horizontal dialogue, he saw *interculturalidad* as more inclusive of others'—*mestizos*'—forms and norms as translated into Kichwa and the school system's organization. He saw the very process of making a national Indigenous school system as premised on the emulation of the preexisting "*Hispano*" school system for *mestizo* students and that this emulation prevented the transformation of state institutions by Indigenous nationalities:[1]

Es un proceso de interculturalidad que están haciendo aquí en la Dineib.	It's a process of *interculturalidad* that they're doing here in the DINEIB.
Lo que han hecho es traducir lo que es la cultura occidental en la que vivimos, al Kichwa.	What they've done is translate what is the Western culture in which we live to Kichwa.

Han traducido el sistema hispano al Kichwa.	They've translated the Hispanic school system to Kichwa.
Entonces, no se ve cambios grandes....	So, big changes aren't seen....
¿Por qué sucede eso?	Why does that happen?
Porque sencillamente creo que estamos pasando por un proceso de reencontrarnos a nosotros mismos	Because I believe that we are simply passing through a process of re-finding ourselves
y lo que está pasando es parte de ese proceso.	and what's happening is part of that process.
Yo creo que ya con las nuevas tendencias que se van dando desde la misma comunidad,	I think that with the new tendencies that continue to emerge from the community itself,
creo que vamos a profundizar más el tema.	I think that we're going to go further into the theme.

Julio emphasized that the interculturality of bilingual education has implied equivalency with "Western culture." While there are national offices to elaborate and plan for Kichwa and its instruction, he saw that they come with peril, such as how intercultural efforts tend to be premised on making an Indigenous school system analogous with the mainstream one (further examined in Chapter 2). According to Julio, the materials and policies made for the school system have been overly influenced by *mestizo* ways, which prevents "big changes." He located those "big changes," necessary given schooling's history of assimilation and current shift toward Spanish, as hard to accomplish in state institutions. He saw efforts from "the community itself"—which are smaller-scale, further from the constraints of state institutions, and driven primarily by enthusiastic or committed civic actors—as promising, yet those would not be as wide-reaching or authoritative as a national school system. Indigenous state agents who occupy roles in which they work in offices and speak to *mestizos* as addressees, thus, experience incongruous subject positions as a double bind (Spivak 2012) like dealing with expectations about being Indigenous, living in a "Western" world, and representing both other Kichwa speakers and the state in their employment.

Although Julio pinpointed the National Directorate (DINEIB) as a site of intercultural policy and planning, his comments did not blame colleagues. Instead, he emphasized that "we are simply passing through a process of re-finding ourselves." This observation closely relates to how Bolivian sociologist Silvia Rivera Cusicanqui (2020, xxvi) describes double binds as matter-of-fact and common in Andean Indigenous worlds as "a sign of Pachakutik, a time of change." *Pachakutik* can refer to a major change, the "overturning of space/time, the end of a cycle and the beginning of another, when the world upside down can get back on its feet" (Rivera Cusicanqui 2018, 85).[2] There is evidence of a significant collision or overturning in how Julio and his colleagues must translate such incommensurate worlds. Northern Andean philosophies (such as in Imbabura, Ecuador, from where Julio's family hailed) see *pachakutik* in daily events, too, since "everything has a *pachakutik*, a change, a transformation for renewal" (Cachiguango and Pontón 2010, 60).[3] Such changes are even modeled in daily activities like sudden changes in direction while dancing in a circle during solstice celebrations (Wibbelsman 2018). In other words, "simply . . . a process" conveys a routine sense of managing state institutions and acknowledging the vast influence of predominant logics. Julio's emphasis on "re-finding ourselves" alludes to the renewal common to Andean life, with part of the world "get[ting] back on its feet." After all, those who established the school system had to do so with practically no other examples from which to learn; perhaps a new phase will be birthed with other ideas and approaches.

As we continued to discuss the school system, Julio described a double bind in how standardizing Kichwa has been based on Spanish and what its use accomplishes in bilingual education. In other words, Julio emphasized how double binds occur in the daily circumstances of communicating as state employees:

No queremos ser esencialistas [en la Dirección Nacional] sino demostrar que estamos en la interculturalidad.	We [in the National Directorate] don't mean to be essentialists but instead to demonstrate that we are in *interculturalidad*.
Prueba de eso es el hecho de tratar de estandarizar el idioma nativo denominado Kichwa, estandarizar en el formato a nivel nacional.	Proof of that is the fact of trying to standardize a native language named Kichwa, to standardize in the national-level format.
Entonces, es por eso que los saludos [ya] son buenos días y buenas tardes.	So, that's why the greetings are [now] good morning and good afternoon.
Es cierto [que en] el español tiene sentido, ¿no?	It's true [that in] Spanish, they make sense, no?
En el inglés también tiene sentido el good morning, *el* good afternoon. . . .	In English, too, *good morning, good afternoon* make sense. . . .
Entonces, algo así pasa con el Kichwa.	So something like that is happening with Kichwa.
Es muy grotesco decir: alli puncha *porque para nosotros, el Kichwa es un idioma de caricia.*	It's very outlandish to say *alli puncha* [good morning] because for us, Kichwa is a language of caress.
Cuando yo te digo que tengas una linda noche, te estoy diciendo de corazón de que quiero que duermas bien.	When I say to you to have a beautiful night, I'm telling you from the heart that I want you to sleep well.
Buenas noches es un poco frío.	Good night is a little cold.

Entonces, nosotros cuando nos topamos, nunca decimos alli puncha, *en el caso de Otavalo.*	So, when we meet up, we never say *alli puncha* in the case of [the town of] Otavalo.
Nosotros lo que sabemos decir es: Imanalla, *¿cómo está?*	What we usually say is *Imanalla,* how are you?
O decimos: minkachiway, imanalla.	Or we say *minkachiway, imanalla.*
[Con] minkachiway *yo estoy diciendo hágame parte de usted, hágame participar.*	[With] *minkachiway* I'm saying make me a part of you, make me participate.
Hágame ser parte de su vida.	Make me a part of your life.

Julio's comments reveal how employment as state agents is organized around conflicting demands, including the need for a "national-level format" of Kichwa that inevitably excludes some local ways of communicating and life philosophies. The demonstration of *interculturalidad* is bound up in the norms, tasks, and contexts of state employment in national offices. This quote, and Julio's use of "demonstrate," which implies an onlooker, suggest the importance of linguistic anthropological research that has shown in other parts of the world how the act of listening is racialized in perceiving and instructing communicators on how they should speak (Alim, Rickford, & Ball 2016; Inoue 2006; Rosa & Flores 2017). As linguistic anthropologists have written, whiter listeners routinely shape expectations of how communication is or is not appropriate in institutional talk (Flores & Rosa 2015; Rosa 2016). For example, teachers in the United States may attempt to get young Black and Brown students to use standardized English and, consequently, denigrate their other ways of speaking as "inappropriate" for use at school and beyond. Such actions ultimately focus on changing the students' behavior while leaving the larger institutional and societal racism that they experience intact (Flores & Rosa 2015).

In this case, in addition to Kichwa speakers having to shift speech to speak to larger, *mestizo*-inclusive audiences, even the most common signifiers of a standardized register (like *good morning*) are more closely modeled on office Spanish. Moreover, Julio emphasized that Unified Kichwa greetings eclipse Kichwa philosophies that are the very essence of how people understand the world. Julio described this in how *minkachiway* ("I'm saying make me a part of you . . . make me a part of your life") is more profound than an office greeting in Spanish ("from the heart").

Intra- and inter-linguistic communication—across and within Kichwa and Spanish—thus sheds new light on double binds and how they function at the intersections of the state apparatus and Indigenous worlds. The contexts of speaking reveal contradictory messages that build upon routine patterns, wherein a first order interpretation ("a message," in Gregory Bateson's terms) may stand in contrast to a second order interpretation (a "metamessage"), thus placing the speaker in a double bind as they follow the very parameters of communication that their jobs entail.[4] For example, the use of Unified Kichwa greetings in public speaking events allows speakers to invoke their Indigenous identities ("a message," in Bateson's terms) for others, a common use for greetings in Indigenous languages (cf. Ahlers 2006; Graham 2002; Viatori 2009). Yet, Julio and others may subsequently be seen by Kichwa speakers as "essentialists" based on their use of greetings.

The greetings put into practice a state-sanctioned ideology of recognition seen throughout the world: that historically oppressed peoples must demonstrate emblematic signifiers of Indigeneity to be seen and heard, yet this expectation means that their actions reinforce multicultural stratus quos that tend to include static, somewhat homogeneous representations of them (Duchene & Heller 2007; Loperena 2016; Muehlmann 2008).[5] In this case, Kichwa use serves to reinforce ideologies about a singular language despite the plurality of communication in the language family (see also Viatori & Ushigua 2007). With greetings, for example, speakers set apart (or, as linguistic anthropologists write, entextualize) specific tokens of standardized Kichwa—from the vast ways of speaking the language family—by foregrounding them in the communicative roles of the state. While such tokens increase Kichwa's presence, through their repeated use, they also enregister or make greetings seen and heard as prime examples of Kichwa as standardized, the intercultural state, and even how state-authorized Indigenous persons ought to speak.

Moreover, Indigenous and non-Indigenous-identifying others can quickly reuse the greetings, which increases Kichwa's overall salience but also changes how the language is heard and viewed in national politics. Although the use of Kichwa forms—especially those equivalent to office Spanish—is not complete or all-consuming, the forms appear that way in their repetition, which demonstrates Bateson's emphasis on repetition or "repeated experience" as common to double binds. The lack of modeling other ways of communicating, what is *not* included in efforts to make Kichwa into a "national-level format" and demonstrate it as such, undercuts the very diversity that ties Kichwa to specific Indigenous experiences, such as *minkachiway* and the union and goodwill implied. As a result, others may also view bilingual education directors as changing Kichwa, as did Julio. Planners' use of intercultural Kichwa even risks fracturing the support of members of Indigenous organizations and, paradoxically, discouraging other speakers' use of Kichwa altogether. Many teachers, parents, and others focus on how Kichwa language use in official contexts is out of step with cultural categories and local expectations for appropriateness. Directors, thus, simultaneously endure, in Bateson's terms, "negative injunctions" from their constituents. The double binds involve "learning to live with contradictory instructions" (Spivak 2012, 3), including about how to communicate for contrastive listeners of which audiences will consist.

Indigenous state agents witness many repetitions of mixed messages and may strategically or even systematically use Unified Kichwa. They may also feel extremely frustrated. However, unlike the "victims" who preoccupied Bateson, their accounts show that all are aware they occupy difficult, mediating positions amid many competing demands. Yet their livelihoods, commitment to the bilingual schooling project, decades of experiencing such contradictions, and aspirations for incremental change keep them involved in circumstances that, if not outright pathological, are persistently problematic.

Intersections of State Politics and Language Reclamation

Julio's comments demonstrate how the rationalities of state-authorized language use, or the logics upheld in Indigenous languages through national planning and promotion, are often at odds with those of language reclamation, especially the need to get people excited about using their languages and to identify with such ways of communicating. Julio and his colleagues' dilemmas show the relevance of Michel Foucault's analyses of power in institutionalized settings like workplaces and schools, such as how resistance is shaped by or refers back to the primary discourses and techniques of governance.[6]

Employees experience governmentality, "an assemblage of techniques, forms of knowledge, and experts," which aims to guide and influence, and not necessarily to force, the conduct and subjectivities of populations and individuals (Urla 2019, 262; Foucault et al. 1991). The directors' actions indicate self-regulation as they make Kichwa more like Spanish as it is spoken in state offices. They also engage in metacultural and metalinguistic labor to influence how others speak and act. In their employment, they draw upon instruments of knowledge-making that manage and influence populations (see also Urla 2019, 263)—what Foucault (1984) calls "technologies." For example, as Foucault (1979) details in *Discipline and Punish*, and later expands upon somewhat differently from the physical training of bodies and the regulation of spaces, technologies include efforts to standardize actions. These standardizations assume stability in recurring sets of characteristics across populations (see Hacking 2015), such as that certain greetings will be representative of, understood by, and used across people who speak Kichwa differently.

Though Foucault focused on larger-scale, historical changes, I consider these effects in daily communication among school system employees. Directors of the school system model what should be said during "official" events. They often extend such expectations to others in their employment, such as in the evaluation of teachers' Kichwa proficiency based around standardized forms. Technologies, thus, tend to yield those who govern and those who are subjects of governance, such as experts and laypeople (Miller & Rose 1990; Lemke 2001), which may further resentment for directors and their speech forms. The norms and regulations for working in state offices entail authority, including the erasure of ways of speaking that are not included (Foucault 1984 [1971], Blommaert 2010, 38).

I foreground three reflections about managing the school system that are related to governmentality in the promotion of Indigenous languages and that draw from linguistic anthropological theory: analogy with more dominant conceptions and forms of communication, recursivity that is fractal in reproduction, and an increase in scale and scope that ultimately frustrates advancement. First, Julio's example of greetings shows how talk is "guided" by the norms of institutional employment and language use. The parallels across linguistic registers exemplify how governmentality in and beyond state-sponsored language use involves *analogy* (see also Agha 2012, 99). If Unified Kichwa is modeled on standardized Ecuadorian Spanish (as in the example of greetings), its syncretism includes degrees of linguistic assimilation by making Kichwa more like Spanish (or even English) in translation, and such expressions sound unusual to many working-class and/or rural Kichwa speakers. Analogies in translation extend across activities beyond speech genres (Agha 2007; Gundaker 1998; Inoue 2006). For example, parts of textbooks in Kichwa reproduce organizations and themes of those in Spanish (Chapter 2)—though not necessarily the entire textbook verbatim. Another example is how parts of lesson plans in schooling call for memorizing Kichwa songs that are translated from Spanish (Chapter 7).

Second, as linguistic anthropological theory would suggest, the doings of governmentality, like using "double-voiced" Kichwa forms like *alli puncha* that are analogous to Spanish, happen recursively and in different magnitudes from gradient to widespread (Gal & Irvine 2019, 43; Heller & McElhinny 2017; Reyes 2017). This insight parallels Jacqueline Urla and her colleagues' (2017) critique of Pierre Bourdieu's (1991) classic work on how "legitimate language" is replicated. They argue that the standardization of minoritized languages like

Basque reproduces the dynamics of state-authorized, comparatively dominant languages like Spanish but not in a simplistic, straightforward fashion. The case of Kichwa is similar. For instance, *alli puncha mashikuna* ("good morning, colleagues") is remarkably thorough in its reproduction of Spanish. The expression uses Kichwa words but is a calque (literal translation) of a Spanish greeting common to office life and podium speech-giving (*buenos días, compañeros*). The greeting modifies Kichwa communication to make it commensurate with standardized Spanish in syntax, reference, and interaction.[7] Such translations are common to Unified Kichwa. Yet there are other contradictions, such as that state-authorized Kichwa communication inevitably uses regional pronunciations or words from Unified Kichwa that coincide with those of other registers. In other words, the analogies of Spanish in Unified Kichwa vary in degree and show contradictions, even if they are systematic.

Third, questions of scale are significant for the self-regulation of activities and speech of directors of bureaucratic institutions (Carr & Fisher 2016). Julio, for example, pointed to a change in scale with Kichwa's state recognition and language planning. He claimed that standardizing a language "named" Kichwa includes a "national-level format." Most of the activities that bilingual education directors engage in as planners, such as promoting the constitutional recognition of Kichwa, elaborating Kichwa as standardized, and then putting that recognition into practice in official use, necessarily involve relatively large audiences (see also Meek 2016). Authoring a textbook or giving a speech for students at one school is vastly different from doing so for a national audience, the latter of which includes many different publics, such as higher-up *mestizo*-identifying audience members and, simultaneously, working-class Kichwa-speaking parents. Planners are, thus, set up to speak to or plan for an impossibly wide set of listeners—for example, *minkachiway* and more extensive Kichwa use is hard to explain to *mestizo* officials—showing the scaled dimensions of these double binds.

This scaled dimension extends beyond Kichwa use, too, and has long been a challenge for Indigenous organizations. As Ecuador's Indigenous organizations emerged in the twentieth century, members tended to support decentralized, local, and regional forms of decision-making (Santana 1987, 130). However, as examined in Chapter 2, those organizations gradually coalesced into national ones and elected leaders for larger ranges of constituents. National initiatives, while yielding more authority and wide-ranging influence, ultimately depend on single representatives to make decisions for many diverse peoples, which means less direct dialogue with organizational members and an array of expectations. These changes present a challenge, as they involve a shift away from more personalized goals (Gal & Irvine 2019, 209).

Who Is Prioritized in Intercultural Efforts?

As I examine in detail in Chapters 3 and 6, Unified Kichwa words like *good morning* (*alli puncha*) have become emblems of intercultural politics and of institutionalized forms of knowledge and power. As Julio implied, their use is associated with Indigenous-identifying speakers who live in cities, have obtained advanced degrees, and/or work in offices. The following vignette indicates who is less included in recognition politics and what emblems of Unified Kichwa like *alli puncha* mean to Kichwa speakers beyond those who work in state offices.

On a sunny Sunday afternoon in 2012, I was in a working-class neighborhood in the Southern hills of Quito, where many Kichwa speakers had migrated from rural areas of the country.[8] For two previous summers, I had lived in the neighborhood with my adopted Kichwa-speaking family who hailed from the Northern Central Highland region of Bolívar. We were spending the day catching up, largely chatting at the dining room table inside their split-level cinder-block home. Unlike many of the houses in the neighborhood, they had painted most of the walls inside the house sea green. But the paint had run out, which meant that, on that day, parts of the walls remained cinder-block gray. The features of their home reflected their incremental upward mobility after moving to Quito in 2009 in search of employment. Over the years, they have seen limited economic stability. When I first lived with them in 2010, there was no paint on the walls, nor were there doors in any room inside the house. But on this day, there were doors, some paint, and a large handcrafted eight-person dinner table in the kitchen where we were standing. I accompanied them to buy the table in 2011 and recall that it cost them more than $200, more than half of what the mother, Yolanda, made in a month's time. Several white plastic yard chairs were set up beside the table.

One reason the walls had some paint and the family owned the table was that a couple of years before, Walter, the father, had enrolled in classes to become a certified driver. His subsequent employment gained through that credential has been largely responsible for his immediate family's stability, including his wife and their three children (and now two grandchildren). Walter worked as a driver in the National Directorate of Intercultural Bilingual Education (until his contract was not renewed), a job that paid better, by far, than any job he previously held. On the day I visited, he was working as a driver and loader for a paper company, physically demanding work that came with a salary that exceeded the minimum wage. His wife, Yolanda, was a domestic worker in a wealthy suburb of Quito and received Ecuador's minimum monthly salary,

$292, in 2012. Walter's parents continued as farmers in his home region and have productive land, though not enough to produce income for their six grown children and their families.

Walter's brothers and sisters, like most Kichwa families in Ecuador, span a range of occupations. For example, his brother, Wilson, who lived in the same neighborhood, had a high school degree but not a professional job. At the time, Wilson was a construction worker, waking early to perform back-breaking labor for considerably less than Walter's wages and contributing to the family income for a wife and three (now four) kids. Wilson had been living in the city for a few years and scraped by month to month. He did not have experience working in offices, as Walter had, and he had never held a job that paid a stable monthly salary.

On that day, as we were talking, suddenly, Wilson burst in with a fresh buzz cut. He formed a wide smile when he saw us, and exclaimed, in Kichwa, with his voice booming, "*Alli puncha, mashi Nicolás!*" (Good morning, colleague Nicolás!). Instantly, he, his brother, the two children in the room, and I all doubled over in laughter. By uttering only these four words, Wilson was showing how Unified Kichwa did not fit with his persona, a joke that everyone understood, given the laughter. The reaction he received—laughs—shows how incongruent the form was. He had clearly heard the greeting, yet he understood that it did not cohere with his identity and surroundings. He was simultaneously greeting me, making himself sound refined, and making fun of himself, and me.

The greeting *alli puncha* paired with the word *mashi* (a Highland and Unified Kichwa term for "comrade," "colleague," or "friend") indexed Unified Kichwa, a register he did not speak with fluency. In this case, his utterance was a joke based on ideologies about the refined—professional and institutionally sanctioned—speakers of Unified Kichwa. Wilson knew that I had learned Unified Kichwa, and he could generate a laugh by trying to speak Kichwa like me. Yet, his joke shows how foreign-seeming Unified Kichwa forms are for those further from the central state apparatus. His joke indicated that, since the forms are pervasive yet ill-suited for most people's talk, they invoke the speech of Indigenous professionals, which demonstrates an incongruence of class with their use as related to Wilson's surroundings. That Wilson and I are the same age and he called me *mashi*, a word he would not typically use and that shows collegial respect for an interlocutor, further added to the joke. His use of these words shows how greetings like good morning have become emblems of Unified Kichwa and the speakers associated with such ways of speaking. In other words, such ways of speaking are comically out of place in the homes of many working-class Kichwa speakers.

Intercultural: Some Origins

Julio's concern about the essentialism of *interculturalidad*, also indexed by greetings like *alli puncha*, was one I rarely heard coordinators of bilingual education express. For many in the National Directorate offices, *intercultural* describes a set of philosophies that emphasize dialogue and learning across differences. Interculturality supports the recognition and tolerance of forms of communication offered or embraced by Indigenous peoples (Dietz 2012; Postero 2006; Rappaport 2005). Yet, Julio's mention of *interculturalidad* ("It's a process of *interculturalidad* that they're doing here in DINEIB") conveys how he saw (1) the predominant form of state-sponsored cultural politics as *intercultural*; and (2) intercultural as, paradoxically, the continuation of a status quo. In contrast, the Indigenous organization CONAIE's more radical stance of *plurinacionalidad* (plurinationality), recognized in the 2008 Constitution in addition to *interculturalidad*, refers to making a new society via the state and attempting to change the "hegemonic," "white *mestizo*" state in the process (Almeida Reyes 2011, 276). The school system could be an example of *plurinacionalidad*, yet Julio cited bilingual education efforts as distinctly intercultural. Other Indigenous organizations and Correa often opposed *plurinacionalidad* as ambiguous, as foregrounding Indigenous nationalities at the expense of other marginalized peoples, and as overly radical.[9] Directors, similarly, were divided, though all agreed with the designation of Ecuador as intercultural. Such processes of translation, including in how they may prioritize *mestizos* and Spanish, convey intercultural efforts.

Another critic of *interculturalidad*, Luis, claimed *intercultural* does not exist in Kichwa, as I wrote in the previous chapter. In so doing, he questioned the origin of the concept. Luis's question and Julio's description of interculturality's double binds indicate an important point about *intercultural*: the word is lexically bivalent; it can be written in the same way in both English and Spanish. It is not, as he said, from Kichwa. This dual nature across languages indicates a trajectory that complicates its current prominence for describing Indigenous philosophies and rights. Research on Indigenous education in Central and South America tends to trace the emergence of the concept to Mexico in the early 1980s, when *intercultural* became ingrained in the official recognition of Indigenous education and language policy throughout the region. However, the use of *intercultural* can be traced to at least the first half of the twentieth century, primarily in academic spaces in the United States.

A genealogy of *intercultural*, especially in Mexico, shows how the concept is more of an *Indigenist* one (see also Galán López & Navarro Martínez 2016). As the term *intercultural* moved to Mexico and to Spanish—as early as 1916 but especially by the early 1970s—it took on *Indigenist* goals for theorizing situations of contact between Indigenous peoples and *mestizos* and, later, for describing forms of Indigenous education (Dervin, Gajardo, & Lavanchy 2011). Indigenism refers, broadly, to a philosophical movement that emphasized the importance of Indigenous knowledge and ideas in the realm of art, medicine, and policy—spaces largely directed by whiter populations. Throughout Central and South America, *non-*Indigenous-identifying advocates tended to promote Indigenism. Despite the name, their projects were often assimilationist.

For example, Mexican anthropologist and indigenist Manuel Gamio (2006, 27) used the word *intercultural* once in his 1916 book to describe cross-cultural *influence* from Spanish colonizers on rural *pueblos* ("*influencias interculturales*," intercultural influences). Similar uses of *intercultural* were also common in US higher education, especially in the first half of the twentieth century, as a euphemism for "cross-cultural." Indeed, Gamio studied at Columbia University with Franz Boas. Throughout the next decades, some of Mexico's most famed anthropologists would study in the United States. Likewise, many US anthropologists would visit, study, and apply anthropology in Mexico, where many were engaged in racist efforts to measure Indigenous peoples or assimilate them through teaching Spanish. These trajectories indicate how exchanges and ideas were flowing between academic research and practice in the two countries.

By the 1930s, *intercultural* was becoming common in the United States in the aftermath of World War I and the beginnings of World War II. It often still meant cross-cultural, but it was increasingly associated with schooling, especially with progressive and anti-racist education. Rachel Davis Dubois, for example, a Quaker educational advocate, began to study for a master's degree in 1932 at Columbia University's Teachers College—coincidentally, my employer. She writes that she developed intercultural education philosophy when she worked in schools in New York City's Harlem neighborhood with Teachers College faculty Mabel Carney, who studied rural and African American schooling. In 1934, Carney, Davis Dubois, and academic and community members founded the Service Bureau for Education in Human Relations to help educators advance intercultural education (McGee Banks 2010, 126).[10] It was the first prominent organization devoted to intercultural education (McGee Banks 2010, 126), and many cite it as the progenitor (Quillen 1955, 106). In 1938 the name was officially changed to the Service Bureau for Intercultural Education.

Davis Dubois also had connections to anthropology and to Mexico. For the former, she encouraged Boas to develop ways of explaining anthropological ideas to high school students (Davis Dubois 1984, 66). For the latter, in 1935, Davis Dubois went with Carney to Mexico as one of eighty students and rural teachers to visit the new rural schools being developed. Graduates of Teachers College working in the Mexican presidential administration facilitated the trip (Davis Dubois 1984, 74). While in Mexico, she gave a talk titled "Problems in Intercultural Education in the United States," showing the increased use of the word. By the 1940s and 1950s, the word was also common in US anthropology, including the anthropology of education.[11]

For example, Cora Dubois (1955) (no relation) published on "intercultural education" and "intercultural learning" in a compendium of talks from a major conference on anthropology and education, which prominent anthropologists, such as Margaret Mead and George Spindler, attended. Her chapter spelled out how *intercultural* education was lacking in US schools, and she concluded by emphasizing how the "elite of the so-called underdeveloped countries" had significant intercultural understanding, since they had studied languages different from their own; lived abroad; had well-formed philosophies that they learned at home that may contrast with those they learned about at school; and did not grow up in countries that sought to become major world powers, thus becoming more understanding of life elsewhere (105). In the United States, intercultural became linked to differences across nation-states that could be a part of post–World War II curriculum.

The work of another Mexican anthropologist, physician, and "second wave" Indigenist, Gonzalo Aguirre Beltrán (1973), would cite Cora Dubois's writing as he defined intercultural education in Mexico as Indigenous education. Aguirre Beltrán's writings represent a change in Mexico from the earlier use of intercultural for describing relationships and "situations" of cross-cultural interaction—from the brief reference in Gamio's writing to much of Aguirre Beltrán's theorizing about people from distinct regions of Mexico—to describing education for Indigenous peoples, too.

Aguirre Beltrán, who studied anthropology at Northwestern University, was one of Mexico's most influential applied anthropologists and oversaw much of Mexican state-sponsored development throughout the mid-twentieth century. He and other Indigenists, as well as US academics and missionaries, were focused on education as one aspect of development for Mexico's Indigenous peoples, alongside health, agriculture, and fishing (Mateos Cortés 2010). His 1955 book *Programas de salud en la situación intercultural* (*Health Programs in the Intercultural Situation*)—published nearly four decades before intercultural became a common referent for Indigenous education in policy throughout the Americas—used the word to describe relationships between *mestizos* and Indigenous peoples. The "intercultural situation," he writes, refers to "the Indigenous zones in which Indians and *mestizos* live together in tight socio-economic interdependence" (Aguirre Beltrán 1955, 7). This use still conveyed dimensions of Gamio's earlier reference—an emphasis on *mestizo* influence.

By 1973, Aguirre Beltrán had expanded intercultural to describe education. His well-known book *Teoría y práctica de la educación indígena* (Theory and Practice of Indigenous Education) begins by using intercultural similarly to previous work in describing a "region" or "situation." Yet, he (1973, 35) spelled out in detail how intercultural education is for "pre-literate" people who "lack schooling" and "academic teaching characteristic of national society," problematically implying that Indigenous peoples should be seen through the lens and institutions of "national" society and its predominant racialized populations.[12]

Much of his writings do not include such deficit discourses. For example, he also emphasizes how all people change (that Indigenous peoples are not timeless or static) and that health and education policy should better reflect the needs and knowledges of those who would be served. There are parallels in his description to current intercultural bilingual schooling, such as the emphasis on language and making use of Indigenous languages for pedagogy and instruction (what he called "vernacular languages").[13] This section of the book contains the reference to Cora Dubois's writing on intercultural experience and learning, and to US anthropological theory, Mexican Indigenism, and an English-language book on foreign-language teaching. That he was interested in teaching in Indigenous languages, instead of just teaching Spanish or employing *castellanización*, an assimilatory form of bilingual education, indicates a major break with the predominant theories of Mexican Indigenism and education that preceded him. His writings also make clear his conversancy in US and Mexican academic and practical domains, especially in how the word *intercultural* merges them.

It was with this trajectory that *intercultural* began to be adopted in the late 1970s and early 1980s to refer to Indigenous education throughout the continents. Research on interculturality and bilingual education traces *intercultural* to the early 1980s, especially to a 1980 regional conference in Pátzcuaro, Mexico (Pozzi-Escot 1991, 137; Walsh 2009, 49; Zúniga & Gálvez 2002).[14] Indigenists from across Central and South America met there to discuss Indigenous education. The name "bilingual and bicultural education" had become a more common way of describing Indigenous education, and they proposed a name change to *educación intercultural y bilingüe* (intercultural and bilingual education).

They emphasized that the status quo of bicultural was a misnomer. Bicultural, according to them, was not like bilingual because culture is more profound and wide-reaching—more "global and integrator"—than languages ("Informe final" 1982, 334). They saw the term "bicultural" as more immutable because it did not seem possible to teach two cultures in a parallel fashion (which they viewed as more likely in "bilingual" language education), and risked positioning one culture as dominant and the other in simplified terms ("Informe final" 1982, 334). Bilingual education scholar and advocate Luis Enrique López (1991, 181) writes that anthropologists also problematized bicultural from its links to missionaries and literacy efforts, which further encouraged them to change the word to move away from goals like conversion and assimilation. Given that the bilingual-bicultural education program in Mexico had become almost entirely assimilatory, they also desired to break from that tradition with a new word (Moya 1998).

Language policy scholar Nancy Hornberger (2000, 178–79) notes that one of the first policy uses of *intercultural* was in Venezuela's 1979 education policy, where the word emphasized Indigenous populations who would "grow and change in contact with the majority national culture." This citation shows that Indigenist meetings and planning had spread *intercultural* out of Mexico and across the continent and reminds of the term's inextricable ties to the "majority." Indeed, Ecuador's president during the early 1980s, Osvaldo Hurtado, described the use of *interculturalidad* at the time to me in the following way:[15]

No estaba en el debate público y sin duda no estaba en . . . el mundo indígena ése tema.	It was not in the public debate and, without a doubt, that theme was not . . . in the Indigenous world.
Esa fue una reflexión fundamentalmente de la sociedad mestiza, de la sociedad política, de los académicos.	That was a reflection fundamentally from mestizo society, from political society, of the academics.

Such emergence from "Western culture" is part of what Julio critiqued.

Though the meanings of *intercultural* have shifted depending on its contexts of use, some early challenges continue today, including the description of Indigenous languages as static, linked to "being essentialists." This genealogy shows a paradoxical way that intercultural state recognition functions: the onus for change continues to be on Kichwa speakers or other historically marginalized peoples to modify their behavior in order to become recognizable to the state and others, which has been an emphasis in intercultural initiatives for a century. It is within this history that directors of intercultural bilingual education reckon with how to halt language shift and promote Kichwa from state institutions and encounter double binds in so doing.

PART II
HISTORICAL AND SOCIOLOGICAL TRAJECTORIES

2

The Intercultural Era

Histories of Kichwa, Literacies, and Schooling in National Politics and Policy

Introduction

This chapter considers how Indigenous *pueblos* and nationalities established intercultural bilingual education in Ecuador. Much research on the rise of social movements in Ecuador, and elsewhere in the Americas, focuses on mobilizations and protest.[1] I combine the analysis of social movements and force with a focus on directors' use of metalinguistic labor to make languages, cultural emblems, and people relatable to others in positions of higher authority. I show that inclusion in the state apparatus entailed demonstrating state-sanctioned forms of language use, literacy, and democracy. In this chapter, I also compare the case of Kichwa in Ecuador with bilingual education in Bolivia to better understand how and why the Ecuadorian case became so special. Here, I make two arguments about language policies, state institutions, and mobilization.

First, Indigenous organizations' pressure on presidents with relatively progressive policies has been integral to shaping and enacting their demands.[2] A thread that runs through the recent history of Ecuador is that major advances in cultural and linguistic recognition came about during the tenure of leftist or centrist heads of state. Schooling and literacy, in particular, fit within the agendas of modernizing state planners who seek to increase "democratic" participation. Literacy and bilingual schooling policies have provided common ground between state officials and activists—more so than, for example, claims to land or water. Despite being spaces to teach state-sponsored values, schools are also some of the first institutions to change based on the demands of social movements (Carnoy & Levin 1985, 108). Indigenous organizations, too, seek to set the terms of literacy and schooling as they repurpose institutions of state assimilation by teaching culturally and linguistically relevant curricula.

Yet, my second argument here, as seen throughout this book, is that intercultural policy has prioritized state-sanctioned forms of communication that are more understandable to *mestizos*, over more radical forms of difference, such as Kichwa philosophies. In activists' efforts to make sense to non-Indigenous state agents, most of whom know little about Indigenous ways of life, they have had to tailor their talk about themselves and their initiatives. Such tendencies shed light on which epistemologies ultimately prevail in state schooling and literacy initiatives, including progressive ones. As members of Indigenous nationalities met with national state officials, they encountered—in addition to straightforward resistance—professed ignorance. Such contexts of interlocution inevitably shape the emergent policy (Inoue 2006; Flores & Rosa 2015). I focus on how members of *pueblos* and nationalities communicated as spokespeople, describing themselves and modifying their speech for heads of state and national planners, as well as how others communicated their expectations.

Ultimately, this chapter shows that interculturality, plurinationality (explained below), and autonomy—the ideals of many Central and South American Indigenous movements for transforming state policy and institutions—can shift in meaning and be used by state agents for the opposite effect. For example, administrators of bilingual education, as well as scholars, have described the school system as "autonomous" by showing how directors elected their leaders, hired employees, managed their budgets, and designed curricula without counterparts in the Ministry of Education having the final say.[3] In Central and South America, Indigenous activists have long built educational and cultural recognition into requests for autonomy, which emphasize: the ability to direct and administer schooling (García 2004, 358), and culturally and linguistically relevant teaching that contributes to students who are not solely steeped in Western or institutional values (Hornberger 1998). As this chapter shows, however, autonomy also extends a metaphor of self-governance, especially of land, to schooling. Detractors of bilingual education invoked "autonomy" to justify a shift in the school system's control from Indigenous organizations to the Ministry of Education. They argued that education, like the land redistributed in agrarian reform, can be subpar and require state management to reach its full potential.

Activists sought to have bilingual schooling throughout the entire country by making a separate school system and by directing state institutions. This chapter is organized around three main periods of this cultural and linguistic planning in Ecuador, each marked by presidential transitions, modernization efforts, and cultural and linguistic inclusion. The first was in 1979 as Ecuador transitioned from military rule with the election of a president who sought to extend modernization initiatives to all and, in particular, Indigenous peoples. As a sign of the inclusive state, Jaime Roldós Aguilera became the first president to give a speech in Kichwa, which signified his multicultural policies. Second, around 1988, after transitioning from a more authoritarian regime, President Rodrigo Borja signed off on the establishment of the Dirección Nacional de Educación Intercultural Bilingüe (DINEIB, National Directorate of Intercultural Bilingual Education) to form a more inclusive state. During this time, Borja and his officials delegated the management of schooling to Indigenous organizations. Third, around 2007, in a period that followed political upheaval and launched efforts to update Ecuador's school systems, the election of President Rafael Correa brought "twenty-first-century socialism" and cultural politics, including his use of Kichwa, to the forefront of national politics. He simultaneously moved bilingual education further within the management of state offices.

The Launch of the Intercultural Era: Kichwa, Literacy, and Schooling in National Politics and Policy, 1979–1985

In 1979, Ecuador transitioned from military rule back to representative democratic governance. Like political currents in Bolivia and in Peru, Indigenism in Ecuador had become a common movement for cultural solidarity and the inclusion of historically oppressed peoples in nation-states. Presidential candidates were forced to reckon with whether or how to bring Indigenous peoples into the realm of policy. Newly elected populist president Jaime Roldós (Figure 2.1) saw literacy rates as important for Ecuador's transitional agenda and supported widespread literacy initiatives (Pallares 2007, 187). This view brought inclusive cultural politics into a presidential agenda as part of a vision for "progress" for the Ecuadorian state.[4] Many people who were considered "illiterate" were also considered Indigenous; thus, Roldós was thoughtful about Indigenous languages and how linguistic inclusion and planning could be linked to social advancement. In his inaugural speech, flanked by military generals with cameras rolling, Roldós broke with the language use of previous presidential administrations when he became the first president to give a speech in Kichwa.

Early in his speech, first speaking Spanish, he asked the question: to whom was he speaking? (¿"para quién hablo"?). He answered the question and showed an emergent model of inclusion in national policy (as opposed to exclusion or outright assimilation): "*sin la exclusión de nadie*" (without excluding anyone). In his next sentence, he described more specific publics that would be included: "*humildes hermanos ecuatorianos*" (humble Ecuadorian

Figure 2.1 President Jaime Roldós Aguilera. This file is licensed under the Creative Commons Attribution-Share Alike 2.0 Generic license.

brothers [and sisters]), "*centenares de miles de indios*" (hundreds of thousands of Indians), and "*mis hermanos indígenas*" (my Indigenous brothers [and sisters])." He also referenced the devastation of the colonial period for Indigenous peoples: "*protagonistas de la novela, materias de poesía, objeto permanente de explotación social.... Para ellos, la historia se quedó en la colonia*" (protagonists of the novel, subjects of poetry, permanent object of social exploitation.... For them, history remained in the colony). While an important acknowledgment of the devastation of colonialism, his comments show how Indigenism had influenced the speech of inclusive politics. His words referenced, and critiqued, how Indigenous peoples were subjects of art—such as in Indigenist poetry—but forgotten when state institutions could make their lives better. Today his words sound antiquated and even retrograde. During that period, they were progressive.

Then, perhaps foreseeing the future of Kichwa use to acknowledge Indigenous peoples, Roldós read three paragraphs in a highland register of Kichwa. He repeated parts of what he said in Spanish and affirmed in Kichwa that he was using the language to speak to Indigenous listeners. "*Kunanka, pikunaman rimani?*" (Right now, to whom am I speaking?), he said. "*Mishukunamanlla? ... Mana.*" (Only to *mestizos*? No.) He went on to name others, not just *runakunaman* (to *runa*, or Kichwa populations) but also listed Indigenous nationalities (and others) who do not speak Kichwa (such as the Shuar, Waorani, and others). Roldós thus evidenced how his Kichwa use was indicative of an emergent form of state recognition.[5] At that moment, he depicted Kichwa as a major emblem of Indigeneity and transformed the language family as a mode for state agents to demonstrate inclusivity. Today many Indigenous activists cite Roldós as a paragon of inclusion. His use of Kichwa in a state address was provocative, as was his naming of racialized others as significant publics for state policies. As progressive as his speech was, however, it thrust a uniform and national notion of Kichwa—one that was Highland and largely standardized—into the spotlight as representative of all Indigenous groups, a predicament that has manifested throughout *interculturalidad*'s history.

Roldós's speech shows how a politics of recognition depended on a president more disposed to inclusivity; how Indigenous peoples and languages were becoming more involved in upper-level state politics; and how a wide array of collaborators and activists made such moments possible. He responded to, in part, increasing political organization among Indigenous peoples and other collaborators who would help facilitate the arrival of bilingual schooling. For example, according to Osvaldo Hurtado, Roldós's vice president,[6] the Kichwa speech that Roldós read was given to him by *mestiza*-identifying linguist and educator Consuelo Yánez Cossío, who was working with other linguists to craft a standardized Kichwa literacy and language education program.[7] Two young Kichwa speakers were working with her, including Luis Montaluisa who would become instrumental in the establishment of the bilingual school system, and they translated the message (Montaluisa 2019, 327). Roldós, who was from Guayaquil, Ecuador's major coastal city located hours from the Andes mountains, struggled to pronounce Kichwa and knew almost nothing about Indigenous ways of life.[8]

After Roldós's sudden death, President Hurtado (1981–1984) continued many of his predecessor's policies. With pressure from Indigenous organizations, Hurtado introduced constitutional reform in 1983 to support bilingual education, building on national Kichwa literacy efforts in the Ministry of Education. The reform emphasized Kichwa literacy and designated Spanish a language of "*relación intercultural*" (intercultural relation) in areas with "*predominante población indígena*" (predominant Indigenous population) (Chiodi 1990, 363). This legislation, too, was significant in naming the importance of Kichwa as the medium of instruction for schools in those areas (Chiodi 1990, 395). These efforts would be undone by the presidency that followed Hurtado, but the wording *intercultural relation* would reappear to recognize Kichwa in the 2008 Constitution.

I now turn to examine two other influences from which this early inclusive state emerged: the establishment of Indigenous organizations in Ecuador and across the Andes; and two major Indigenous education and literacy projects launched by other institutions connected to the Roldós regime, including the center run by Yánez Cossío.

Indigenous Organizations and Bilingual Education

At the beginning of Roldós's term (1979), which coincided with a rise in Indigenism and Indigenous organizations, it was difficult to carry out any national development project without negotiating directly with regional and local organizations (Santana 1987, 129). Roldós's inclusion conveyed how Indigenous organizations throughout the Americas were seeking schooling as a platform through which Indigenous-language speakers could transform state institutions (Dietz 2004). In Bolivia, too, Highland Aymaras and Lowland Guaranis organized around literacy and schooling in the 1970s and 1980s (Gustafson 2009). For example, in 1982, lowland Indigenous groups organized and founded the regional Confederación de Indígenas del Oriente de Bolivia (Confederation of Indigenous Peoples from the Bolivian Amazon) to unite against settlements on their land (Postero 2004, 195). In 1990, the organization marched and joined with Highland groups as they negotiated with the president who, in turn, recognized seven Indigenous territories. Activists also sought better schooling, though an educational congress and comprehensive reform plan did not foreground bilingual education until 1992 (Luykx 1999, 55–56).[9]

In Ecuador, activists emphasized inclusive schooling in the 1980s and cited and built on the efforts of Dolores Cacuango in the 1940s. Cacuango was a well-regarded, Kichwa-speaking communist activist and progenitor of Kichwa medium of instruction schooling in the mid-twentieth century. She was also one of the first Kichwa activists who, in collaboration with class-based and Indigenous organizations, systematically drafted policies and proposals for modern state institutions (Becker 2008, 84). Organizing, including beyond schooling, has routinely invoked her efforts.

Immediately after Roldós's election, in 1980 the First Regional Conference of Indigenous Nationalities of the Ecuadorian Amazon was held, during which Indigenous organizers asserted *nacionalidad* (nationality) to emphasize the political and territorial rights of Native peoples. Drawing from Russian ideals of group formation, the term *nationality* became a tactic to remake Ecuadorian society and the state. Self-identifying as nationalities foregrounded collective membership among those who preceded the state—many Indigenous peoples—and a means to unite in the contestation of predominant society (Altmann 2014; Becker 2010, 16–17). The arrival of *nationality* also saw the emergence of *Indigenous*-identifying regional organizations (as a shift from, e.g., class-based organizations). For instance, activists at the 1980 meeting established the pan-Amazonian Confederación de Nacionalidades Indígenas de la Amazonía Ecuatoriana (Confederation of Indigenous Nationalities of the Ecuadorian Amazon). Then, building on such advances, Amazonian Indigenous activists worked with Highland Indigenous activists to form the Consejo Nacional de Coordinación de las Nacionalidades Indígenas del Ecuador (CONACNIE, National Coordinating Council of Indigenous Nationalities of Ecuador), which organized with small associations, unions, and town councils, which, in turn, gradually expanded into regional and national political organizations (Almeida et al. 2005, 22).

The emerging organizations emphasized Indigenous education and literacy, which became a meeting point between Roldós and representatives of Indigenous movements. Early on, the Roldós administration proposed to establish a Dirección Nacional de las Culturas Aborígenes y Acción Comunitaria (National Directorate of Aboriginal Cultures and Community Action) to be located within the Ministry of Education and Culture. However, representatives of the organizations wanted a decentralized office they would direct from different regions, not a centralized, government-controlled institution (Santana 1987, 130). In fact, they preferred no institution at all to the government's proposal and, ultimately, negotiations fell through. Geographer Roberto Santana (1987, 130) describes the breakdown not just as a disagreement but as fundamentally different epistemologies about literacy: "The conversations showed that the mark of reference in which literacy was inscribed was very different for some than for others, that the pluriculturality of Ecuadorian society was not translated in the same way [between representatives of the Indigenous organizations and the government])."[10] The state agents wanted to follow a national development plan while offering descriptions that were "reductionist" and "a tool of acculturation" (Santana 1987, 131).

In 1986, 500 delegates from nine Indigenous nationalities and twenty-seven organizations launched the Confederación de Nacionalidades Indígenas del Ecuador (CONAIE, Confederation of Indigenous Nationalities of Ecuador), which would become Ecuador's most powerful and prominent organization up to the present day. CONAIE was a large pan-Indigenous organization that united peoples and smaller organizations from across the Andes, Amazon, and the Coast and was essential to the development of bilingual education. Over the following decade, CONAIE members led large-scale mobilizations that forced presidential administrations to negotiate with them and wove bilingual education—including a national office—into their demands. From its founding, CONAIE aligned with the workers' movement, going on to express itself as "anti-colonial, anti-capitalist, and anti-imperialist" (Becker 2010, 19). CONAIE (and other) activists were increasingly frustrated by state policy, offering that policies "folklorized" cultural markers by promoting those markers in presentations and displays for others and detaching them from those who produced them. While activists avoided supporting political parties (Almeida et al. 2005, 22), they sought increased control over policymaking and a rethinking of economic direction within the state (Pallares 2007, 147).

CONAIE's efforts further oriented state policy toward social programs for Indigenous peoples. In addition to working against unemployment, agricultural industrialization, and racism, the organization sought the recognition of Indigenous languages and the development of bilingual education (Becker 2010, 19). Many of CONAIE's organizers, including Luis Montaluisa, the organization's secretary of education, science, and culture in 1986, had experience in Kichwa literacy and pedagogical initiatives, which I examine below. CONAIE's stance of *plurinacionalidad* (plurinationality), in addition to interculturality, meant that activists encouraged a strategic paradigm for self-identification, evidenced literally in the *nationalities* present in CONAIE's name. Wroblewski (2014, 69) describes *plurinacionalidad* as more radical by referring to the rights of historically separate nations, which contrasts with *interculturalidad* as a set of practices generating more equitable communication and learning between groups (see also Chapter 1). I more closely examine *intercultural* in this book because such racialized dimensions of knowledge are precisely what have *not* been systematically changed in state-authorized Kichwa use and because it is the name of the school system. In later years, the organization Confederación Nacional de Organizaciones Campesinas, Indígenas, y Negras (FENOCIN, National Confederation of Peasant, Indigenous, and Black Organizations) and the religious-based organization Consejo de Pueblos y Organizaciones Indígenas Evangélicos del Ecuador (FEINE, Council of Evangelical Indigenous Pueblos and Organizations of Ecuador) also became prominent national-level organizations that supported bilingual education, though FENOCIN generally has not supported CONAIE's efforts to organize through *plurinacionalidad*.

International and Domestic Collaborating Institutions

Another factor in the emergence of state-sponsored Indigenous schooling is that international organizations, non-governmental organizations, and multinational corporations established and augmented transnational ties with Indigenous movements. This, too, was a tendency emerging across the continent. As early as 1940, non-Indigenous-identifying anthropologists and planners met at the First Interamerican Indigenist Congress in Barbados where their discussions centered on how to modernize and assimilate Indigenous citizens, especially through schooling and literacy (Barros 1995). A later Barbados conference in 1971 aimed to correct some of the earlier assimilatory efforts and would serve as a launching pad for the Indigenous rights movement, where Latin American anthropologists denounced human rights violations against Native peoples, called for anthropologists to advocate on behalf of those with whom they did research, and crafted statements that Indigenous movements could use to organize (Brysk 2000, 18). The United Nations also sponsored conferences on NGOs and Indigeneity throughout the decade (Brysk 2000, 86). For example, the 1977 UN International NGO Conference on Discrimination against Indigenous Populations in the Americas marked the first time that Native peoples from all parts of the world united and represented themselves in a singular voice (Niezen 2003, 2). International organizations also advised Indigenous peoples on transnational organizing, such as how the International Work Group of Indigenous Affairs participated in the formation of the World Council of Indigenous Peoples (Brysk 2000, 87).

Throughout Central and South America, Indigenist policy included schooling. One of the main institutions in Ecuador for launching Indigenous education was the Centro de Investigaciones de Educación Indígena (Center of Research on Indigenous Education), housed in the Pontificia Universidad Católica del Ecuador (Pontifical Catholic University of Quito, "the Catholic University"). An early step toward establishing the Center occurred when members of the Summer Institute of Linguistics and the Ministry of Education and Culture organized the First Seminar on Bilingual Education in 1973 (Von Gleich 2006, 49). This session launched Kichwa planning initiatives at the Catholic University where, at that time, mainly *mestizo*-identifying linguists began to write pedagogy, among other materials, for learning to read and write in Kichwa (Montaluisa 1980b, 129). In 1975, the University established the Department of Linguistic Research in its language institute. This institute proposed the development of Kichwa literacy materials, which was supported the following year by hiring two young Kichwa speakers (Rodríguez Cruz 2018, 66).

The Center's approach to Kichwa literacy contrasted with the Ministry of Education's and international organizations' pedagogies in the 1970s and early 1980s, since the status quo tended to transition and assimilate readers from Kichwa to Spanish (Yánez Cossío 1997, 44). In 1978, the Ministry of Education and Culture signed a contract with the Catholic University to run a subprogram for Kichwa literacy within the Programa Nacional de Alfabetización (National Literacy Program), for which the Center would eventually be responsible (Conejo 2008, 67; Krainer 1996, 45). The program was not without contestation in the University. Some faculty members and administrative staff complained that the first two Indigenous employees did not have the educational credentials for the job, and others made overtly racist comments about Kichwa-speaking employees (Yánez Cossío 1991, 46–47).

Bilingual education scholar and practitioner Matthias Abram (1992, 66) notes that the Center's literacy program still struggled for two reasons: first, most Indigenous people wanted to learn to read in Spanish and, second, because of the Center's affiliation with the Ministry of Education, most Indigenous organizations were opposed to the endeavor and boycotted it. Schooling, as a state-sponsored project, has long yielded tensions with Indigenous parents (Rockwell 2007; Sumida Huaman 2020).

In 1982, the Center stopped the adult literacy program and began to work on primary schooling. Its employees established around 500 programs in schools throughout Ecuador for students through the third grade (Abram 1992, 67). Those programs used preexisting literacy materials and authored new ones as they operated inside Ecuador's public schools. Through involvement with the Center and by studying in higher education (Conejo 2008), Indigenous peoples assumed teaching positions and other positions of institutional authority, even if Indigenous-identifying teachers would often deal with routine confrontations by parents and Spanish-speaking teachers who did not want Kichwa-speaking children to attend. This effort continued until the Center closed in 1986, and afterward many of its employees would move on to author national educational policies and curricula in the National Directorate or assume leadership positions within CONAIE.

The second major organization that set the framework for the school system had more international ties, but it too began within national state offices: Proyecto Educación Bilingüe Intercultural (Project EBI), coordinated by the German Agency for Technical Cooperation (GTZ, Deutsche Gesellschaft für Internationale Zusammenarbeit). GTZ launched internationally funded experimental education throughout the Andes during the 1980s. GTZ (now called GIZ) built a large schooling infrastructure and was instrumental to preparing Indigenous teachers and developing curricula in Indigenous languages in Ecuador and Peru (Cortina 2014), including the famed Quechua and Spanish bilingual schools in Puno, Peru (Hornberger 1988).

This project exemplifies another key difference between Indigenous education in Ecuador and Bolivia, the states with the most comparable national cases. For Bolivia, the experimental pilot project for bilingual education was located on the Peruvian side of the border, not in Bolivia. Unlike in Ecuador, emerging professionals left the country to participate (López 2005, 118), which ultimately increased their distance from national policies and offices. It was not until 1988 that international organizations like UNICEF, in collaboration with the Bolivian Ministry of Education, implemented an experimental intercultural bilingual education project in three languages (Aymara, Quechua, and Guarani) (López 2005, 128), and actual classroom teaching did not begin until 1990 (López 2005, 131). In Ecuador, GTZ signed an agreement with the Departamento de Educación Rural (Department of Rural Education) within the Ministry of Education and Culture; the project began in 1982 (Abram 1992, 85) and was also preceded by CIEI's project. The project was, thus, linked to national state offices and policy, as its offices were inside the Ministry in Quito for the first four years. It was codirected by an Ecuadorian national coordinator (named by the Department of Rural Education) and a German expert (Abram 1992, 90). Another difference is that, in Ecuador, efforts were focused on Kichwa (instead of being divided across other major language families like Aymara in Bolivia). The project in Ecuador was also relatively horizontal in its organization in comparison to the Center at the Catholic University, prioritizing the participation of Indigenous organizations and courting CONACNIE.

Like the Center, Project EBI began with little precedent and faced challenges. It required, for example, research on previous projects and their successes; institutional contacts from state and non-state institutions; cooperation from provincial Indigenous organizations; curricula, especially bilingual resources, that largely did not exist; and teachers, administrators, and schools. There were also interpersonal tensions. Project EBI's sponsorship by the state contributed to problems with the Indigenous organization CONACNIE, which, in addition to concern about state involvement in general, rejected the human rights violations of President León Febrés Cordero's mid-1980s governing regime (Abram 1992, 94). There were also tensions between the two major bilingual education projects. As the Center was increasingly on the outs with the Cordero regime, Consuelo Yánez-Cossío, its director, denounced Project EBI as the outsourcing of Indigenous education to the German private sector (Abram 1992, 94). The Project further faced the wrath of Indigenous parents who were concerned, again, with the state educating their children. Moreover, many employees self-identified as *mestizos* and did not speak Kichwa, yielding further divisions within the project. Though there was only one Indigenous-identifying member of the team in the early years, over time that number steadily grew, often drawing from those formerly employed by the Center (Abram 1992, 96).

Despite such difficulties, the Project established more than seventy schools within the first two years and maintained most of them until its conclusion in 1990 (Abram 1992, 104). Though employees sometimes borrowed materials from the Center, they produced many of their own, such as books in regional varieties of Kichwa. This marked a different approach to language instruction from the Center, which tended to use standardized Kichwa. Project EBI considered Unified Kichwa to be "artificial" and opted for local registers (Abram 1992, 106). Furthermore, although the Center trained several Indigenous professionals who would go on to leadership positions in CONAIE and bilingual education, it perennially lacked funds and did not award tenure to teachers. In contrast, Project EBI emphasized that its teachers would receive tenure from the state and focused on securing long-term jobs for its employees. In fact, many Project EBI employees would go on to have tenure in the National Directorate offices.

The Beginning of National Indigenous Schooling: The Early Years of the National Directorate (mid-1980s to mid-1990s)

The rise of Indigenous movements and the prominence of Indigenous literacy and bilingual initiatives continued throughout the mid-1980s. However, major advances in national policy were stymied until Rodrigo Borja, a left-leaning candidate with a focus on representative democracy, national unity, and bettering economic conditions for the poor, won the 1988 presidential election. The start of the previous administration of León Febrés Cordero in 1984 had brought structural adjustment policies, privatization of state agriculture and fishing organizations, rising unemployment, social repression, and forced disappearances. Before Cordero, the Ministry of Education and Culture had been responsible for publishing the Center's teaching materials. However, in part, because of how restrictive the Cordero regime had been with curriculum, Kichwa-speaking planners and activists sought the institutionalization of an Indigenous school system that did not require Ministry approval.[11]

Indigenous organizers had backed Borja in his unsuccessful 1984 run, and its members played a major role in his 1988 election, even as CONAIE rejected endorsing a candidate. In his campaign speeches, Borja described Ecuador as consisting of "multiple nationalities, multiple cultures, and multiple ethnic peoples" (Whitten & Whitten 2011, 101). Yet, tensions would later erupt, as seen in CONAIE's remarkable marches in 1990. In seeking a more inclusive state, Borja, like Roldós, emphasized modernization. Borja also saw concessions of self-determination as threats to sovereignty (Whitten 2003, 6). These challenges were compounded by Borja being a member of Ecuador's white, elite class. Although he generally promoted more inclusive discourses, he knew little about forms of Indigeneity and bilingual education (Whitten 2011, 101). His ignorance—which could also be considered self-interest—forced Indigenous activists to routinely explain their goals and their differences and likely influenced the commensurate project that emerged.

Luis Montaluisa, the prominent Kichwa activist who had worked in the Center and became a director within the Indigenous organization CONAIE, noted that his own nomination for an academic position at the Catholic University helped him establish authority for the president's policymakers (Montaluisa 2019, 328). He and others saw Indigenous schooling as a less controversial institution (e.g., than territorial sovereignty) for achieving governance. During the congress that led to the establishment of CONAIE, he proposed the establishment of Indigenous education within the state. CONAIE and members of other organizations were weary of how national state offices might begin to control social movements but, ultimately, they voted for the initiative (Rodríguez Cruz 2018, 74).

Montaluisa also had to convince those in the Ministry of Education. In conversations with the minister of education, Montaluisa told him, "*Si usted está de acuerdo, lo que hay que hacer es crear la Dineib*" (If you agree [with inclusion and bilingual education], what one has to do is create the DINEIB." But the Minister responded, "*Yo no sé que es la Conaie, entonces, quiero tener una reunión pasado mañana con toda la directiva*" (I don't know what CONAIE is, so I want to have a meeting with all of the directorate the day after tomorrow). The meeting in July 1988 included most of the higher-ups from the Ministry, almost all of whom, according to Montaluisa, were against establishing bilingual education (Montaluisa n.d., 17–18). There was a document with thirty-seven arguments against bilingual education, such as that the school system "*iba a dividir al país*" (was going to divide the country). Montaluisa emphasized prior legislation in response, such as the 1983 amendment to the constitution (Rodríguez Cruz 2018, 76). The minister of education decided to organize a debate between three representatives of CONAIE and three representatives of the Ministry of Education who were against the project. Again, CONAIE members had to demonstrate rational forms of discussion.

Ministry expectations drove the need for activists to describe bilingual schooling in ways that made it familiar and understandable to state agents, especially when talking about their organizing as "democratic." When the representatives from CONAIE arrived, they brought more than the three allowed representatives. When the minister protested that they were only allowed to have three, a leader of CONAIE responded that, "*Señor Ministro, estamos en democracia y por eso permita que todos los compañeros presencien el debate*" (Mr. Minister, we are in democracy and so permit all the comrades to be present at the debate) (Montaluisa n.d., 19). Only three would participate, but the others would watch and report back to their communities. The minister relented. When the national director of education spoke, she supported the establishment of the Dirección Nacional de Educación Indígena Intercultural Bilingüe (National Directorate of Indigenous Intercultural Bilingual Education, the institution's original name) to govern and administer the school system: "*Señor Ministro es verdad que estamos en democracia y por eso puede crearse la Dirección Bilingüe*" (Mr. Minister, it is true that we are in democracy and that's why the Bilingual Directorate can be created) (Montaluisa n.d., 19). Operationalizing and demonstrating "democratic" engagement, as well as invoking constitutional recognition of Kichwa and schooling, were essential to the National Directorate's founding.

Borja's minister of education asked an assessor to develop an executive decree to establish the school system who, in turn, tasked Luis Montaluisa with the job (Montaluisa n.d., 19). The president signed Montaluisa's decree as an executive order in November 1988, legally establishing the National Directorate as an entity within the state earlier than in Bolivia and Peru. The decree was upheld for more than twenty years, despite other state actors' efforts to overturn it.[12] As a national school system for Indigenous students, intercultural bilingual education would run parallel to the principal school system.

Executive Decree No. 203 proclaims:

Esta Dirección cuyo personal deberá poseer a más del dominio de la lengua castellana el de alguna de las lenguas indígenas del Ecuador, tendrá a su cargo la planificación, organización, dirección, control, coordinación y evaluación de la educación indígena en los subsistemas escolarizado y no escolarizado.	This directorate, whose personnel must possess, in addition to the command of the Spanish language, the [command] of one of the Indigenous languages of Ecuador, will be responsible for the planning, organization, oversight, control, coordination, and evaluation of Indigenous education in school-based and not school-based subsystems.

The decree yielded substantial self-direction to Indigenous-language speakers ("planning, organization, oversight, control, coordination, and evaluation"). Indigenous activists in Ecuador saw the importance of linking proficiency in Indigenous languages with employment in a major institution of state power. A challenge was how to inscribe this requirement, as a modernist ideology of bilingualism was simultaneously written into the legal recognition of the school system by requiring those in the directorate to "possess one of the Indigenous languages." While exceptional in the range of responsibilities it accorded, the decree invoked the language ideology of European nation-building and modern linguistics that languages are stable, countable, equitable wholes (Bauman & Briggs 2003). Kichwa and Ecuador's other Indigenous languages were inscribed, literally, as possessions like a singular colonial language (manifest in the parallelism of the phrase "in addition to . . . the Spanish language"). They were situated through modernist descriptions common to state documents.

The decree describes some of DINEIB's functions, such as producing linguistically and culturally appropriate teaching materials; planning, directing, and carrying out bilingual education; establishing communication channels with representatives of Indigenous nationalities; and preparing teachers throughout the nation-state. It names the national director of Indigenous education as the highest authority. In 1992, another law (Law 150) officially established the Indigenous school system that would run parallel to the *Hispano* school system and further specified the technical, financial, and administrative autonomy of intercultural bilingual education. It added to CONAIE's management of the school system (Rodriguez Cruz 2018, 85) and tasked the organization with the development of educational materials in Indigenous languages (Conejo 2008, 68). Throughout the country, directors sought and established provincial directorates of Indigenous education, equivalent to the Hispanic system's organizational structure, to administer the school system in sixteen of Ecuador's twenty-one provinces, those where Indigenous peoples resided (Abram 1992, 110). Founders established the national and regional scales based, in part, on the Ministry of Education's preexisting institutional model and, in part, on the structure of Indigenous organizations, which also had regional organizations affiliated with national ones.

Though now legally sanctioned, the school system prompted other forms of resistance. For example, *mestizo*-identifying teachers from the *Hispano* system worried about losing their jobs and often demanded that the Indigenous school system be dissolved. They also accused directors of the school system of not engaging with them about whether their schools should become "bilingual," and were then alarmed when, seemingly overnight, their schools were converted to "bilingual" ones (González Terreros 2011, 59). They conducted strikes, petitions, and demonstrations supported by the National Educators Union (Abram 1992, 111). As one former employee of Project EBI put it, the regional protests were inseparable from white supremacy "*porque en provincias, los jefes mishus no querían que se les quite su poder sobre los indígenas*" (because, in the provinces, the *mishu* [*mestizo*] bosses didn't want their power over Indigenous people cut off)."[13]

As Montaluisa recounted, as DINEIB's first director, he was once even sequestered by protestors for a day on a visit to the province of Cotopaxi:[14]

Entonces, me invitan diciendo:	So they invite me [to Cotopaxi to speak with regional coordinators of the *Hispano* system], saying,
"vea, mis supervisores quieren que usted les explique en qué consiste eso de la Dineib."	"Look, my supervisors want you to explain to them what that of the DINEIB consists of."
Yo cogí el bus y me fui. . . . Entonces, ahí me secuestraron.	I took the bus and left. . . . Then, there they sequestered me.
Más de quinientos profesores habían bajado de las escuelas del campo, profesores hispanos.	More than 500 teachers had come down from the schools in the *campo*, *Hispano* teachers.
Entonces, me encerraron. Me tuvieron todo el día insultando.	So, they locked me in. They kept me there all day, insulting [me].
Yo les hablé en Kichwa, eso les daba más coraje.	I spoke to them in Kichwa, and that made them angrier.
Lo que ellos querían es que se derogue la Dineib. Que desaparezca.	What they wanted was to destitute DINEIB. That it would disappear.
Habían llevado algunos compañeros indígenas engañándoles diciendo que van a tramitar un camino.	They'd [also] brought some Indigenous colleagues [to protest against me], tricking them [by] saying that they were going to build a road [for them if they turned against the school system].
Entonces, ya en la tarde, después de que me tuvieron insultándome, amenazando todo el día, me dicen:	So, then in the afternoon, after having me there all day insulting and threatening me, they say,
"y para que te des cuenta que tu propia gente te rechaza, aquí están los compañeros que te van a decir lo que te mereces."	"And so that you realize that your own people reject you, here the comrades are going to tell you what you deserve."
Entonces, los compañeros [indígenas] como me conocían, dicen:	So, the [Indigenous] colleagues, since they knew me, say [to the *mestizo* teachers],
"porque ustedes [los profesores mestizos] vienen el martes a dar clases y el jueves ya se van dejando la escuela,	"Because you come on Tuesday [to the school just] to teach [despite living elsewhere] and [already] on Thursday you go home abandoning the school,
porque ustedes vienen a las nueve de la mañana y a las once ya se van.	because you come at nine in the morning and at 11 A.M. you already leave,
Por eso, estamos de acuerdo con la educación bilingüe."	that's why we're in agreement with bilingual education."
Se fueron saliendo ese rato.	They [the sequesterers] left at that moment.

Montaluisa's story indicates how threatening the school system was to the status quo, so much so that he experienced physical coercion by those seeking the school system's destruction. Accustomed to the self-professed ignorance of others about Indigenous education, he readily accepted invitations to publicize and explain the school system. Teachers and teachers' unions, concerned about the potential loss of control and jobs, used such "ignorance" to detain and threaten him. Yet, the *Hispano* teachers did not reside where they taught and were unfamiliar with community norms.

At the national level, though linguistic and cultural recognition had become more mainstream, even the *name* National Directorate of Indigenous Intercultural Bilingual Education was controversial. A major part of the controversy was that bilingual education presented an *Indigenous* project. As Montaluisa put it:[15]

Comenzaron a criticarnos diciendo que éramos indigenistas,	[Others in the Ministry] started to criticize us saying that we were indigenists,
racistas, enemigos del blanco.	racists, enemies of the white person.
Entonces, me pareció que esa palabra indígena	So, it seemed to me that the word "Indigenous"
era el motivo de la polémica....	was the motive of the controversy....
En la ley que hice, yo ya me imaginé que venía otro presidente y nos borraba.	In the law that I made, I imagined that another president would come and erase us.
Entonces, yo mismo redacté la ley 150,	So I myself redacted Law 150,
ahí le quité la otra "i" [del cambio de DINEIIB a DINEIB].	There I took out the other I [for *Indigenous*, making DINEIIB from then on DINEIB].

In addition to its other functions, Law 150 changed the name of the directorate. "Indigenous" implied not just difference from *mestizos* but, at the time, was also a more radical and threatening label. "Intercultural" and "bilingual" became acceptable forms of state recognition. As Kichwa linguist Alberto Conejo put it, *Indigenous* tended to imply an overly inward focus in contrast to interculturality:[16]

Al inicio la Dineib no era muy intercultural,	At the beginning, DINEIB wasn't very intercultural,
más bien era desde los indígenas, para los indígenas, con los indígenas....	it's more like it was from Indigenous people, for Indigenous people, [and] with Indigenous people....
También era un trabajo político de las organizaciones indígenas,	It was also a political work on behalf of the Indigenous organizations,
de intelectuales indígenas, dirigentes indígenas.	of Indigenous intellectuals, Indigenous directors.

Conejo described a group of employees grappling with how to maintain a project within state institutions. Implicit in his comments is figuring out how to proceed and what to do within the difficult circumstances that Montaluisa described. Conejo contrasts intercultural as safer than indigeneity because the former included more of a focus on *mestizos* and white people who occupied positions of greater authority.

Some of CONAIE's historic marches in the 1990s emerged through and around bilingual education, such as Montaluisa's sequestering and other similar events. As Montaluisa put it,[17]

¿Cuál fue nuestra respuesta?	What was our response [to his sequestering]?
Hacer marchas en cada ciudad.	To hold marches in each city.
En Latacunga a las tres semanas respondieron las comunidades con una marcha de más de cinco mil indígenas.	In Latacunga [the capital city of the Cotopaxi region where the sequestering took place] in three weeks communities responded with a march of 5,000 Indigenous people.

Furthermore, while the establishment of bilingual education was a remarkable advance, CONAIE's second congress in 1988 had proposed the Ley de Nacionalidades Indígenas (Law of Indigenous Nationalities), which did not come to fruition. Indeed, in the stunning national 1990 uprising against the Borja administration, Indigenous mobilizers paralyzed parts of Highland Ecuador for more than a week by blocking highways, leading marches, and conducting sit-ins and a hunger strike. As the protests grew, activists refused to cease until the presidential administration negotiated with them. The efforts also included detaining police and military members and holding wealthy *hacendados* (landowners) captive (Becker 2008; Whitten and Whitten 2011, 96–97). Borja decried the uprising as "*regionalista*" (regionalist) with "*agitadores irresponsables . . . manipulando a los indígenas de la Sierra*" (irresponsible agitators . . . manipulating Indigenous people from the Sierra) (Kowii 2017, 218).

A little over a week after the first protests, Borja relented to a meeting but still did not acquiesce to Indigenous activists' demands for land rights, schooling, economic development, and maintenance of traditional judicial systems. In fact, many of CONAIE's requests emphasized recognition of Indigenous peoples by nation-states across the South American continent, a demand more likely to spur larger-scale awareness than immediate results. But after the uprisings and the meetings, directors of Indigenous organizations pronounced 1992 the year of self-determination as it also marked 500 years of colonialism (Whitten & Whitten 2011, 97).[18]

As Indigenous organizers across the Andean nation-states sought legislation during that period (the late 1980s and early 1990s), they had contrastive listeners in heads of state and educational planning, again showing Borja's importance for bilingual education. In Bolivia, neoliberal policymakers implemented some of the most severe structural adjustment policies in the region, exacerbating poverty even while meeting with Indigenous organizers (Lucero 2008, 122). While Bolivia's Indigenous movements tended to be somewhat more radical than in Ecuador, including demands for "decolonizing" the state, Bolivia's efforts for bilingual education and interculturality were ultimately folded into an emerging development industry that made Bolivia a site for testing neoliberal policies and an influx of foreign aid (Gustafson 2014, 79). In 1992 the Asamblea del Pueblo Guaraní (Assembly for the Pueblo Guarani) sued the federal government to establish a national educational governing body like Ecuador's, which the president established with a Supreme Decree in 1992. However, authorities in the Bolivian Ministry of Education and other critics, especially those in charge of rural education, were against the office and the decree was never carried out (López 2005, 133–34). Ultimately, a 1994 law that yielded national Indigenous education policy set precedent for intercultural bilingual education, vastly altering the schooling landscape even while focusing on assessment, teacher evaluation, and anti-union policies (Gustafson 2014, 77). The reform finally made its way to classrooms in 1996 (López 2005, 134).

Ecuador marked a significant contrast. When CONAIE's prominent uprisings began in the 1990s, bilingual education was already established and operating. The pilot projects for Indigenous schooling had been ongoing throughout the 1980s, providing an infrastructure of intercultural bilingual schools. Furthermore, neoliberal reforms in Ecuador were much less aggressive than in Bolivia, and heads of state were generally hesitant or unable to halt Indigenous mobilization (Lucero 2008, 122), making the school system somewhat less controversial even as it endured constant challenges.

As the school system expanded, employment within it was controlled by Indigenous organizations and, thus, became a significant source of jobs (Martínez Novo and de la Torre 2010, 16). Employees of DINEIB would manage much of the school system from the national level, including making language policy decisions, preparing and evaluating teachers, authoring curricula, and promoting Indigenous languages. Regional offices would also manage the school system for respective provinces, including conducting similar tasks as directors in DINEIB.[19] National and regional Indigenous organizations served as gatekeepers for employment. At the national level, the largest and most prominent organizations—CONAIE, FENOCIN, and FEINE—were the gatekeepers of employment, deciding which candidates to sponsor for jobs in DINEIB, and regional organizations similarly regulated hiring in provincial directorates. CONAIE tended to hold more influence in the national offices and when the system of regional directorates was established, directors awarded tenure to more than 1,000 Indigenous educators (Montaluisa n.d., 22), vastly increasing institutional employment possibilities. The school system also hired administrators, accountants, pedagogy experts, secretaries, and drivers. At the time, few candidates had the schooling credentials for the jobs, and not many of them identified as Indigenous.

A main purpose of the system was to strengthen and support Kichwa since schools had long been institutuions of linguistic assimilation. However, there were also questions of how to reclaim long-marginalized ways of speaking in the school system and whom to hire. A longtime administrator put it this way:[20]

Habían dirigentes que nos decían:	There were directors who would tell us:
"nosotros luchamos con nuestras vidas para obtener educación bilingüe porque a nuestros hijos les maltrataban	"We struggled with our lives to obtain bilingual education because they mistreated our children,
porque [nuestros hijos] sabían Kichwa y no entendían el español."	because [our children] knew Kichwa and didn't understand Spanish."
Entonces, decían, por esto nosotros queremos que la educación bilingüe surja y haya profesores, pero que sean verdaderamente y netamente indígenas.	So, they said that's why we want bilingual education to surge and that there are teachers but that they're truly and purely Indigenous.
Pero ... [después] ya la mayoría [de los profesores] fueron hispanos [con títulos]. . . .	But [afterward] the majority [of teachers] were hispano [because they had the degrees]. . . .
La educación bilingüe estaba sirviendo a los mismos hispanos.	Bilingual education was serving the hispanos themselves.

A main goal was to teach students in languages they spoke at home and to promote Kichwa as a language worthy of schooling. Kichwa-speaking educators were ideal for those tasks. Yet, the process of obtaining the degrees required for entry into the school system, combined with ongoing language shift and historical lack of access to schools, meant that non-Indigenous peoples and non-Kichwa speakers were increasingly hired to fill open positions.

Although the emerging project advanced through years of negotiations and activism, directing national offices also presented challenges, including interpersonal ones. When DINEIB was established in 1988, many of its employees were associated with CONAIE and had worked previously in the Center of Research on Indigenous Education at the Catholic University. When Project EBI was winding down in the early 1990s, authors and planners from the Project were hired into DINEIB. The arrangement was remarkable in how it united an emerging group of professionals with experience in Indigenous education in Ecuador, but it also merged different approaches to schooling and claims to expertise, such as language standardization. Employees who had worked on Project EBI tended to have more schooling, credentials, and institutional work experience but found themselves inserted into a new order run by CONAIE members and some former employees of the Center. Some members belonged to contrasting Indigenous organizations and were resentful of CONAIE's influence. All of this was compounded by employment in bureaucratic spaces. For example, employees received different pay grades, which contributed to hierarchies among employees. The new administrative offices were run much like other state institutions (Conejo 2008, 80), and they replicated many aspects of the preexisting *hispano* school system, as Francisco mentioned in Chapter 1.

Authoring materials for an entire school system also presented an enormous scope to work toward. One way that DINEIB authors and curriculum developers dealt with this challenge was to borrow some materials from earlier work in the Center and Project EBI. The Center, for example, had elaborated around sixty-four types of materials in Indigenous languages, including literacy notebooks, math workbooks, history lessons, maps, and dictionaries (Montaluisa n.d., 6). Another strategy was to model some of the Spanish-language materials on those used in the *Hispano* school system (Yánez-Cossío 1997, 63), and some of the Kichwa-language ones, too. One person involved in the start of the school system said: "*Los materiales que hemos hecho, hemos copiado del otro sistema queriendo hacer muy rápidamente*" (The materials that we've made, we've copied from the other system, wanting to do them very quickly).[21]

A major source of pride of school system employees was when DINEIB published its well-known Modelo del Sistema de Educación Intercultural Bilingüe (Model of the System of Intercultural Bilingual Education) in 1993, a curricular model of standards for producing pedagogy. The document lists goals and strategies for Indigenous schooling in Ecuador, spelling out the philosophies and principles of the school system for teaching agricultural techniques and Indigenous linguistic and cultural "*cosmovisiones*" (worldviews) (Martínez Novo 2014a, 106). The model emphasizes that Indigenous languages should be the primary means of communication in education, with Spanish taking on a secondary role in the early years of schooling, even as, in practice, bilingual schools have mainly taught in Spanish (see also the Introduction and Chapter 7).

Funding for the school system was another major factor to think through, in addition to curriculum development. State administrative offices did not designate a fund for the school system and instead depended on international organizations for daily operating costs (Krainer 1996). During the development of bilingual schools in the 1990s, the school system received significantly less than the *Hispano* school system, which also meant lower teacher pay (Krainer 2010, 40). From the beginning, intercultural bilingual education was underfunded and endured ongoing marginalization by those in central state offices and others (Gustafson 2014, 83; Kowii 2011, 182). Given such financial constraints, the school system made a vast number of materials and has reached a remarkable number of students since its beginning.

Mid-2000s to Today: Cultural and Linguistic Recognition, Standardizing Education, Dividing Movements

The mid-2000s was the start of the third consequential period for national politics and Indigenous language recognition, schooling, and literacy. On the heels of six different presidents during a five-year period, of which Indigenous mobilizations helped remove at least two, the last short-term president, Alfredo Palacio, appointed Raúl Vallejo as minister of education. Vallejo was the former director of Ecuador's prior literacy campaign and former minister of education and culture from 1991 to 1992 during the Borja administration. By 2005, Vallejo also had a doctorate in literature and history and had received a Fulbright scholarship to study in the United States. Vallejo had a long and distinguished career as a literacy advocate, poet, novelist, politician, and, of particular relevance here, modernizer. As he moved from his academic appointment at the Simón Bolívar Andean University to the Ministry of Education and Culture in the midst of political turmoil, he began a legislative project to standardize education, centralize administration, evaluate teachers, and make the nation-state "literate."[22] Known as the Plan Decenal de Educación del Ecuador (Ten-Year Educational Plan of Ecuador) scheduled to run from 2006 to 2015, some of the main policy goals included universal preschool, universalized education for students from first to tenth grade, "*erradicación*" (eradication) of illiteracy, bettering "*la calidad y equidad de la educación*" (educational quality and equity), and "*revalorización*" (revalorization) of the teaching profession (*Plan Decenal de Educación del Ecuador*, 5).[23] A picture of Vallejo dressed in an embroidered shirt linked to Indigenous populations appears in the Plan, foreshadowing how Vallejo would display markers of Indigeneity while shifting control of the school system away from the long-standing bilingual education directors.

During the Palacio administration, Vallejo hired Ariruma Kowii (Figure 2.2), a colleague from the university and a well-regarded Kichwa poet and academic, as assessor in the Ministry of Education (Montaluisa 2011). The two attempted to reorganize the school system as a part of Vallejo's reform efforts. They focused on establishing a Subsecretariat governing body that would supersede the DINEIB's long-standing control over the school system's administration and curriculum design. Subsecretariats reported directly to the minister and vice minister of education, so a new subsecretariat would extend the Ministry's current bureaucratic organization to oversee the long-standing bilingual education offices. In 2006, Vallejo and Kowii established, through Accord 425, the Subsecretaría de Educación de los Pueblos Indígenas (Subsecretariat of the Indigenous *Pueblos*' Education) as an organizational and administrative office of higher rank than DINEIB (Montaluisa, "Derogatoria"). Vallejo then named Kowii subsecretary.

At the time, DINEIB still had widespread support from Indigenous organizations, especially the powerful CONAIE. Montaluisa and others from the office immediately sounded the alarm, noting that a "war," as one interlocutor who worked for the new Subsecretariat offices put it, was occurring

Figure 2.2 Ariruma Kowii in 2010. This file is licensed under the Creative Commons Attribution-Share Alike 2.0 Generic license.

against DINEIB. Ultimately, Vallejo and Kowii agreed to change the name to the more ambiguous Subsecretariat of Intercultural Dialogue. Again, *intercultural* proved to be a meeting point of state control. Vallejo and Kowii still tried to restrict DINEIB's administrative body through the directors that it would appoint. However, organizational backing and support in the National Assembly allowed a committee of Indigenous peoples, most from DINEIB, to appoint another long-standing employee of the office, Mariano Morocho, to the position of DINEIB's director.[24]

But the 2006 election of Rafael Correa (to assume the presidency the following year) brought another salient era of cultural and linguistic recognition to the presidency, along with technocracy and severe repression. Correa, who identifies as *mestizo*, would speak briefly in Kichwa in public events, building on Roldós's example and signaling alignment with Indigenous efforts (Figure 2.3). An era of Indigenous-inclusive states extended beyond Ecuador with Bolivia's presidential election of 2005, where Aymara-identifying Evo Morales won. Correa also prioritized health and education, increasing state control over these areas and establishing new policies, hospitals, and schools. He was first elected with the support of Indigenous organizations and, ultimately, served until 2017.

After Correa's election, his relationship with Indigenous organizations, especially CONAIE, soured. For example, many directors decried Correa's

Figure 2.3 President Rafael Correa in Otavalo, Imbabura in 2011. This file is licensed under the Creative Commons Attribution-Share Alike 2.0 Generic license.

expansion of oil and mineral extraction (Riofrancos 2020). Morales saw similar dissent in Bolivia, where policies of extracting natural resources infringed on Indigenous territories and sovereignties and led to marches and blockades (Gustafson 2014, 81). Correa's political party prioritized a development model of "good living" (*buen vivir* in Spanish and *Sumak Kawsay* in Kichwa) that involved extracting natural resources and using that extraction to fund social programs and even some economic renumeration for vulnerable citizens. These policies generated protest by many Indigenous *pueblos* residing near mines or petroleum fields (Ortiz-T., 2016). In other words, they appropriated a Kichwa term to describe a national development plan, which has since become common policy throughout the Andes (Rodríguez Cruz 2018, 109; Quick & Spartz 2018).

Correa tended to have fervent fans and sharp critics throughout the country. Many people who identified as Indigenous were increasingly drawn to Correa's discourses of progress for all. Yet, he also ridiculed those who directed Indigenous movements, especially CONAIE, and attempted to curb their influence. Directors of organizations decried that Correa manipulated their cultural emblems for political gain, including his use of Kichwa in speeches.[25] His administration responded to protests with repression, including the persecution of political dissidents as "terrorists," among them Indigenous activists.[26]

Correa also set forth a rewriting of the Constitution to further remake Ecuador in the aftermath of years of presidential turnover. The 2008 Constitution saw major forms of intercultural recognition, such as the designation of Kichwa (and Shuar, another Indigenous language) as "*idiomas oficiales de relación intercultural*" (official languages of intercultural relation) and a commitment by the state to "*respetar*" ("respect") and "*estimular*" (stimulate) their "*conservación y uso*" (conservation and use).[27] Even the designation, however, conveyed the ambivalences and contradictions of Correa's administration. That designation fell short of what some Indigenous legislators proposed by demoting Kichwa (and Shuar) from "official language" to the modified "official language of intercultural relation" in a dramatic pre-dawn showdown between the president's political party and others.[28] Furthermore, during the height of the disagreement, Correa pushed hard against naming Kichwa as official with an argument about it being a minority language. He even called the possibility of recognizing Kichwa as official a "*novelería*," a superficial romanticization or novelty of what he deemed a small group of speakers who did not fully understand the repercussions of the act. Directors of Indigenous organizations rebuked the paternalist and racist nature of his comment.[29]

The 2008 Constitution saw disagreement around *plurinacionalidad*, too, as the president's party and the other major Indigenous organization, FENOCIN, wanted a less radical change and to focus solely on *interculturalidad* (Ortiz-T.

2016, 61). To the president's dismay and with the pressure of CONAIE and Indigenous mobilizers, Article 1 of the 2008 Constitution came to stipulate: "*El Ecuador es un Estado constitucional de derechos y justicia . . . intercultural, plurinacional*" (Ecuador is a constitutional state of rights and intercultural, plurinational justice). Plurinationality was threatening as a reference point for collective rights and obligations (Resina de la Fuente 2012, 61).

Bilingual education experienced similar contradictions and ambiguities during Correa's tenure. He regulated intercultural bilingual education more than, perhaps, any preceding administration, even as he increased investment in the school system. A primary route of this regulation was in 2009 when Kowii and Vallejo resumed efforts to supersede the National Directorate's authority. Correa signed Presidential Decree 1585 on February 18, 2009, that would "*apoyar y fortalecer*" (support and strengthen) the school system under a "*rectoría . . . del Estado a través de la autoridad educativa nacional*" (rectory . . . of the State through national educational authority). The decree used the very advances in the Constitution to justify the erosion of their authority, citing *interculturalidad* and *plurinacionalidad* as guiding principles for the change.[30] The decree spelled out the structure of the school system, establishing the Ministry of Education as the "*máxium instancia*" (maximum agency) and the Subsecretariat as the "*instancia de coordinación*" (coordinating body) between the intercultural bilingual school system and the National System. The National Commission of EIB, which had previously chosen directors, and the National Directorate would be demoted to the third and fourth governing bodies. The Decree stated that the previous bureaucratic chains of command, in which the DINEIB was at the top, "*quedan derogadas*" (are hereby repealed).

Vallejo was the second signer (after the president) of the Decree. The Decree specified that further details of the emergent organizational structure would be spelled out in Ministry Accords, and so Vallejo became a primary authority and author of the details for administering Indigenous schooling within the instruments of the state. CONAIE directors protested Correa's usurpation of the "autonomy" of EIB (Martínez-Novo 2014a, 107). DINEIB's offices—formerly in a house in the historic center of Quito—were moved to the Ministry of Education from that time on. The Minister of Education could then appoint a subsecretary to the office who would have authority over the director of the school system and the National Directorate offices.

One way that Kowii and others justified the change is based on criticism of the prior arrangement. Kowii (and others throughout the system during my research, including in the national offices) criticized a small group of CONAIE-affiliated planners, including Montaluisa, for years of choosing national and regional directorates while claiming the process was "democratic." Kowii also justified the change through notions of "autonomy" and the very-Indigenous-led designations in the 2008 Constitution, much as Correa did:[31]

Desde la visión de un sector de la dirigencia y de los técnicos de la Dineib, ellos ven el tema de la interculturalidad y la plurinacionalidad como una cuestión autónoma.	From a part of the DINEIB directorship's and technicians' vision, they see the theme of *interculturalidad* and *plurinacionalidad* as a question of autonomy.
Entonces, en este caso, el sistema intercultural está aparte de lo que sería el sistema educativo nacional.	So, in this case, the intercultural [school] system is apart from the national school system,
Que esté aparte gobernado por los propios indígenas, ¿no?	that it's separate, governed by Indigenous peoples themselves, no?
Y lo mismo en el tema de territorio.	So, the same for the theme of territory,
O sea, tener una autonomía territorial, por lo tanto también tener un sistema de gobierno propio de los pueblos indígenas....	Like having a territorial autonomy, and therefore also having a system of self-government by Indigenous *pueblos*....
Este sistema, lamentablemente, no rinde cuentas a nadie.	This system, sadly, [was] not accountable to anyone.
Entonces, creo que ahí hay un problema de visión de cómo pensamos el estado intercultural, plurinacional.	So, I think that there's a problem of vision there of how we think about the intercultural, plurinational state.
A mi me parece un error pensar en una autonomía territorial, cuando históricamente sobre todo en la sierra,	It seems to me like an error to think about territorial autonomy when, historically, above all in the Highlands,
el sistema colonial designó las tierras que no eran buenas a los pueblos indígenas.	the colonial system designated the land that wasn't good to the Indigenous *pueblos*.
Eran lugares marginales porque las mejores tierras se han quedado los hacendados.	They were marginal places because the *hacendados* (landowners) kept the best land.
Entonces, hacer una autonomía en unos espacios así tan deprimentes,	So, to make autonomy in those spaces that are so depressing,
creo que significaría condenarles a las poblaciones a un estado de pobreza.	I think that would mean condemning those populations to a state of poverty.

Definitions of autonomy, interculturality, and plurinationality are at the heart of who is allowed to direct bilingual education. Kowii flagged that, in conceiving of the school system, *autonomy* was understood by those who direct the school system as a metaphor that applies the governance of land to the governance of the school system. This, ultimately, raises questions of who governs and how authority is situated with other forms of state governance. He emphasized that, on the surface, state recognition, such as of interculturality and plurinationality, includes questions of autonomy. Yet, he said that, in practice, autonomy—including the redistribution of land—is not as promising as it seems for arrangements that are "depressing," "marginal," or "condemning...to a state of poverty," reiterating criticisms of the school system. He offered that bilingual education directors had maintained autonomy to avoid "accountability" and argued that autonomy is not inherently beneficial, especially depending on what is controlled and who is controlling it. He, thus, positioned the state and "accountability" as neutral, a contestable claim given the history of state violence and paternalism toward Indigenous peoples.

Further complicating the state's commitment to Indigenous autonomy, ministers of education since that time have tended to pick subsecretaries who respond more favorably to the Ministry's proposals. All have been members of Indigenous nationalities and, usually, with extensive experience in the school system.

When I was researching in the National Directorate from 2011 to 2013, the other directors of the school system had worked in hostile conditions for several years. But there was also a range of perspectives among employees of the National Directorate office. Some were in favor of the president, his social-spending and public-works projects, and what they saw as his disruption of some Indigenous directors' insular control of the school system. Others decried repressive policies, the dismantling of leftist political parties, and the expansion of state management. Many employees in the office had tenure and continued in the jobs they had held for more than a decade, even as they worked in contentious conditions. Ministry of Education officials forced others, including some dissidents with tenure, to retire soon after this research concluded. Others were employed on one- or two-year contracts and tended to have a more favorable stance toward the Correa administration's policies.

The forms of "accountability" that Kowii mentioned were seen throughout the rest of Correa's time in office and were promoted by Vallejo.[32] Although Vallejo left in 2010 following controversy around his echoing UNESCO's declaration of Ecuador as *"libre de analfabetismo"* (free of illiteracy), his reforms continued to be controversial, such as bringing Millennial Schools to Ecuador. The Ministry planned to construct up to eighty-eight centralized, technology-driven schools by 2015. In the process, officials shuttered hundreds of other schools, including intercultural bilingual community-based educational institutions. The Millennial Schools divided those who lived in rural areas, with some appreciating the disappearance of *unidocente* schools that have just one teacher for all grade levels, and others lamenting the erosion of rural jobs, short commute times to school, and local values.

In the evaluation of the school system that Vallejo began, the Ministry determined *"baja calidad y cobertura de los servicios educativos"* (low quality and coverage of educational services).[33] This designation concluded that Indigenous languages were rarely being used in schools. Correspondingly, the school system's budget increased in the Correa era. Each year, from 2007 to 2010, EIB's budget was between $1.1 million and $1.8 million. The Ministry established the Proyecto de Fortalecimiento de la Educación Intercultural Bilingüe (Project for the Strengthening of the Intercultural Bilingual Education) and budgeted $16 million from 2011 to 2014 as this research was underway. Some of the Project's goals included to "*socializar el eje de la interculturalidad y plurinacionalidad*" (socialize the axis of *interculturalidad* and *plurinacionalidad*)" make materials in Indigenous languages, train teachers, and audit and assess the school system.[34] From 2008 on, the school system's documentation shows several initiatives toward teaching Indigenous languages and more concentration on teaching English throughout the school system (Rodríguez Cruz 2018, 112). There were also fewer schools and personnel coordinating the school system. In 2011, when I first started research in the office, there were more than seventy employees.[35] In later visits, such as in 2015, there were half that number, in part due to relocations and retirements, some of them forced by the Ministry of Education.

Before he stepped down in 2010, Vallejo began efforts to pass an education reform law, which was ultimately ratified by the National Assembly in 2011. The Ley Orgánica de Educación Intercultural (LOEI, Organic Law of Intercultural Education), like the 10 Year Plan, continued efforts to centralize education, including emphasizing one National System of Education of which the "*Sistema de Educación Intercultural Bilingüe*" (Intercultural Bilingual Educational System) is a "*parte substancial*" (substantial part) (Article 77; see also 1, 78). The Law further affirmed the changes so contested by many in the system, including that the Subsecretariat contributed to the decentralization of the school system (from the National Directorate); a name change for the Subsecretariat to that of Intercultural Bilingual Education (Article 89); and a decree that assets of the National Directorate of Intercultural Bilingual Education belong to the Subsecretariat (p. 81). These designations, unquestionably, tightened state control.

The Subsecretariat was also tasked with "*transversalizar la interculturalidad en el Sistema*" (transversalizing interculturality in the System) (Article 89), which implies responsibility for making interculturality a part of the entire National System beyond the bilingual school system. What was before called the *Hispano* school system is now often described as intercultural, and the LOEI also states that "*al menos un idioma ancestral*" (at least one ancestral language) will be taught "*en todas las instituciones educativas que comprenden en Sistema Nacional de Educación*" (in all the educational institutions that comprise the National System of Education (p. 44), a change that would be sweeping if enacted.

During the years I was an ethnographer in the office, there was also turmoil caused by changing directors, employees, and roles, to which the Law contributed. The minister would suddenly replace subsecretaries depending on their actions, political dispositions, and alliances in the National Assembly. While, in the past, a select group in the office would determine the new director (the previous head of the school system, now the director of the coordinating offices that reported to the subsecretary), the subsecretary and others of political influence, such as politicians in the National Assembly, had far more control. At the regional level, the subsecretary would sometimes appoint new directors of those institutions, as well. Appointing directors from the centralized unit as part of the changes to the school system sometimes spurred backlash, such as when members of a regional organization enacted community justice on a new director by whipping him with a spiny *ortiga* plant.[36]

Many employees experienced employment uncertainty. Articles 25 and 27 of the LOEI stipulated the reconfiguring of bilingual education's offices as "*cuatro niveles de estion*" (four levels of management), one that is centralized and three with "*gestión deconcentrada*" (de-concentrated management) as zones, districts, and educative circuits, which altered the previous institutional structure of provincial directorates since the start of the school system. These arrangements meant that people currently working in bilingual education, including in the National Directorate, could be moved elsewhere and that some regional offices would close or be merged. Political and organizational changes thus led to employees' concerns about their future employment.

Conclusion

In examining the arrival of Indigenous education to national state offices, this history has shown how members of Indigenous *pueblos* and nationalities appealed to and protested against relatively progressive presidents as they gained state recognition for Kichwa and for bilingual education. They leveraged their experiences with institutions, educational planning, and national politics to present bilingual education in a way that gained acceptance by certain presidential administrations, accomplishing a nearly impossible feat. Yet, those presidents and other *mestizo*-identifying interlocutors' expectations, ignorance, or self-interest shaped the project that emerged. Ultimately, the policies adopted some of the epistemologies of modernist institutions even as they rejected most mainstream approaches to teaching literacy and policy that would assimilate students through Spanish.

Many of the challenges seen in establishing the school system were also linked to the emergence of national-scale organizing and policy. Around the time that Kichwa became an emblem of a more inclusive state in the late 1970s and early 1980s, Indigenous organizations were moving from local and regional aspirations to national ones. National goals, however, inevitably erased vast differences: Unified and Highland Kichwa came to represent many ways of speaking; policy initiatives were labeled intercultural (and not Indigenous) to be less threatening; and making a curriculum for use across the country required expediency and borrowing forms and ways of understanding the world in the limited number of preexisting textbooks.

At the heart of the difficulties for establishing and sustaining bilingual education is how autonomy is and is not situated within state institutions, how closely Indigenous education resembles predominant education, and who makes planning decisions. Over time, the very philosophies put forth by Indigenous organizations, such as plurinationality and interculturality, were used to justify the augmentation of state control. This recent history of the school system and those who direct it show how metalinguistic labor has been key for presenting proposals to others. Others have responded by confronting how the school system exists and who directs it. As this book's epilogue shows, many of these same challenges continue today.

3

Unified Kichwa?

Unions, Divisions, and Overlap in the Making of a Standardized Register

Introduction

Efforts to reclaim Indigenous languages often foreground standardization as a first step.[1] One reason is that standardization facilitates planning and prestige. For instance, efforts to agree upon linguistic norms, invent new words, and conventionalize an alphabet all aid in the production of schooling materials for use throughout a population, which helps to promote Indigenous languages and plan for their instruction. Yet, Luis Montaluisa, a Kichwa scholar who was instrumental in establishing the school system, writes that there was "no other alternative" but to standardize Kichwa (Montaluisa-Chasiquiza 2019, 367). His comments indicate that there were difficult decisions to make in unifying Kichwa.

Indeed, standardizing initiatives are increasingly contested by speakers. Language standardization in Ecuador, as is the case elsewhere, is double-edged: the act of making some linguistic forms "standard" means that other ways of speaking or writing are *not* standard and, usually, viewed as deficient or wrong in comparison (Gal 2006; De Korne & Weinberg 2021). Standardization can even result in reactions that exacerbate language shift, as many speakers are already embarrassed about speaking their languages and, upon standardization, have trepidation for doing so as speakers of a register not considered the correct or official one (Costa et al. 2017, 2; Hill 2002; Zavala 2019).

This chapter examines such challenges and builds on the presentation of Unified Kichwa in the introduction. I consider: which Kichwa forms are standardized and how are they used, understood, and contested? I argue that "unifying" Kichwa has involved, paradoxically, translating much Spanish into Kichwa and basing a unified variety on ways of speaking in select regions of Highland Ecuador. I begin with a teacher's concern about Unified Kichwa and consider its implications for current research on language standardization. I then describe the development of a standardized version of Kichwa and some forms that many Kichwa speakers attribute to it, such as alphabets, lexicon (especially calques—literal translations from Spanish), grammar, and ideologies about writing. This focus bolsters the arguments that many speakers make in their rejection of language standardization.

For linguistic anthropologists, this closer examination of linguistic forms, like vocabulary or verb endings, in addition to considering ideologies about them, may seem unusual. Recent research on language standardization focuses more on how people perceive and talk about standardized languages, such as how standardization is "best approached as an ideological phenomenon" (Gal 2017, 222) or through studying "social actors, [and] their ideologies and practices, rather than ... language per se" (Costa et al. 2017, 1). In this case, the overlap of words and grammar across languages and across registers—as well as how people react to standardization—sheds light on why standardized ways of speaking and writing are prominent and contentious in Indigenous language politics.

Though speakers may describe standardized registers as "neutral" or "anonymous" in some contexts, not invoking social categories like region, race, class, or gender (Woolard 2016, 25; De Costa et al. 2017; Gal 2006), research increasingly emphasizes that perceptions of neutrality are racialized and classed (Bonfiglio 2013; Flores & Rosa 2015; Rosa 2016). As raciolinguistics research in the United States has shown, listeners—especially white ones—affect the speech of speakers of nonstandardized registers (Rosa & Flores 2017; Alim 2016). For Indigenous languages, in general, and in Ecuador with Unified Kichwa, language standardization strongly indicates social position, yet also has dimensions of sounding "neutral." On the one hand, as I show in this chapter, planning for Unified Kichwa involved putting scientific theories about universal, unmarked languages into practice. On the other hand, speakers of Unified Kichwa are marked as different in several ways that are anything but neutral. To better understand these subtleties, I also diverge a bit from a goal in raciolinguistics research of "shift[ing] from privileging individual interactions and speaking practices" (Rosa & Flores 2017, 622), since in Ecuador how Kichwa is spoken in the presence of others who understand Kichwa offers insight into the construal of racialized, classed, and urbanized speaker identities that vary among speakers of the language family.

Though shared forms and meanings among registers of Kichwa and between Unified Kichwa and Spanish are part of the controversy surrounding language standardization, their overlap holds potential for undoing the double binds of public speech in Kichwa and appealing to different Kichwa-speaking audiences. Michel de Certeau (1984, 30) notes how, in describing the effects of modern institutions like workplaces on people, some ways of operating can be "in-between" the norms to yield an unexpected result from the situation. I conclude this chapter by focusing on one bilingual education director's linguistic example of speaking on behalf of the school system while using such practices. This director, Gloria, whose recent migration to the capital Quito positioned her in somewhat different ways from others in the office, combined forms from Unified Kichwa with those that were clearly from a different register. This strategy, which I call "offsetting," provided an alternative that Kichwa-speaking audience members appreciated. Such register variation in the same speech holds promise for animating an array of publics in Kichwa-speaking politics.

Perspectives on Language Standardization

Why is Unified Kichwa so contested? For one thing, Ruth, a teacher in Quito with whom I worked closely, expressed the common concern that standardized Kichwa was quite different from how she would speak. To her surprise, over her young life (she was in her mid-thirties), she encountered not only another way of speaking and writing Kichwa from when she was growing up in the rural hills of the Central Ecuadorian Andes but, also, learned that it had a different name. Ruth described the register of Kichwa that was common in her community as "Quechua." In her words, she later met "made-up Kichwa." Her comments convey an exasperation about language standardization that is similarly expressed by speakers of many different Indigenous language families. She also called attention to the need to better analyze what constitutes language standardization to understand people's concerns more fully. In her bright classroom, as her young students played outside at recess, she noted the following about named linguistic varieties:[2]

Yo digo ¿de dónde sacan que nosotros hablamos Kichwa?	I say, from where did they come up with that we speak Kichwa?
Nosotros hablamos Quechua, en Bolívia y en Perú [también].	We speak Quechua, in Bolivia and in Peru, [too].
No sé a quién se le ocurrió quitar todo eso porque nosotros hablamos en Quechua.	I don't know to whom it occurred to take it all away because we speak in Quechua.
En las comunidades hablamos en Quechua.	In the communities we speak in Quechua.
No sé porque ahora dicen que hablamos en Kichwa.	I don't know why they now say that we speak in Kichwa.
No sé quién hizo Kichwa.	I don't know who made up Kichwa.
Más antes sabían decir, "¿en qué idioma hablas?"	Years ago it was customary to say, "In what language do you speak?"
"En Quechua," yo sabía decir.	"In Quechua," I used to say.
Sabían decir estos mashis mismos, "nosotros somos Quechuas." Así era.	Those same *mashis* [directors of bilingual education], used to say, "We are Quechuas." That's how it was.

Like cases of language standardization elsewhere (e.g., Guerrettaz 2019; Lane et al. 2017), Unified Kichwa has been divisive and many lament that they cannot understand it (Wroblewski 2021). Here, Ruth made a distinction between "Kichwa" and "Quechua" and noted that she did not know why "*they* now say *we* speak Kichwa." I have never heard another person in Ecuador say that "Kichwa/Quichua"—an orthographic distinction that I briefly describe in this chapter—used to be called "Quechua," and records indicate the use of the word Quichua. However, it is likely that Ruth heard talk of Quechua as she was growing up during the 1980s. Quechua is the common name in Bolivia and Peru for varieties of the language family and may have made its way to her region of birth as Kichwa-identifying linguists and educational planners were promoting the unification of ways of writing Quechua throughout the Andes. An early Ecuadorian constitution (1945) also described the language as Quechua, perhaps also drawing from the name of the language family in other countries.[3]

While most Kichwa speakers in Ecuador use the word "Kichwa" today to refer to the language, one sometimes hears *runa shimi* (human speech), *ñukanchik shimi* (our speech), or *yanka shimi* (worthless speech), the last being a testament to years of marginalization. After colonial agents invaded Peru, they likely derived the name Quechua from mis-hearing speakers of a regional variety refer to *qheswa simi* (valley speech), adapting "valley" for the language's name (Mannheim 1991, 6). Before the Spanish arrived, there was no fixed name for ways of speaking across the Incan Empire. The most common referent was *runa shimi*, a more general term that may have referred to all talk by people (Cerrón-Palomino 1987; Mannheim 1991, 6). There have been a plurality of names for the language family over time and across regions, as well as in Spanish and Kichwa.

Ruth's description teaches us several important lessons about Kichwa as standardized and about language standardization more generally. First, her description divided Kichwa-speaking membership into those who regulate and promote Kichwa as "they" and everybody else or "communities." She questioned "to whom it occurred to take it all away," indicating division and hierarchy attached to standardizing Kichwa over the use of other forms. She aligned "they" with the Kichwa term *mashi* ("friend," "comrade," or "colleague,") assimilating *mashi* to Spanish grammatical categories with the plural suffix -*s*. Her description is not unusual. For Kichwa speakers, *mashi* has become a word emblematic of Unified Kichwa and those who make it, such as bilingual education directors. This specific reference is probably why Ruth used *mashi* while speaking Spanish: as a means to invoke *Unified* Kichwa; to link those who developed it—Indigenous professionals in charge of the school system—with refinement;

and to, simultaneously, critique authority. The brief history of Unified Kichwa in this chapter, however, shows that many of the earlier standardizing efforts came from non-Indigenous-identifying academics and missionaries, which ultimately shaped the possibilities for language planning.

Second, the term *mashi* is not common to all registers of Kichwa, which tells us more about where Unified Kichwa forms have come from. *Mashi* is commonly used in Imbabura Kichwa, spoken in the Northern Highland province with the prosperous artisan town of Otavalo just two hours from Quito, which is located in the province of Pichincha (See Figure 3.1). Ruth's use of *mashi* conveys a predicament of Unified Kichwa more generally: many forms associated with it are also identifiable with Kichwa as spoken in parts of the Northern and Central Ecuadorian Highlands.

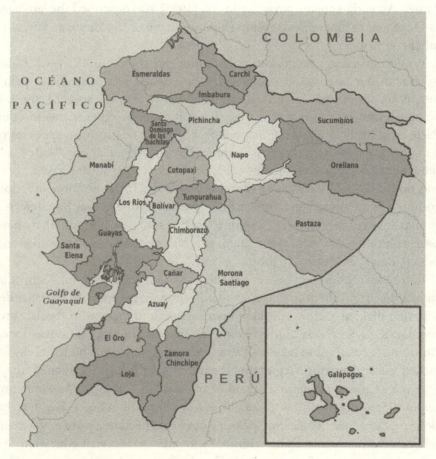

Figure 3.1 Map of Ecuador. This file is licensed under the Creative Commons Attribution-Share Alike 2.5 Generic license: https://creativecommons.org/licenses/by-sa/2.5/deed.en.

Some efforts to standardize languages aim to make a variety that is "nobody's spoken language" and thus less politicized, as is the case of Basque (Urla et al. 2017, 26). And, other times, academic claims are incorrect that such registers are neutral, as Montaluisa (2019, 364) critiques in the academic study of Ecuadorian Kichwa. Planning meetings are rarely unshaped by the language use of those who plan.

For example, in unification meetings in the late 1970s and early 1980s, Kichwa speakers from Imbabura were overrepresented (Hornberger & King 1998). Imbabura is the region with the second highest number of Kichwa speakers. Bilingual education planning and research also drew much from Kichwa as spoken in the Central Highland province of Chimborazo, where the largest number of Kichwa speakers reside. This overrepresentation also has to do with the demographics of the National Directorate offices and of academic and professional work more generally. There are more Indigenous professionals who are from and live in those regions, including people with degrees who are interested in Kichwa linguistics. Most employees in the National Directorate, and most employees dedicated to language policy, teacher workshops, or curriculum planning, have historically been Kichwa speakers from these two provinces.

Some even view these registers, especially from Imbabura, as "high prestige," perhaps because Imbabura Kichwa speakers are more commonly viewed as successful artisans (Muysken 2019, 211). However, Imbabura Kichwa has undergone immense and calquing from Spanish (Fauchois 1988; Gómez-Rendón 2008). A third point to take away from Ruth's comments is that *mashi* is an example of how Unified Kichwa maintains lexical "purity" from Spanish by avoiding the use of Spanish words or particles. However, instead of borrowing Spanish words, many references of the forms associated with Unified Kichwa have been *translated* from Spanish. *Mashi* is an example of this process. On the one hand, *mashi* is a Quechua word, as it was likely adapted from a Bolivian and Peruvian Quechua particle *masi*, meaning an association among people in a shared activity (Howard 2008, 16). On the other hand, with *mashi*'s use in bilingual education in Ecuador, its reference has shifted—is calqued—to be roughly equivalent to the reference of *compañero* (comrade or colleague) in Spanish. *Mashi* is an example of how a pan-Quechua lexeme, now associated with Unified Kichwa, has a parallel meaning from Spanish. *Compañero* is a word long used for leftist organizing in Spanish (Howard 2008, 16). In the National Directorate offices, *mashi*'s use tended to coincide more with *compañero* as used in office Spanish that would translate to English as "colleague."

Fourth, *mashi* is a word now widely known even by some *mestizo*-identifying citizens, indicating how Unified Kichwa calques can become representative of that register and even emblems of the entire language family. Ruth expressed her concern (as further examined in Chapter 6) that Kichwa consisted of words like *mashi*, which she saw as obscuring immense linguistic diversity in state-authorized multilingual communication. For Kichwa speakers, *mashi* often indexes Unified Kichwa, Imbabura Kichwa, and/or elitism. Especially for those in state offices and speakers of Unified Kichwa, *mashi* also serves as an honorific to maintain a respectful distance toward an interlocutor (see also Wroblewski 2012, 78). Even former president Rafael Correa routinely used the word, self-descriptively, as the handle of his active Twitter account (@MashiRafael). As president, he would also speak, selectively, in Kichwa in many political speeches despite not self-identifying as Indigenous. His use shows how *mashi* signifies Indigeneity and the intercultural presence of Kichwa when embedded in communication in Spanish. These examples illustrate how such forms change depending on how, when, and by and for whom they are used.

Ultimately, while Ruth lamented a change in the name of the language and the arrival of Unified Kichwa, I believe that she was getting at a more troubling concern: such ways of speaking Kichwa are shaped by the largely *mestizo*-identifying and Spanish-speaking world of educational degrees, professionally waged labor, and feelings of individualism that many Kichwa speakers describe as foreign (see Chapter 4). Research has shown how Unified Kichwa has emerged from "intellectual layers of the *mestizo* world" (Muysken 2019, 380; Floyd 2004; King 2001). As Ruth shifted from describing speech in Quechua to how directors would say "we are Quechua," she showed that many speakers see ways of communicating as part of who they are (Ennis 2020; Montaluisa 2019). In the quest to demonstrate a language distinct from Spanish, but with the competing (political) motivation of making a version of Kichwa that could be recognized and planned for, planners tended to exclude signifiers of many Kichwa registers that are vastly different from Spanish, and speakers feel this difference.

In the same conversation after lamenting Kichwa as imposed, Ruth further distinguished how she saw "Kichwa" as linked to standardization. She expressed her disagreement in shorthand as *unificado* (unified) with concern that speaking it would reduce linguistic diversity to a single, emblematic register:

Yo no estoy de acuerdo con el [Kichwa] unificado porque de aquí a un rato toditas [las maneras de hablar]	I don't agree with the Unified [Kichwa] because from here on, in a while all [the ways of speaking]
se van a perder porque vamos a hablar toditos en [Kichwa] unificado.	are going to be lost because we're all going to speak in Unified [Kichwa].

Ruth worried about *intra*-language shift in standardization, especially away from contrastive registers across the nation-state. She equated invention with efforts to *unify* many ways of speaking into a (newly) named, single, static language ("Kichwa" in the previous interview excerpt).

Where Did Unified Kichwa Start? Early Years of State Policy

Ruth, in her comments above, lamented language planners while not knowing precisely who changed Kichwa or when it changed:

"From where did they get that we speak Kichwa?"
"I don't know to whom it occurred to take it all away."
"I don't know why they *now* say that we speak in Kichwa."
"I don't know who made up Kichwa."
"Years ago . . ., that's how it was."

Ruth's uncertainty about Unified Kichwa's origins is common, as various meetings and numerous actors over several decades, often from different institutions, have contributed to Unified Kichwa.

A major pathway to standardization was the legislative struggle that earned constitutional recognition. Spurred in part by Kichwa organizers Dolores Cacuango's and Tránsito Amaguaña's networks of activists in the northern highland region of Cayambe who sought to teach students in Kichwa, the 1945 Constitution named Spanish "*el idioma oficial*" (the official language) while specifying that "*Se reconocen el quechua y demás lenguas aborígenes como elementos de la cultural nacional*" (Quechua and other aboriginal languages are recognized as elements of the national culture) (Article 5). Luis Montaluisa (2019, 325) sees this constitution as significant in also recognizing schooling for Kichwa, since the constitution stipulated that "*En las escuelas establecidas en las zonas de predominante población india, se usará, además del castellano, el quechua o la lengua aborigen respectiva*" (In schools established in zones of predominant Indian population, people will use, in addition to Spanish, Quechua or the respective aboriginal language) (Article 143, Number 8). That constitution, however, was replaced the following year, eliminating the legal basis for linguistic and educational gains.

In the 1979 constitution, which also granted universal suffrage, Spanish was again named official.[4] In the years following some major efforts to standardize Kichwa, the constitution declared that "*se reconocen el quichua y demás lenguas aborígenes como integrantes de la cultura nacional*" (Quichua and other aboriginal languages are recognized as components of the national culture) (Article 1). Speaking to Ruth's point, the official characterization of the language family was now "Quichua" (a change from "Quechua" in 1945). That 1979 constitutional recognition resulted from and bolstered efforts across Bolivia, Ecuador, and Peru to plan for policy and schooling in Quechua. In the 1970s and 1980s, state planners and academics (then mainly non-Indigenous-identifying professionals known as Indigenists, or *Indigenistas*) began to develop and promote a pan-Andean writing system as they considered how to bring Indigenous peoples further into state "modernization." They emphasized standardized registers and alphabets as steps toward unification. As Ruth mentioned with her emphasis on Quechua, one source of Unified Kichwa is from cross-Andean policy and politics. Ecuadorian linguists and educational planners had a referent in Peru, where Quechua was named an official language in the 1975 Constitution, though it was repealed by the end of the decade.

Another source of Unified Kichwa is that, beginning in the early 1970s, Consuelo Yánez Cossío, a linguist and faculty member at Quito's Pontifical Catholic University, carried out research on Kichwa phonology in Colta (a canton with many Kichwa speakers in the Central Highland province of Chimborazo) and in Otavalo (in the Northern Highland province Imbabura). Based on her research, she and a colleague at the University elaborated, perhaps, the first textbook and systematic pedagogy for teaching Kichwa (Montaluisa 2019, 356). This textbook was made for and used in higher education for learners at the university who did not speak Kichwa. It continues in use today and was one of the first efforts to standardize Kichwa for schooling. That pedagogy, and its standards for writing, became a reference point for elaborating Unified Kichwa in the years that followed. Yánez Cossío's work, her involvement in national policymaking, including later becoming the minister of education and culture, and her work with *mestizo*-identifying linguists and young Kichwa speakers all contributed to the register that emerged. Like her research, the unification in that textbook also drew heavily from the Highland Kichwa spoken in those regions.

Despite cross-country unification goals, the Quechua languages in general, and registers of Kichwa more specifically, are widely different. Mannheim (1991) documents a major division across the Andes between Central Peruvian Quechua and "periphery" varieties of Quechua, the latter including Southern Peruvian, Bolivian, and Ecuadorian varieties. Central Peruvian registers of Quechua are largely unintelligible from Southern Peruvian Quechua, and Central Peruvian Quechua speakers do not necessarily find those varieties to be mutually intelligible, either (see also Luykx et al. 2016). Ecuadorian varieties of Kichwa have syntactic and phonological differences from Southern Peruvian Quechua, and they range in their mutual intelligibility. There is significant variation among ways of speaking in Ecuador, especially between Andean and Amazonian varieties (King 2001; Uzendoski 2008; Wroblewski 2014).

Sociolinguist Marleen Haboud (2004, 70) further divides Highland Ecuadorian varieties of Kichwa to those of the Northern Andes (provinces of Imbabura and Pichincha, where Quito is located); Central Andes (including provinces of Bolívar, Cotopaxi, Chimborazo, and Tungurahua); and Southern Andes (provinces of Azuay, Cañar, and Loja). Amazonian varieties, too, have further regional divisions (Grzech, Schwarz, & Ennis 2019), and Montaluisa (2019) divides them into North, Central, and South, as well. Based on years of experience working with bilingual education employees across Ecuador, Montaluisa writes that, though fewer differences appear in the study of Kichwa linguistics, there is the vast *perception* across Kichwa speakers that major differences exist. Questions of intelligibility are asymmetrical, and speakers of Central Highland varieties profess to understand speakers of other registers well but not vice versa (Montaluisa 2019, 205). Ruth is a speaker of a Central Highland register and is also conversant in Unified Kichwa. She has relatives, however, with less schooling and who continue living in Central Highland Ecuador. They have struggled with various aspects of Unified Kichwa (Limerick 2020).

What Is Unified Kichwa?

Given the difficulty of streamlining and bounding language use, a standardized linguistic variety is more an ideal than an actuality (Silverstein 1996; Urla 2012). Linguistic anthropologist Asif Agha (2005) focuses on how registers manifest when speech forms or repertoires cohere, and wider groups of speakers come to view them as linked to social roles or identities. Register names, such as "Unified Kichwa," emerge out of such processes of sameness and differentiation (Gal & Irvine 2019; Reyes 2017). Speakers identify contrastive sets of forms with identities and register names (Gal 2017), such as how *mashi* is one of many forms that stand apart for Ruth as indexing Unified Kichwa and its elaborators. As Ruth's example showed, *mashi* is often associated with both Unified Kichwa and with Imbabura Kichwa, and so the same form can be tied to multiple registers.

Anthropologist Michael Wroblewski (2012) spells out some areas in which linguists have elaborated signifiers of Unified Kichwa: orthography and its relationship to sounds, lexicon, and morphological suffixes. I add to these syntax and its importance for writing. These areas clarify how the standardization of forms continues and contrasts across registers.

Orthography

Standardizing a language requires writing, and alphabets are a primary focus of standardization. For languages with a Roman orthography, letters are perhaps the most easily identifiable markers of standardized registers in written form for several reasons. First, as opposed to the innumerable words and grammatical forms of a spoken language, a small number of letters (twenty or so in the Unified Kichwa alphabet) facilitates a more stable and finite set of markers that readers can identify with a standardization project. Second, though standardized alphabets are sometimes wholly different from other alphabets, the Unified Kichwa alphabet, like the Spanish alphabet, is based on Roman orthography but includes some letters that rarely occur in Spanish (such as *k*). As a result, readers immediately notice contrastive letters in texts, and this can even turn readers off from reading (Limerick 2018). Third, alphabets account for sounds, including register variation. Alphabets, and their connections to sounds, inevitably prioritize some ways of speaking over others regardless of planners' aims toward neutrality.

A brief history of the current Unified Kichwa alphabet better demonstrates who decided on key elements of standardization and when and why they did so. From the time of its arrival in Ecuador in 1953, US missionary linguists of the organization Summer Institute of Linguistics (SIL) contributed to writing in Kichwa. The missionaries focused on translating the Bible to Kichwa while using Spanish graphemes to transcribe regional Kichwa varieties for reading materials (Montaluisa 1980b, 126): *a, b, c, ch, d, f, g, h, i, j, l, ll, m, n, ñ, p, q, r, s, t, u, y, z*. Historian Franklin Barriga López (1992, 72) notes that the Summer Institute of Linguistics' goal in Ecuador was "global preparation" of Indigenous communities through bilingual education, literacy, and training Indigenous teachers. Bilingual education scholar and advocate Matthias Abram (1992, 63) describes SIL's goals differently: as assimilatory practices for the Spanish-speaking world. Though any offering of Kichwa-based education was somewhat progressive at the time, Kichwa was a language of transition in SIL's educational institutions. Indigenous languages were to be eliminated from schooling by the third grade.

In the 1970s and 1980s, state planners, academics, and some missionaries throughout the Andes sought to use a unified alphabet across all Indigenous languages to promote "science" and "order," which they said could ameliorate stigmas around not being able to read in Indigenous languages (Weber 2005). These efforts tended to contrast with on-the-ground initiatives throughout Central and South America, such as missionary work that used the Spanish alphabet to more closely represent local ways of speaking. For instance, at the First Seminar on Bilingual Education in 1973, Consuelo Yánez Cossío and her research team at the Pontifical Catholic University emphasized a unified alphabet as essential for researching and understanding the phonology of the language (Montaluisa 2019, 258), and which contrasted with the Spanish alphabet that missionaries (and others) were using throughout the country.

That collective at the University gave way to the establishment of the Centro de Investigación de la Educación Indígena (Center of Research on Indigenous Education, "the Center") (Von Gleich 2006, 49), where linguists began to write the aforementioned pedagogy for learning to read in Kichwa. The Center's program adopted a version of the alphabet that was officialized in an earlier conference in Bolivia in 1954 as Pan-Andean for Quechua and Aymara: *a*, *ch*, *i*, *j*, *k*, *k'*, *l*, *ll*, *m*, *n*, *ñ*, *p*, *p'*, *r*, *s*, *sh*, *t*, *ts*, *u*, *w*, *y*, reserving "Spanish" letters *b*, *d*, *g*, and *f* for Spanish loanwords. In Ecuador, they saw the united letters as a way to showcase Kichwa as an "international" language consistent across the state borders (Montaluisa 1980b, 126). The Center's language planners in Ecuador further promoted the Unified Kichwa graphemes to reject the Spanish alphabet, which they linked to religious assimilation and Spanish.

The unified letters, however, were not without controversy, and they were soon changed. While the Center's planners included mainly *mestizo*-identifying linguists with a few members of the Kichwa nationality, other planning meetings in the late 1970s and early 1980s included largely Kichwa representatives from different parts of the country. Montaluisa describes immediate criticisms that surfaced among those attendees for standardizing letters, including, for example, that *k*, *y*, and *w* are "*letras gringas . . . no son letras quichuas*" (gringo letters . . . they are not Quichua letters) and they're employed to "*hacer que consumamos más wisky y tabacos king*" (make us consume more whiskey and King tobacco) (Montaluisa 1980b, 128). For many Kichwa speakers, the ways of writing that the Summer Institute of Linguistics missionaries used had become normative. While for some individuals, letters like *k*, *w*, and *y*—not in the earlier alphabet—pointed to making Kichwa a more international, scientific alphabet, for others they indicated Western ways of writing and capitalist consumption.

After a series of meetings in 1980, mainly Kichwa-speaking planners voted to eliminate several letters that were more closely linked to Spanish, such as *b* and *d*, and they also voted not to include letters that might index English, like *k* and *w*. The elimination of *b* and *d* constituted ongoing "unification" to condense voiced and unvoiced stops to single letters that formerly represented only the unvoiced version (Montaluisa 1980b), with those sounds now merged into *p* and *t*, respectively. Although voiced and unvoiced stops are perceived as separate phonemes (that distinguish between different words) in most Kichwa registers, they are often allophones of the same phoneme in Imbabura Kichwa (Gómez Rendón 2007, 483). This means that the erasure of those significant differences modeled even the *alphabet* more closely on Imbabura Kichwa. They established the first official alphabet, rejecting *k* while still reducing the number of letters: *a, c, ch, h, i, j, l, ll, m, n, ñ, p, q, r, s, sh, t, ts, u, y, z* (Chango Juarez 2007, 11).

In the late 1990s, new talks began about the alphabet. At that time, nearly all Kichwa language planners were Kichwa speakers themselves, and most were bilingual education employees who had completed high school or other credentials. According to an interview with one employee in the National Directorate, materials were coming out of various bilingual education regional directorates with contrasting orthographies. He said that at that time they needed a unified alphabet "*de una manera urgente*" (in an urgent way) to produce national schooling materials and for administering Kichwa proficiency exams.[5]

The Second Meeting for the Unification of the Kichwa Alphabet, following the meetings in 1980, was held on July 21, 1998, and included members of Indigenous organizations, DINEIB and regional bilingual education office employees, Kichwa and *mestizo*-identifying linguists, and teachers (Quishpe Lema 2013). The Indigenous organization Confederación de Nacionalidades Indígenas del Ecuador (Confederation of Indigenous Nationalities of Ecuador, CONAIE), to which many in the National Directorate claim affiliation, was especially influential at the meeting. They and other organizations had already printed materials with contrastive alphabets, and no one wanted their materials deemed irrelevant in the meeting's aftermath. For example, the Consejo de Pueblos y Organizaciónes Evangélicas del Ecuador (FEINE, Council of Pueblos and Evangelical Organizations of Ecuador) is said to have been worried about stacks of Bibles printed with the Spanish alphabet that would no longer matter, with FEINE representatives concerned that they might have to destroy the Bibles.[6]

Ultimately, the graphemes selected were: *a, ch, i, j, k, l, ll, m, n, ñ, p, r, s, sh, t, u, w,* and *y*, with *ts* and *z* sometimes needed for sounds in words remaining from pre-Incan languages. This alphabet was a version of the Bolivian 1954 standardized alphabet for all Andean Indigenous languages that, in theory, could be used across Quechua/Kichwa-speaking territories. Two significant changes from the 1980 Ecuadorian alphabet included: the adoption of *k*, which replaced multiple graphemes, including *c*, *g*, *q*, and in some circumstances *j*; and the implementation of *w* and *y* for diphthongs, for instance, *guagua* became *wawa*. The new alphabet had overlapping letters with the previous one, but some spellings changed. In 2004, there was one more change made when those of the Academy of the Kichwa Language met and decided on using the grapheme *h* in place of *j* to further distinguish the Kichwa alphabet from Spanish and to draw from standards for Indigenous languages across the continent, among other reasons (Chango Juarez 2007, 19).

The overlap and contrast of "new" Kichwa letters with others has brought challenges for present-day readers, as Ruth indicated. The following quote demonstrates these challenges. Yolanda, a Kichwa speaker who worked in the National Directorate for years, told me how changes such as *k* offered a practical difficulty:[7]

[El alfabeto de Kichwa unificado] me dio mucha pena de lo que ahí se perdió,	[The latest alphabet] made me so sad because of what was lost there,
muchísimos vocabularios que había.	many vocabularies that there were.
Por ejemplo, la k unió la g, la c, [a veces la j,] y la q.	For example, the *k* united the *g*, the *c*, [sometimes the *j*] and the *q*.
Fusionan las tres letras.	The three letters are fused.
En esas tres letras, habían diferencias de vocabularios,	With those three letters, there were vocabulary differences
que no eran alófonos. Eran significados diferentes.	that weren't allophones. They were different meanings.
No es lo mismo killa y jilla,	It's not the same to say *killa* and *jilla*
porque killa es la luna y jilla es la pereza....	because *killa* is "moon" and *jilla* is "laziness."...
En el momento que reduce el alfabeto en una lengua,	In the moment that reduces the alphabet in a language,
no está ayudando a fortalecer la lengua.	it's not helping to strengthen the language.
Está fortaleciendo la eliminación de una lengua.	It's strengthening the elimination of a language.

The new alphabet shared letters with the Spanish alphabet, but other letters were condensed and eliminated, resulting in changed spellings (Wroblewski 2012, 75) based more closely on Imbabura Kichwa sound patterns. Such changes systematically altered literacy in Kichwa even as the unification project continued. Since the changes are harder for many to read, newer official letters have contributed to reader frustration with Unified Kichwa.

Lexicon

As the *mashi* example shows, expanding Kichwa's lexicon has been key to making Unified Kichwa, and speakers often associate neologisms with the register. Luis Montaluisa (1980a, 99) estimates that at the time of the 1980 alphabet meeting, between 10 and 20 percent of words in most Kichwa registers were Spanish loanwords. That number has certainly increased in the forty years since the meeting, which has yielded a challenge for Kichwa speakers who want to avoid loanwords like *libru* (from *libro* "book" in Spanish) or *pizarrun* (from *pizarrón,* "blackboard") (Montaluisa 1980a, 105). In the years following the 1980 alphabet meeting, various actors published dictionaries that attempted to invent new Kichwa words in light of shift to Spanish (King 2001, 42).

For example, at the aforementioned Center of Research on Indigenous Education, Montaluisa himself led this effort during the late 1970s and early 1980s. Their strategies to *"enriquecer"* (enrich) the vocabulary included taking words from less spoken regional varieties and aiming for their use elsewhere, looking for now uncommon words in old dictionaries and by conducting interviews with elders, looking for older meanings of words whose references had changed, and reasoning new words based on the semantics of others (Montaluisa 1980a, 105–8). Authors borrowed loanwords from Spanish as a last resort and sometimes calqued or translated forms and references from Spanish into Kichwa.

Another noteworthy time period for inventing new Kichwa words started in 2003 when National Directorate employees and nine directors of bilingual education regional directorates launched a project that focused on Kichwa education.[8] The *Kukayu* textbooks (see Chapter 5), for which many new words were coined, came out of this initiative (MOSEIB 2013, 19). Those textbooks became notorious for how difficult they were for people to read, a challenge compounded by the many words readers had never seen before. I routinely heard teachers comment that linguists must have made up words haphazardly, using whatever ideas occurred to them. That said, many *Kukayu* textbooks had mini-dictionaries in their last pages that listed uncommon words. This project also established the short-lived Academia de la Lengua Kichwa (Academy of the Kichwa Language), responsible for *"normatizar y estandarizar el desarrollo y uso de la Lengua Kichwa"* (normatizing and standardizing the development and use of the Kichwa language) (Academia de la Lengua Kichwa n.d., 2). One of its responsibilities was to make and analyze new terms. Most of its members were employees of the National Directorate or regional bilingual education offices, and its main council included the national director of bilingual education, in addition to a president of the academy (Academia de la Lengua Kichwa n.d., 3).

The elaboration of dictionaries also contributed to the development of additional neologisms. The Ministry of Education sponsored dictionary workshops, such as for the principal one used by school system, *Kichwa Yachakukkunapa Shimiyuk Kamu* (Ministerio de Educación 2009, 13). My experience was that many who used this dictionary found it to have more unknown neologisms than others, though it was available for free as a PDF online, making it accessible.

Morphology

Another important area of Unified Kichwa is how planners have attempted to standardize grammar, such as suffixes. Actors from the Center of Research on Indigenous Education, Academy of the Kichwa Language, the National Directorate of Intercultural Bilingual Education, and independent Kichwa academics have published grammar tables and lessons in books or dictionaries over the years. For instance, the aforementioned dictionary lists and defines verb conjugations, tenses, and other infixes and suffixes (Ministerio de Educación 2009). There is also a small number of independent Kichwa linguists who publish similar books. As with vocabulary, there are various disseminators of sometimes-inconsistent grammatical norms, even as the school system is the most authoritative publisher.

Wroblewski (2012, 79) describes standardized morphemes as a "constant source of confusion" for Kichwa speakers in the Amazonian province of Napo. He lists examples of Unified Kichwa morphemes and contrasts them with an Amazonian or Lowland variety spoken in the region of Napo:

	UK	Napo	Examples		English gloss
Progressive tense infix	-ku-	-w-	kallpakuni	kallpawni	"I am running."
Locative suffix	-pi-	-y	wasipi	wasiy	"at home"

Two of the five morphemes in the original chart are listed in this adaptation. When compared to Kichwa as spoken in Napo, these Unified Kichwa forms (and two others of the five) offer significant contrast. These Unified Kichwa forms are also common to most varieties of Highland Kichwa in Northern Andean Ecuador, which shows the extent to which Unified Kichwa prioritizes certain regional speakers over others. These morphemes are thus examples of register bivalency, where many standardized forms are also used in other varieties of Highland Kichwa, in addition to the calquing that occurs across languages, where Spanish grammar is translated and paralleled in Kichwa. Chapter 5 further considers translation and shows how standardized Spanish syntax shapes expectations for how to write or translate in Kichwa, yielding dissent as Kichwa grammar is made more equivalent to Spanish and other common ways of speaking are judged as "incorrect."

Some of the morphemes that are less common in Unified Kichwa are even those that are closely tied to Kichwa philosophies for understanding the world. For example, Kaarhus (1989, 184) provides an insightful example from Imbabura Kichwa with *-ntin* and *-wan*, noting that *-ntin* is falling out of use. Each morpheme expresses "accompaniment," but the conceptions of what that entails are different.

> Ñukaka wambra-***wan*** purini
> I   adolescent-**with**   walk (first person, singular, present tense)
>
> "I go with the adolescent" in a more casual sense, as in walking together or having bumped into the person along the way and then continued and perhaps parted ways before the going was complete.
>
> Ñukaka wambra-***ntin*** purini
> I   adolescent-**with**   walk (first person, singular, present tense)
>
> "I go with the adolescent" in that they do something collectively, or as in walking together or having bumped into the person along the way and then continued and returned together.

The latter example, *-ntin*, is a more transformative category that implies "togetherness" in a deeper sense. It refers to an action and even people who are united, who "belong to the same category" (Almeida 1979, 729, cited in Kaarhus 1989, 186). It expresses relations "outside of the possibility of expression" in Spanish (Kaarhus 1989, 188). But use of *-wan* is becoming more common in Imbabura Kichwa and, subsequently, in Unified Kichwa as most speakers of Unified Kichwa are bilingual in Spanish and tend to speak that language more routinely. It is one example of how forms and ideas more like those in Spanish are multiplying in Kichwa (Gómez-Rendón 2008). Unified Kichwa depends upon such commensuration, such as more frequent use of particles like *-wan*, even replacing case markers from Kichwa beyond that of *-ntin*. These are the kinds of grammatical expressions that demonstrate changes in social worlds and further justify Ruth's concerns.

Syntax and Writing

Routinely in the National Directorate, as some directors explained the importance of "writing well," their comments would often compare dialectal variation in Spanish with that of Kichwa. They emphasized that Kichwa, like Spanish, should have one correct way to write. For instance, at the translation workshop that I consider in Chapter 5, one bilingual education coordinator focused on the rules of writing in his directions for attendees:

Para la escritura tienen que observarse ciertas reglas.	For writing people have to observe certain rules.
Lo mismo en el Kichwa, también tenemos esas reglas.	The same [happens] in Kichwa. We also have those rules.
Hablamos con los dialectos.	We speak with dialects.
Para escribir ya hay un Kichwa unificado.	For writing, there's now a unified Kichwa.

In the comments, a director equated Unified Kichwa with grammatical rules for writing. His remarks demonstrate how planning has standardized goals and how writing tends to be an important conveyor of those goals. His comments make Kichwa equivalent with other languages in written form.

At first glance, efforts to unify Kichwa syntax and writing defy influence from Spanish. A legal document from the school system, *Ministry of Education Accord 289*, declares that any teacher certified as proficient in Kichwa "*estructura las oraciones de acuerdo a la sintaxis de la lengua indígena*" (structures sentences according to the syntax of the Indigenous language) and "*emplea la ortografía de su respectiva lengua*" (employs the orthography of [the examinee's] respective language [and not Spanish's alphabet]). However, as the workshop speaker demonstrated in framing Kichwa through Spanish, "the same" "rules" from Spanish apply to standardization in Kichwa. Many Kichwa speakers who do not have extensive Unified Kichwa experience use somewhat more fluid syntax distinguished by case markers, rather than a rigid SOV word order, which, as the most long-standing syntactic ordering in many Kichwa registers, became a rule in its standardization. Even though the accord focuses on Indigenous languages, stipulating a word order also imposes an ideology about fixity onto Kichwa, as its case markers render word order less important. For those who speak other varieties of Kichwa and have less experience with standardization, the new norms can be especially difficult and contribute to frustration.

Gloria, "Kichwa-Kichwa," and Language Use between Worlds

Though some employees of the National Directorate coordinating offices were influential in the elaboration of Unified Kichwa, people in the offices also disagreed about whether Unified Kichwa was important and/or how to speak it. While some critiqued the register's unintelligibility, most employees saw Unified Kichwa as important and connected it to speaking Kichwa "well." Imbabura Kichwa, the regional register most like the standardized register, was also often described as "good Kichwa." However, those from outside the national office, such as friends transcribing speeches, regional directors, and teachers, routinely praised the speech of Gloria Yungaicela. She was one of the National Directorate employees less proficient in Unified Kichwa, and she spoke Kichwa with Spanish mixed in most routinely for daily communication.

Gloria became one of the foremost directors of the National Directorate when, before this research started, she arrived in Quito to run the national-level bureaucracy from a Southern Highlands region from which no other employees in the office had grown up. Her hiring was unusual and came about after the Ministry of Education, under Correa, had more influence over the school system. She had not previously worked in the National Directorate. In her home province, she had worked as a teacher, principal, director of a regional network of schools, and a councilwoman. This background was atypical since most people in the National Directorate had either been employed there for years or were young adults just beginning their careers. She was unusual for the office in other ways, too. Like most national directors, Gloria had a college degree; however, unlike most national directors, she was a graduate of the bilingual school system, as many teachers were. Before she went on to work in the school system, she received a teaching degree from one of the system's higher education institutes and later earned a bachelor's degree from another university. Gloria had grown up routinely speaking Kichwa, including in her adult years, and her everyday Kichwa use was nonstandard (see Chapter 6).

Commentary on her daily talk and podium speeches shows how Kichwa use has long marked its speakers as racialized, rural, or classed (Zavala 2011). For example, Marlon, another director, described Gloria's Kichwa as more closely linked to Kichwa-speaking worlds. As he explained to me one day in an interview at his cubicle in the Ministry of Education, "*Ella es Kichwa Kichwa. Ella habla más Kichwa que español*" (She's Kichwa Kichwa. She speaks more Kichwa than Spanish).[9] Here he connected extensive Kichwa use to a certain kind of person—one racialized as more Kichwa—and contrasted Gloria with himself and other colleagues. He professed that those who speak Kichwa more routinely are viewed as more Kichwa than others, showing how routine language use is associated with the essence of an identity (Rosa 2019).

Most other employees in the office had lived in Quito for years. Gloria moved to Quito with the start of her employment, indicating that the "Kichwa-Kichwa" description also had rural dimensions that differed from many other employees. Unlike many educational planners in the office, she had recently learned Unified Kichwa. She did not speak Unified Kichwa before arriving to her position but quickly went to work learning and consulting linguists in the office. Though the vice minister of education decried the speech (analyzed in the next section) that she gave as transgressive, the example shows one unusual instance of how to combine standardized and nonstandardized registers for wider approval by everyday Kichwa speakers.

A Pathway for Further Inclusion in Kichwa-speaking: Offsetting Unified Kichwa

I now turn to a speech Gloria gave at an anniversary event for the National Directorate. Her speech was exceptional, in part, for how long she spoke Kichwa; few public speeches used Kichwa for more than opening remarks (see Chapter 6). But it was also a "good" speech, according to several people in the audience who were not employed in the National Office, a rare compliment. And it contained a minimal number of forms associated with Unified Kichwa.

On the day of her speech, in the large auditorium in the basement of the Ministry of Education, the school system's flags lined the two walkways that divided the seats into three sections. Shirtless young men from the Amazonian lowlands and young Highland Kichwa women with round, white hats lined the auditorium, each holding a white bilingual education flag. A packed audience was seated in reclining chairs included nearly every employee of the National Directorate, students, representatives from various nationalities, teachers, and others. On the stage the vice minister of education, a representative of UNICEF, the subsecretary of intercultural bilingual education (the highest position), and Gloria were seated at a table. There was also a podium for the speeches. After Marlon, the subsecretary, spoke, the masters of ceremony called Gloria to address the crowd. Both MCs also served as translators and carefully alternated between Spanish and Kichwa during the entirety of the event (a process further examined in Chapter 6). Gloria, dressed in a white hat, a black shawl, and a long skirt, slowly approached the podium. She pulled the microphone down and began to speak in Spanish. Because of the length of the speech, I elide much of the Spanish language parts to focus on her talk in Kichwa. Segments that may be construed as Unified Kichwa are placed in bold, and there is annotation about the use of grammatical forms associated with Unified Kichwa in brackets.

1 *Estimado Doctor Pablo Cevallos, Vice Ministro del Ministerio de Educación,*
Esteemed Doctor Pablo Cevallos, Vice Minister of the Ministry of Education,

[Welcomes all other attendees, omitted because it is not integral to analysis]

2 *en primer lugar, quisiera saludar a todos ustedes*
in the first place, I'd like to greet all of you all

3 *ya que este día es tan especial para todos y todas.*
since this day is so special for all (men and women).

4 *La interculturalización inicia*
Interculturalization begins

5 *desde la gestión de los mismos indígenas*
from the efforts of Indigenous people themselves

6 *a partir de los años cuarenta,*
From the 1940s on,

7 *aparecen algunas iniciativas al nivel del país,*
initiatives appear at the level of the country,

8 *especialmente en la zona de Cayambe,*
especially in the zone of Cayambe,

9 *promovido por Dolores Cacuango y Tránsito Amaguaña*
promoted by Dolores Cacuango and Transito Amaguña,

10 *entre otros líderes,*
among other leaders,

11 *y más adelante se desarrolla en Cotopaxi, Bolívar, Napo, Cañar, Loja.*
and from then on developed in Cotopaxi, Bolivar, Napo, Cañar, Loja.

12 *En este contexto, el objetivo de crear una educación*
In this context, the objective [is] to create an education

13 *con congruencia cultural y lingüística*
with cultural and linguistic congruence

14 *para el sector indígena.*
For the Indigenous sector.

[She then references the historical establishment of EIB and efforts to institutionalize Indigenous education, which I have omitted.]

[She then switches to Kichwa.][10]

15 **Kikin** *shimipi rimashpa,*
Speaking in your[honorific, no possessive suffix] language,

16 *kuyashka apukkuna,* **yachakuy***manta,*
dear leaders, because of schooled knowledge,

17 *ñawpaman apak,*
leaders of years past,

18 *warmikuna, karikuna,*
women, men,

19 *kay* **ishkay chunka kimsa** *markamanta,*
from these twenty-three provinces,

20 *wawakuna, yachachikkuna,*
children, teachers,

21 *kankunamanmi shunkumanta* **napayta karani**,
to you all[without honorific] a greeting from the heart I send,

22 *kay Ecuador mama llakta* **ishkay** *shimipa shutipi.*
in this Ecuador country's[no possessive marker] two languages'[not pluralized, with possessive suffix] names
[non-literal gloss: in the name of Ecuador's bilingual education]

23 *Maypimi ñukanchik shimipi* **kikin** *yachayta,*
Where[emphatic marker] in our[no possessive suffix] language, your[honorific, no possessive marker] knowledge,
[non-literal gloss: Where we learn in Kichwa, your knowledge]

24 *mikuyta, takita, tukuy sumak raymikunata,*
food[not pluralized], song[not pluralized], all of the great celebrations[pluralized],

25 *ñukanchik kay llaktapi ñawpaman yachachishpa*
in our[no possessive suffix] this country to move forward through teaching,
[non-literal gloss: to advance our teachings in Ecuador]

26 *shamunchik.*
we come.

27 *Chaymanta, kunan puncha,* **ishkay chunka kimsa** *watatami paktachinchik.*
Because of that, today, we complete twenty-three years.

28 **Mashi** *kashkata rikuchishpa,*
Showing that we're comrades,

29 *Runa kashkata rikuchishpa,*
making it seen that we're human beings,

30 *ñukanchikpa sumak yuyaypika,*
in our[possessive marker] brilliant ideas,

31 *ñukanchikpak,*
for us,

32 **kikin** *kawsayta sinchiyachinami kan.*
your[honorific, no possessive suffix] life needs to become strengthened[emphatic marker].
[non-literal gloss: to strengthen our identity or culture]

33 *Shinapish, kunan pacha*
But nowadays

34 *ñukanchik* **ishkay** *shimi yachayta alli [apankapak, yachankapak] killkashkami kan.*
our[no possessive suffix] bilingual education is well written.

35 *Kay hatun* **mama kamachik**pi *shinallatak,*
In this Constitution, it's like that [recognized in the constitution],

36 *kay* **yachakuy kamachik**pipish.
and in this Organic Law of Intercultural Bilingual Education, too.

37 *Maypimi ayllu llaktakunapi, markakunapi,*
Where[emphatic suffix] in communities, in provinces,

38 *ñukanchik wawakunawan,*
with our[no possessive suffix] children,

39 *uchilla munayta [paktachikunchik] shinallatak ñawpa pacha imashinami*[11]
to [carry out] the small desires, similar to in times past

40 *ñukanchik taytakuna, yuyashpa tapurkakuna,*[12]
like our[no possessive marker] ancestors thought and asked,

41 *shuk **yachakuyta kikin** shimipi [yachankapak],*[13]
[to learn] lessons in your[honorific, no possessive marker] own language [Kichwa],

42 *shinallatak shuktak shimikunapipish ruranata.*
too, like lessons in whatever other language.

43 *Chaymanta kunaka kaypimi kanchik.*
That's why today, we are here[emphatic suffix].

44 *ñuka **yupaychani**.*
I thank you.

45 *Ñukanchik yachaymanta pushak katik apuk Pablo Cevallos,*
Our[no possessive suffix] second-in-command for education, Pablo Cevallos,

46 *payka **mashi** Gloria Vidalpa shutipi,*
in she, colleague Gloria Vidal's[possessive suffix] name,

47 *kaypimi kanchik.*
we are here[emphatic suffix].

48 *Kaymi kan ñukanchik **yachakuy**,*
This[emphatic suffix] is our[no possessive suffix] lesson,

49 *ñukanchik wasi,*
our[no possessive suffix] house,
[non-literal gloss: the Ministry of Education is ours]

50 *maypimi runakuna, **mashikuna**, mishukuna,*
where[emphatic marker] Indigenous people, friends, *mestizo*s,

51 *tantarishpa kay sumak yachakuytaka kawsachishpa shamunchik.*
are meeting to make this great knowledge [of the *pueblos*] live, we come.

52 ***Ishkay chunka kimsa** watapika, tawka kushikuykunatami charinchik.*
In twenty-three years, we've had a lot of excitement.

53 *Kankuna chay yachana wasikunapi,*
You all[without honorific] in those schools,
[addressing the teachers]

54 *sumakta, wawakunawan, taytamamakunawan,*
meeting well with children and parents,

55 *shuktak yanapak tantanakuykunawanpish*
with those other organizations[pluralized] that support, too,

56 *llamka**shpa katishkanchik*.
working we have continued [up to today].

57 *Shinashpa, kaypimi kan*
That's why, here are[no third person plural suffix],

58 *chay **mashikuna**pish.*
these colleagues, too.
[non-literal gloss: That's why NGO employees are present at the event]

[Switches to Spanish, omitted: thanks funders and others briefly before concluding the speech in Kichwa]

[Switches back to Kichwa]

59 *Shinaka **mashikuna alli shamushka** kaychik.*
So, friends, be welcomed[without honorific].

60 *Kaypimi kanchik ñukanchik **ishkay shimi yachay**manta.*
Here[emphatic marker] we are because of our[no possessive marker] bilingual education.

61 *Huyayay **ishkay shimi yachay**!*
Long live bilingual education!

62 *Yupaychani*.
Thank you.

Unlike the quiet applause after the subsecretary and others' speeches at the event in which little to no Kichwa was spoken, the crowd erupted with yells of *kuyayay* ("long live"). Gloria's Kichwa use was extensive and unusual in comparison to other public speeches made on behalf of the school system. The content of her speech resonated with Kichwa-speaking audiences, too, because of *how* she spoke Kichwa. While Gloria compartmentalized the two languages (separating Kichwa from Spanish) and followed conventions for speech-giving in Spanish, common strategies seen throughout the event (and in other public speeches) that make Kichwa use less threatening to *mestizo-*identifying audience members, she also used register contrasts to offset standardized Kichwa. Such blending of Kichwa registers contributed to a speech that was well received by Kichwa speakers.

On the one hand, Gloria did not use loanwords from Spanish when speaking Kichwa, thus adhering to purist ideology and producing "good" Kichwa for listeners who favor Unified Kichwa. She even used neologisms with which many audience members were likely unfamiliar, for example, *hatun mama kamachik* ("constitution," or "big mother law" in line 35). Another is *llamkana* ("to work" line 56 as *llamkashpa*), for which many speakers borrow the verb *trabajar* from Spanish and assimilate it to Kichwa grammatical categories to produce *trabajana*. She used a number of words associated with Unified Kichwa, the use of which Kichwa-speaking listeners would typically decry. But they did not. She tempered her use of Unified Kichwa by employing scant calqued formulaic phrases from Spanish. She used *alli shamushka kaychik* ("welcome," or "be well having come," which translates directly from *sean bienvenidos* in Spanish in line 59) at the end of her speech, but did not open it with *alli puncha* ("good morning"). Rather, she began in line 1 by noting that she is speaking Kichwa as "your" (*kikin*) language, which is closer than "good morning" to how many Kichwa speakers communicate and avoids use of the Unified Kichwa emblem.

The example of *kikin shimi* (line 15) is also important because it shows how she offsets Unified Kichwa forms with others. *Kikin* (second person honorific in lines 15 and 23) is routinely indicative of Highland and Unified Kichwa and is calqued from *Usted*/you formal in Spanish. It likely developed long ago through language contact and is used in fewer varieties than the non-honorific *kan* ("you") (Gómez-Rendón 2008, 505). *Kan* and *kikin* are parallel with the *tú/Usted* distinction in Spanish, but *kikin* is conjugated in the second person as opposed to the third person in Spanish. Gloria used *kan* instead of *kikin* for the second person pronoun twice in the speech in the plural *kankuna* (lines 21 and 53), showing how she varied use of the forms. Moreover, she most commonly avoided *you* altogether by frequently using *ñukanchik* "we" or "our," which all Kichwa registers would deploy. In other words, this example of pronouns shows how she varied her use of standardized Kichwa speech forms with more common ones, thus increasing comprehension and offsetting formality, standardization, and forms overly associated with one region. The use of "we" also aligned her with addressees.

Moreover, the example of *kikin shimi* shows that although she at times employed the Unified Kichwa form *kikin*, she generally did not follow the most common Unified Kichwa grammatical norms for indicating possession. The possessive suffix (-pa) (kikin*pa* shimi, as the alternative would be) is common to Unified Kichwa, but in various other varieties (e.g., non-Northern Highland Kichwa) -pa is routinely omitted as redundant since possession is implied by the preceding noun. Unified Kichwa's morphological differences between a pronoun and a possessive exist, albeit not as suffixes, in Spanish (e.g., *yo* "I" instead of *mi* "my"). In her speech, Gloria varied her use of -*pa* as a possessive suffix, exemplifying both forms in how she spoke. For example, in line 22 "in this Ecuador country's two languages' names," the possessive inflecting "country" is inferred from context, whereas the possessive inflecting "languages" is marked.

"*Ecuador- mama llakta ishkay shimi-pa shutipi.*"

Ecuador mother town[no possessive] two language[possessive] name[in]

Note here within the same sentence that she alternated between the forms. She more commonly used the possessive suffix with nouns (twice) than with pronouns (once). In line 30, she used *ñukanchik-pa* for "our" but, in line 34 and throughout the remainder of her talk, she used the bare form *ñukanchik*. In her 14 uses of possessive pronouns, she added *pa* only once.

Gloria also varied her use of Kichwa plural suffixes. For example, in her one conjugation of a third person plural (line 57), she did not use (*-kuna*), the third person plural form common in Unified Kichwa that more closely parallels Spanish. Instead, she used the bare form, a common third person singular conjugation in nonstandardized Kichwa. In other parts of her speech, she did use the form. She also exhibited regional phonetic variation in line 58 (*mashikuna-pish*), using *-pish* ("and") instead of the Unified Kichwa form *-pash*. Again, she did not strictly adhere to standardization based on Northern Highland Kichwa, but instead she alternated standardized forms with ones that were clearly nonstandard.

Carlos, a friend transcribing her speech who is conversant in Unified Kichwa noted that she spoke "formally," a common description of Unified Kichwa, but not "overly formal." Throughout the speech, he said, the formality dropped off somewhat, which he attributed to "winning the trust of the listeners." This illustrates a common belief about Kichwa that it confers trust between interlocutors. However, Gloria's rapport-building contrasts with the lack of "trust" people associated with many standardized forms, as Ruth described at the start of the chapter. Her speech's referential content, such as repeating various times that "we are here," he said, also built trust with listeners. Another friend conversant in Unified Kichwa, who is from the Central Highlands, commented that Gloria is a "very good" speaker (*habla muy bien*). Her speech sounded formal to him due to the use of some signifiers of Unified Kichwa, such as *alli shamushka kaychik* ("please be welcomed") and *yupaychani* ("I am grateful"), but not overly so.

For Kichwa speakers, the content of Gloria's words in Kichwa (and Spanish) is not especially controversial, though it does show commonalities with describing and modeling intercultural citizenship that I unpack later in this book. In the first section of her speech in Kichwa, she emphasized notions of language, among other markers of Indigeneity, as an emblem of identity ("in your language" in line 15, "in this country's two languages" in line 22). She largely focused on the successes of recognition through "writing" bilingual education into the Constitution and the Law (lines 33–36). And although non-Indigenous identifying Ministry officials did not understand her, she named them (Pablo Cevallos and Gloria Vidal) and then aligned herself and Indigenous knowledge and its knowers, as represented *here* in the Ministry of Education (in the "house") (lines 45–46). Her inclusive description of *runakuna, mashikuna,* and *mestizos (mishukuna)* offered an image of a citizens in intercultural Ecuador (line 50), and she named many regions, recognizing them and their inhabitants (line 11). However, as Chapter 6 shows, the vice minister of education became concerned after hearing her speech because so much of it was in a language that he did not understand. Her Kichwa was not curtailed and was less commensurate with Spanish. An effective part of her speech for Kichwa speaking listeners was the use of standardized Kichwa mitigated by blending in forms from contrastive Kichwa registers.

In her speech, Gloria's separation of Kichwa from Spanish while including seemingly contradictory forms from different registers is somewhat different from many cases of language mixing that scholars have considered. She was not producing "Kichwañol," a form of language mixing that, similar to contexts in other languages, is viewed as "bad" by some bilingual education directors. Instead, how she combined forms from different registers demonstrates linguistic prowess for many listeners. Gloria's linguistic efforts included offsetting as a strategy of pluralism that "goes-between" registers. She used forms that clearly signified contrastive registers. This way of communicating helped overcome some of the alienating effects of unification for the Kichwa speakers that the project of bilingual education must serve.

Conclusion

The standardization of Indigenous languages occurs within a history of linguistic alterity and domination. As such, advocates aspire for standardization to help overcome shame for speaking marginalized languages and as a route to recognition (De Costa et al. 2017). Yet, *how* languages are standardized and used is worthy of further examination. Jacqueline Urla and her colleagues (2017) challenge the idea that standardization practices for comparatively oppressed languages reproduce those for dominant languages in any simple way. This chapter, too, has examined the diverse ways and forms of reproduction from Spanish in less dominant languages. Though standardizing Kichwa has systematically reproduced practices and perceptions of standardized

Spanish—such as the proscription of Kichwa syntax and ideologies about "good" writing—it offers contradictory dynamics. For example, planners made the Unified Kichwa alphabet so that writing in Kichwa would not be wholly based on the Spanish alphabet. The Unified Kichwa alphabet also has a looser connection between letters and sounds than what exists in Spanish. Yet, ideas driving the elaboration of the Kichwa alphabet, such as that just one alphabet should be used for writing across the country, are based on for writing in Spanish and other more dominant languages. Many of the actual Spanish letters overlap, too, and adult readers lament the alphabet as harder to read.

This close examination of different registers calls attention to how bivalency is a defining feature of Indigenous languages and a significant component of language standardization. Linguistic forms can and do belong to more than one register. Ultimately, even in an especially technical and planned register of Kichwa, more forms overlap with some Northern and Central Highland varieties than others, and teachers like Ruth lament Unified Kichwa as wholly contrastive with how they speak. Bivalency is not limited to shared lexicon across registers of Indigenous languages, either, as forms may not be lexically borrowed from colonial languages but instead calqued based on syntax, reference, and/or use. As this book will later show, calqued expressions in Kichwa are readily deployable for public speaking even as they are also some of the most contested forms. Calquing helps to explain why many Indigenous-language speakers contest Unified Kichwa for sounding "foreign," and it shows that standardization in this case is not neutral.

The blurred boundaries between languages and registers also have potential for speaking in Kichwa for larger audiences with an array of Kichwa speakers and people who identify as *mestizos*. For Kichwa speakers who are somewhat further from the centralized state apparatus, blending contrastive forms from different registers and offsetting Unified Kichwa can make the difference between "good" and "too formal" or overly standardized Kichwa. In Gloria's case, she demonstrated expertise and formality while also showing a concern for intelligibility by using contrastive Kichwa forms that built solidarity with everyday Kichwa-speaking audience members. For agglutinative language families like Kichwa, pronouns, infixes, and suffixes tied to distinct registers become important forms for managing and appealing to distinct publics.

Offsetting is important for how Indigenous-language speakers like Gloria work within the parameters of their jobs. De Certeau (1984, 30) considers the art of "going-between" through a wide array of contrastive norms and behaviors and strategically using what could be considered register differences to do socially consequential things. As he put it, "just as in literature one differentiates 'styles' or ways of writing, one can distinguish 'ways of operating'—ways of walking, reading, producing, speaking, etc." De Certeau calls attention to ways of speaking within and across a language to understand the non-normative and blended ways of operating that occur across differences. Ruth distinguishes *"mashis"* from all others, indicating some of the identities associated with Unified Kichwa—those closer and more conversant in the middle-class, urban, *mestizo*-identifying Spanish-speaking world of offices and schools (see Chapter 4). A closer look at the actual linguistic forms—alphabets, particles, words—and how they are used has shown how a standardized register makes Kichwa like Spanish. That use is tied to the kinds of speakers more conversant in the institutions of the state. Yet, Gloria was able to speak Kichwa publicly and better connect with her Kichwa-speaking audience members. Her example offers a strategy for pushing back against office norms and expectations, albeit one in a major event celebrating bilingual education and one that came with the concern of her bosses.

4

Employment as Professionals

Promise and Predicament

Introduction

An encouraging consequence of state recognition is that members of Indigenous *pueblos* and nationalities are more involved in authoring policies and managing the development projects that affect them. Intercultural bilingual education is led by directors and educators who hold high school, bachelor's, master's, and, occasionally, doctoral degrees and are salaried employees of the state. Employees are commonly referred to as "professionals." This chapter considers two related questions: what does it mean to become a professional? And how does schooling affect the pathways of members of Indigenous *pueblos* and nationalities?

Schooling—necessary for obtaining the credentials to become a professional—in Ecuador and elsewhere has been a major focus of demands for equality, yet it involves several challenges and double binds. Given that state planners have long viewed schools as sites to assimilate citizens, education research and practice have shown the changes in identities and behaviors that routinely occur in state institutions like schools (Brownell & Parks 2022; García-Sánchez 2014; Wortham 2005), which is one reason activists seek to oversee those institutions. However, these schooling experiences of assimilation may extend all the way up to directing a bilingual school system. For example, as current professionals were growing up, they were routinely taught not to speak the languages of their parents in institutions like schools. Teachers even attempted to inflict physical violence on students for speaking Indigenous languages (Lomawaima & McCarty 2002; Reyhner 2015), which is one reason children became used to speaking Spanish in institutional spaces. Most directors of the school system now use Spanish more routinely than Kichwa, which other members of the social movement for bilingual education may cite for their loss of confidence in bilingual education.

Professionalization has been at the center of discussion and disagreement around bilingual education, even as many Kichwa parents aspire for their children to follow similar paths as current employees. Despite language shift, most members of the Kichwa nationality see schooling as a primary route to stable employment and upward mobility, much like ideas about education throughout the world (Benei 2010; Vavrus 2021).

At the same time, during my research, teachers, parents, and even planners themselves routinely critiqued professionalization as contributing to Western or *mestizo* views of the world, the use of Spanish, and even setbacks to Indigenous organizing. Indigenous professionals tend to have more access to and conversancy in the *mestizo*-identifying worlds that are predominant in higher education and urban life than other family members or constituents. While secondary and higher education can provide career and economic stability across urban and rural communities (Martínez Novo 2014b, 222), other family and community members may subsequently see Indigenous students and professionals as marked by socioeconomic differences and changing ways of understanding the world (Brayboy 2005; Waterman 2012). The challenges of professionalization show the vast adversity that members of Indigenous *pueblos* and nationalities overcome to study, continue to speak Kichwa, and work in offices, and that these efforts may come with double binds.

The case of professionals in the school system speaks to a larger tension with professionalization: professionals often decide what happens, for whom, and how to enforce their decisions (Illich 1977). Their status implies authority, and their decisions for others may contrast with the ways that others learn or make sense of the world. This chapter seeks to better understand the alignments and divides that occur among participants in this movement for social change as linked to professionalization. I begin by drawing from life history interviews with two bilingual education coordinators who worked in the National Directorate, Josefina and Carlos. I show the vast odds that many professionals overcame in completing their schooling and whose early years of work involved organizing, unpaid labor, racist disdain, and assimilation efforts, including demands to stop speaking Kichwa and to become "less Indigenous." Their cases demonstrate the determination and complexity behind their pathways to political struggle and economic stability, and their cases also show how wealth is relative. I then examine some frustrations about the school system through the words of teachers and planners. At the heart of these concerns is that many Kichwa speakers decry professionalism and its influence on Indigeneity. I juxtapose these two sections to show the double binds around schooling, employment, and change that many who work in the office experience.

Pathways through Schooling and Beyond

Anthropologist María Elena García (2005, 135) notes that just a few decades ago, an "educated *indígena*" struck many Peruvians as unusual but cites Ecuador as noteworthy in comparison to the rest of the Andes for having "an Indigenous elite [that] emerged around the development of bilingual education programs" (2005, 144). Her comments show how the official recognition and development of the school system served as a pathway for members of Indigenous *pueblos* and nationalities to study and secure employment that far exceeded efforts in other Andean nation-states.

Elite, though, is contingent and relative. Directors of bilingual education receive a relatively stable monthly salary, which may differ from family members who farm or sell artisan goods. However, as with Indigenous professionals in Colombia (Rappaport 2005) and Guatemala (Warren 1998), employees in the National Directorate of Intercultural Bilingual Education constitute an Indigenous middle class. Only those in the foremost positions of leadership receive salaries that rival the highest earners of Ecuador's *mestizo-* or white-identifying professional class. "Indigenous professional" is also somewhat of an umbrella term. Jobs in the National Directorate were varied but specialized and included policymakers, linguists, curriculum designers, administrative assistants, managers, and accountants. Principals and teachers would be considered professionals, too.

Josefina, an employee in the office in her early sixties who retired in 2013, was among the first generation of educational activists employed to direct the school system. Many threads of her life are common with her colleagues in the office. For instance, her pathway to graduation and employment was challenging. Josefina spent years with principals and teachers who viewed schools as a means for racialized and linguistic assimilation. After graduation, she often experienced labor exploitation. Her case is also different based on how often she spoke Kichwa and how she tended to speak in a nonstandard fashion.

Josefina was born in the province of Imbabura, one of ten children.[1] Her dad kept cattle, farmed, and did small jobs for nuns. Her mom worked at home and made clothes. Her parents spoke Kichwa and Spanish, and her dad tended to speak to her in Spanish while her mom spoke to her in Kichwa, a gendered difference commonly professed in Quechua language ideologies (de la Torre 1999; Rindstedt & Aronsson 2002). Her parents mainly spoke Kichwa to one another.

Even though Josefina was an avid student, she experienced setbacks early in her studies. She almost failed the third grade because she would write

Spanish vowels as Kichwa vowels, only to be marked wrong by the teacher. Furthermore, though her father emphasized his children's studies, her mom did not share her dad's emphasis. Once, while her dad was in Quito buying yarn, her mom took her to pick beans, causing Josefina to miss the week of her final exams and, as a result, fail seventh grade: "*Mi papá siempre quiso que estudie. Y quería que sus hijos estudien. Y más las mujeres que los hombres porque decía que las mujeres no se separan de los maridos aunque les pegue porque el marido le mantiene*" (My dad always wanted me to study. He [also] wanted his children to study and the women even more because he would say that women don't leave their husbands even if they hit them because the husband maintains them.) Her story shows the struggle to attend school and how many parents consider schooling a pathway to upward mobility and even to avoid domestic violence. In many families, boys but not girls were sent to school, so her father may have been unusual in emphasizing her schooling. However, her studies had to be arranged according to her family's work needs, and her mother did not support her schooling.[2]

With her father's financial help and insistence, she attended several schools with Spanish speakers, including a boarding school. When she graduated from high school with a teaching degree, she was assigned to teach in a high school in the mountains of the province of Imbabura. Upon graduation, however, her own teachers instructed her not to speak Kichwa in professional settings, even though Josefina spoke Kichwa often. Her teachers equated speaking Kichwa with being Indigenous—which she clearly was. Accordingly, they attempted to limit her Kichwa use. For example, as Josefina received her diploma, school officials told her:

Y ahí a usted [a ella misma] no le dejan hablar el Kichwa.	"And there they don't let you speak Kichwa.
Usted no es indígena. Repita: no soy indígena.	You are not Indigenous. Repeat: I'm not Indigenous.
Usted no sabe kichwa. Repita: no sé Kichwa.	You don't know Kichwa. Repeat: I don't know Kichwa.
Ustedes ya no son indígenas ¿Entienden?	You all are no longer Indigenous. Understand?
Así nos hicieron graduar. En el momento de entregar el título decían así.	That's how they graduated us. In the moment that they handed out the degree that's what they said.

But then she arrived at the school and saw how children were Kichwa speakers and the problems to which such policies were contributing. Around sixty-five students began the year, but by the time the year finished only twenty remained. So, she told the students, "*ñuka yachani kichwapi. Rimaylla.*" ("I know [what you're saying] in Kichwa. Speak without worry." And the parents were much happier [with that change]), she reported.[3] Thus, Josefina spent most of her life enduring Kichwa censorship, much of which was enforced in institutional domains of talk. Others equated her Kichwa use with demonstrating Indigeneity and aimed to restrict and erase those contours of her life. Even more troubling is that educators expected her to work in various rural Indigenous areas yet attempted to limit how she did so by instructing her to not speak Kichwa. The conflicting priorities—between the institution and the students and families she served—entailed either ignoring the former and risking her job to benefit the latter or being obedient to the former to the detriment of the latter.

For years, she served as an educator across Ecuador and found that such work was often unpaid, "*Nos mandó a que trabajemos ad honorem. ¿Ad honorem que será?*" ([An official] sent us [her cohort of students] to work *ad honorem*. What could *ad honorem* be?). The children's parents organized and gave them breakfast, lunch, dinner, and fares to go home for major holidays, but "*y años fuimos a trabajar gratis*" (and for years we went to work for free). Teaching did not include even a small monthly salary.

She wanted to keep studying and eventually got a scholarship to study textile production in Santiago, Chile, in the 1970s through one of Chilean president Salvador Allende's scholarship programs. While there, she saw a city oriented around schooling and reading and noted a stark contrast to her experiences in Ecuador, where access to books and schooling within her family was limited. While she was on scholarship, Allende was overthrown and died by suicide, plunging the entire country and her studies into despair:

Luchamos hasta el último momento para terminar la universidad.	We fought until the last moment to finish studying at the university [there.]
Pero estaba muy feo eso.	But that was very ugly.
Para que no nos encuentren,	So that [the military coup] wouldn't find us,
nos escondíamos a lo máximo que podíamos.	we hid as much as we could.
Nos quedamos ahí en la embajada, no sé cuántos días.	We stayed in the embassy, who knows how many days,
Ocho, quince. Encerrados como una cárcel.	Eight. Fifteen. Locked in like a jail.
Veíamos que venía un carro,	When we saw that a car was coming,
nosotros salíamos por otra puerta.	we would run out another door.
No nos pescaban hasta el último.	They didn't fish us out until later.
Los capitanes nos revisaban todita la maleta,	The captains looked all through our suitcases,
así libros sospechosamente,	looking suspiciously [for] books,
pero eran de historia de educación.	but they [the books] were about the history of education.

Una de Paulo Freire.	One of Paulo Freire's.
[Los] quemaron. En nuestra presencia.	They burned [them]. In front of us.
Nos regresaron.	They returned us [to Ecuador].
Nos vinieron a botar a Guayaquil.	They came to Guayaquil [Ecuador's other major city] to throw us out.
De ahí venimos acá a Quito, sin pasajes, sin nada.	From there we went to Quito, without tickets, without anything.
Nadie tenía plata.	No one had money.
Nuestros padres preocupados	Our parents worried
porque no salen ni en las listas de muertos.	because [our names] didn't even show up in the lists of dead people.
Y mis papás ya dando misa, que estemos bien.	My parents were at mass praying that we were okay.
Cuando ya llegamos a la casa, lloraron.	When we got home, they cried.
Nos decía mi mamá: ¿pero tú mismo eres?	My mom told us, "But is it you?
Ustedes mismos son.	It is indeed you all.
A mi me dijeron que estaban muertos.	They told me you all were dead."

Josefina loved books and studying, but her time in Chile was met with censure and repression. She was so shocked by her experiences in Chile that she suspended her studies. In 1980, she went to work for Ecuador's Ministry of Education under Jaime Roldós's government and served as a national literacy promoter for Kichwa. She finally earned a salary and was headquartered in an office, noting her earlier years of sacrifice for bilingual education.

Nosotros hemos sacrificado los sábados y domingos	We've sacrificed Saturdays and Sundays
para que esta Dirección [Nacional] nazca.	so that this [National] Directorate would be born.
No es que he venido por la linda cara que tengo,	It's not that I've gotten here because of this beautiful face that I have,
sino más bien cuando hemos estado ligados a la organización	but rather when we've been linked to the organization,
porque todo ha sido un proceso organizativo.	because everything has been an organizing process.
Si yo estoy en Ilumán	If I'm in Ilumán [in Imbabura],
mi papá para conseguirse la luz eléctrica	my dad, in order to get electricity,
tenía que juntarse con toda la gente y aportar con postes.	had to come together with everyone and support the posts.
Entonces, todo hemos conseguido es a base de organización.	So we've gotten everything on the basis of organization.

The advancement of historically marginalized peoples, she noted, has depended on collective support and struggle ("organization," "com[ing] together," and mutual "support") and around-the-clock work beyond the hours at the office. Josefina emphasized political organizing, lest anyone now think that advancement happened serendipitously. Indeed, she has long been a member of Indigenous organizations, joining CONAIE after its founding in the 1980s.

Eventually, the Universidad Andina Simón Bolívar (Simón Bolívar Andean University) in Quito offered her a scholarship, and she studied a *diplomado* (certification program) and obtained a master's degree. Although she studied extensively, others in her family had not, which is common. Professionalism was rarely experienced across all siblings of her generation. Kichwa-speaking families often consist of siblings with different jobs and levels of schooling. Some of her family members are artisans and sell handicrafts and clothes while others are professionals, such as a sister who is a nutritionist and another who is an elementary school teacher. Some have high school diplomas or college degrees and others do not.

She noted that, in contrast to popular opinion, the ones who are not professionals are better off economically. In her case, one artisan sister "*tiene una linda casa en Otavalo de tres, cuatro pisos*" (has a beautiful house of three, four floors in Otavalo) and another has two houses in Otavalo. "*En cambio, la profesión no le da el sueldo y es limitante*" (On the other hand, the profession doesn't yield a [large] salary and is [economically] limiting). She said, "*Yo, una suite que compré todavía estoy pagando*" (I bought a studio apartment, and I'm still paying it off). At the time of our conversation, her mother, her daughter, and her grandson lived with her. She would talk to her Mom in Kichwa, but her daughter struggled to speak, showing how difficult it is to raise children who speak Kichwa in the city. Her mom would request that she "*jubílate rápido*" (retire quickly) to spend more time with her, to which Josefina reminded her with a laugh, "*Usted que no me dejó terminar rápido el colegio. Ya hubiera estado jubilada, le digo. Usted que no me manda a dar el examen*" (You didn't let me finish high school quickly. I'd already be retired [by now], I tell her. You that didn't send me to take the exam [in the seventh grade]).

Josefina's life shows a complex and difficult past in which schooling involved constant conflict but from which a relatively more stable present emerged. As critics of Indigenous professionals routinely mention, she (and others in the office) received scholarships and traveled to study in other nation-states. She was a passionate student and educational activist.

She came to love schooling, even if it brought significant challenges (such as with her mother, or with teachers) or heartbreak and threats of violence (such as what curtailed her time in Chile). From her conflicted educational history to her love of reading, these histories are common across those who coordinate policy in the National Directorate. A passion for reading also manifested in her employment as a national coordinator of literacy in Kichwa.

Another part of her arrival to the Ministry of Education offices was that she, like nearly all employees of the National Directorate over the age of forty, worked for years without pay as an educator. Work in rural areas was closely linked to political organizing. Most others in the office also had experience with Indigenous organizations and, when the school system began, were only able to start work through the sponsorship of an organization. Josefina's case is not unusual.

Her straightforward assessment of economic differences between herself and her family members also shows that those who coordinate the system do not necessarily earn exorbitant salaries. A middle-class salary is not necessarily more income than from artisanship or sales, but the professional status has more respect (and potentially more transformation in terms of where one lives and from ideas common to schooling). In the Ministry of Education, only those at the very top of the school system were the economic exceptions. For example, when I was carrying out this research, the subsecretary position came with a salary of $5,000 a month—an amount of money so astonishing to others in the office that one employee brought me paperwork, mouth open and finger plastered on the total amount of the director's salary to show me the economic discrepancies. That said, professional salaries are still significantly higher than other community members and parents of students who work in farming, domestic work, or construction, common careers for Kichwa speakers in Ecuador for which the minimum monthly salary in 2013 was $318.[4] Most in the office had stories of working years "*ad honorem*," often until late at night and on weekends, showing the financial struggle out of which stability emerged.

One part of Josefina's story that differs from others in the office was her routine communication in Kichwa. Josefina was one of the few employees who spoke Kichwa for an array of interactions, including for daily conversations with others in the office. In these circumstances, she tended to speak a form of Imbabura Kichwa with words from Spanish mixed in, somewhat different from Unified Kichwa. She would also break Spanish-speaking norms in office meetings by using Kichwa for lengthy periods of time, sometimes to applause and sometimes to frustration. As she put it:

Yo sí desde chiquita rapidito hablamos en Kichwa estando en reuniones, estando...	Since I was little fluidly we've spoken in Kichwa, being around others, being—
Puede estar el señor ministro. No puedo evitar.	The esteemed minister [of education] can be there. I can't avoid it.
Ya no puedo evitar, aunque me hayan sancionado.	I can no longer avoid it even though they've sanctioned me.
Es bien duro, peor en el colegio.	It's really tough [to speak in Kichwa] and worse in high school.
¿Quién me va a decir que hable en Kichwa?	Who's going to tell me to speak Kichwa?
En la casa nomás con mi mamá, con mi papá, con nuestros familiares.	Only at home with my mom, with my dad, with our relatives.

Despite years of schooling that attempted to stop her use of Kichwa, Josefina lived with her mother and spoke Kichwa daily. She was more widely viewed by her peers as having strong links to Kichwa-speaking worlds, more so than others in the office, even if she was conversant in modernist institutions. As Chapter 6 will show, other officials, such as the minister, may view Kichwa use in meetings or events as threatening. They do not understand what is being said, especially when Kichwa is spoken outside of intercultural parameters. Speakers may also be embarrassed and "avoid" using Kichwa. Her speaking "fluidly" and uncontrollably illustrated that she routinely spoke Kichwa outside of office spaces.

I now turn to the life history of another National Directorate planner with a slightly different profile. Carlos's life history is more like that of many *mestizo*-identifying employees, even if, like most people in the office, it was closely intertwined with Kichwa experiences.[5] He worked for years in educational projects across Kichwa-speaking parishes. Carlos was born in a small town close to Quito. His father was of Cayambi (Kichwa) descent, a *pueblo* that was ravaged by haciendas. His father was a laborer in an *hacienda* and, in turn, a farmer, a construction worker, and a caretaker of a school. His mother identified as *mestiza*; her family had migrated from Colombia, and she worked around the house. To avoid becoming an *"objeto de discriminación"* (object of discrimination) and because of his mom's influence, he said, he and his siblings wore what he described as *"una forma de vestir mestiza"* (a *mestiza* way of dressing). His Spanish last name was probably given to his father at the *hacienda*. His grandparents spoke Kichwa, but his father did not. Carlos attributed this to his father having been punished in school for any attempt to speak the language. In Carlos's community, people self-identified as *mestizo* or *mestiza* and largely spoke Spanish, too.

Carlos attended a Spanish-language elementary school oriented toward *mestizos*. He began to realize the severity of discrimination when he studied at an agriculture and livestock high school in the small northern highland city of Otavalo in Imbabura. This period was memorable to him for collisions between Indigenous-identifying and *mestizo*-identifying students. He noted that for the students from the *campo* (countryside), the discrimination they experienced was "terrible" and that "*era frontal el insulto, la agresión*" (the insults, the aggression were head-on). He said that others equated a rural upbringing with being Indigenous, so he more closely identified with his Indigenous peers.

Carlos became involved in organizing. He gradually met leaders of social movements and, in 1981, he went to Semiátug, located in a different Central Highland region of Ecuador (Bolívar). There he taught and helped foster a network of future administrators who would manage and teach in a network of rural schools as part of a well-known educational experiment. There, a community elder told him, "*Si usted va a trabajar con nosotros debe vivir y pensar como nosotros, solo ahí nos va a entender*" (If you're going to work with us, you must live and think like us. Only like that are you going to understand [us]). His interlocutor emphasized that understanding and taking on the philosophies and daily lives of members of Indigenous communities should be an integral part of the job.

Carlos became involved in the Confederación Nacional de Organizaciones Campesinas, Indígenas, y Negras (FENOCIN, National Confederation of Peasant, Indigenous, and Black Organizations), which supported him as he began to work in the national bilingual education directorate after it was founded. As he put it, "*Nosotros como no éramos de ahí debíamos migrar y eso precisamente sucedió conmigo*" (Since we weren't from there, we had to migrate [to Quito], and that's precisely what happened with me). He learned Kichwa through his years of work in the countryside and could speak during those years. When he started work in the National Directorate in 1991, however, "*practicamente se perdió*" (it was practically lost).

Carlos's profile gives a sense of his intertwined Kichwa- and Spanish-speaking worlds. In his case, school was key for bringing him together with those who would bring out his Kichwa heritage. He also moved to rural areas to work and later ended up in the city, largely because the school system provided jobs for organizers from across Ecuador, many of whom had been essential to getting rural schools off the ground. Like many others (including

Josefina), he worked long hours for little pay.[6] As mentioned above, when he was working in Kichwa-speaking regions with families and students, he became conversant in the language family. But those abilities faded after years of work coordinating from offices in Quito, where Spanish proliferates the workplace. His shift to Spanish was also motivated by widespread expectations about speaking Kichwa "well" and "properly," even as some employees were just learning the language or were trying to practice what they had learned. As he put it, those with differing levels of proficiency would try to say one thing, but "*se dice una cosa totalmente diferente e inmediatamente salen a flote las risas. Eso es como tener una especie de bloqueo de vergüenza, del miedo a equivocarse para no ser objeto de burlas*" (They would say something totally different and immediately people start laughing. That's like having a kind of mental block due to shame, due to the fear of making a mistake, in order to not be the focus of jokes).

His point shows that language shift also occurs because of how one is speaking and how others respond to their speech, including by applying the norms of correctness common to educational institutions. One way of understanding Carlos's story is that there existed such a preference in office spaces for speaking Unified Kichwa and not making mistakes that Carlos simply preferred not to speak, which exacerbated his lack of practice. Sometimes language shift occurs as a result of violence for speaking the language at all and other times it occurs alongside regulation and ridicule about how registers are spoken.

The Dilemmas of Professionalization

The previous section showed the odds that bilingual education professionals overcome to work in an office and to speak Kichwa, as well as how professional employment has been coupled with Indigenous organizing. This section further considers the question from the chapter's introduction: what does it mean to become a professional? As I talked to teachers, parents, and policymakers, I was struck by how often they aspired for their children to become professionals. Given the protracted and systemic oppression of Indigenous peoples, that parents view professional employment as a means to economic stability and respect is hardly surprising. However, their educational goals tended to be coupled with criticism of current professionals.

The use of Kichwa often figured into comments about professionalization. For example, when I asked Elena, an educator at the other school (not Ruth's) where I carried out research and with whom I spent much time (see

Chapter 7), about her son not speaking Kichwa ("You told me that your son doesn't speak Kichwa. Can you tell me a little more about that?"), she immediately expressed concern that Kichwa use implied exclusion from an office job.[7]

Es que tiene que saber muy bien castellano.	The thing is that he needs to know Spanish really well.
Y también inglés.	And also English.
Son idiomas con más influencia en la sociedad.	They are languages with more influence in society.
Kichwa, claro pues debe saber,	Kichwa, well sure he should know it,
pero con Kichwa no puede ir a las oficinas.	but with Kichwa he cannot go to the offices.
Tiene que saber castellano.	He has to know Spanish.

Elena described how Spanish has become the daily language of institutions and employment. Despite Kichwa's official recognition, Spanish still has greater "influence." For her, prioritizing another language would involve English, not Kichwa, even though she would not mind if he learned Kichwa. She was also teaching Kichwa at the school, though in a restricted way (as examined in Chapter 7). She explained her emphasis on Spanish as a means of finding "office" employment, something she presumed would exclude Kichwa. Since even in the National Directorate most employees found it difficult to speak Kichwa at the office, her concern was not unfounded. She also supposed that speaking Kichwa would make her son less likely to know Spanish "very well." Marked ways of speaking Spanish have long served as pretexts for discrimination against Kichwa speakers and against learning Kichwa, even if research on multilingualism has long shown that speaking one language or register proficiently is not prohibitive of being proficient in another (e.g., Bartlett & García 2011; Benson 2005).

Even though she aspired for her son to work in an office, in another interview, as Elena rued the problems that she saw with the school system, she focused her criticism squarely on "professionalizing":[8]

Yo no comparto con el sistema bilingüe	I don't share [the goals] of the bilingual [school] system
porque muchas autoridades han buscado por ellos [mismos].	because many authorities have looked out for themselves
Ellos se graduaron. Ellos se educaron.	They graduated. They were educated.
Ya están viejos, son grandes profesionales,	They're now old. They are grand professionals.
tienen grandes títulos,	They have grand degrees,
pero no han hecho nada.	but they haven't done anything.
El bilingüe es solamente membrete.	"Bilingual" is just a letterhead.

Eso es profesionalizar—profesionalidad de la persona,	[But] that's professionalizing—the professionalism of the person,
puede identificarse donde quiera, como tal, sí.	they can be identified anywhere as such, yes.
Yo no estoy de acuerdo,	I don't agree.
por eso me da gusto que acabe la educación bilingüe	that's why I'm happy that bilingual education is ending,
porque ya se acabó.	that it's over.

Elena summed up her comments about authorities by claiming that professionalization in bilingual education is a process of self-advancement, especially in the context of schooling and credentials. While *professional* continues to imply schooling and employment, for her, it also carries the negative connotation of some people's success that others do not experience. She noted that directors received scholarships to study and earn advanced degrees, and she described these credentials as self-beneficial rather than as contributing to the school system's improvement. Many would argue that having well-versed people who plan the school system is an important advance. Yet, similar perspectives about directors of Indigenous organizations (such as CONAIE in Chapter 2) are routinely seen in Facebook comments on the school system's and CONAIE's posts. Elena linked such changes to professional positions in bilingual education, yet they are also common to schooling and office work more generally.

Elena's use of "professional" also implies a fluidity in identification, from the "graduation" to the "trips." Professionalism conveys ascent among those who gain degrees and work in offices, which I further examine later in this chapter. While she also held a bachelor's degree, she noted that "they" can "be identified anywhere as such," showing how she sees that being a professional comes with access to more spaces, people, and respect. Teachers, it seems, are viewed somewhat differently from other office-working professionals. As someone who spent her entire adult life working for the school system, Elena supported the loss of its autonomy ("that it's over") because of how she understood the management of the school system to include self-interest.

Her critique of bilingual education directors was not unlike some of the former president's characterizations of the directors of Indigenous movements. Correa, who supported moving the National Directorate into the Ministry of Education, routinely criticized directors of the organization CONAIE for being elitist, using insults like "*ponchos dorados*" (golden ponchos).[9] In the process of calling directors of Indigenous organizations names, he co-opted the discontent of some teachers and parents for his own racialized and classed criticisms of Indigenous movements. In response to protest of his administration's far-reaching policies, he maligned directors of Indigenous organizations for having economic advantages that they largely do not have but which resonated with the concerns of many Kichwa speakers. He also vastly increased monthly salaries for teachers with bachelor's degrees to be on par with many national office workers, which degree-holding teachers appreciated. Others who did not meet the degree requirement, however, especially in rural areas, faced job insecurity.

I now turn to another interlocutor's words to examine the links between professionalization, Kichwa use, and classed and urbanized differences. Professor Ariruma Kowii greeted me and two DINEIB employees—an academic director and a communications and media manager—with a *"buenos días"* in Spanish and a straightforward assessment of how Kichwa is minimized in urban professional life. He focused on professionalism as the death knell of Kichwa. Kowii did not mince words: "*Sí, estamos fregados con la lengua*" (Yeah, we are screwed with the language). Wearing a rounded black hat and pressed white dress shirt with matching white pants and black and white slippers, he received us in his office at the Simón Bolívar Andean University for a planning meeting for the upcoming international conference, the Congress on Endangered Languages.[10] Over cups of tea and water, he told a story that critiqued language shift among Kichwa professionals, including himself and directors of the school system.

As I noted in Chapter 2, Kowii served as the first subsecretary in 2009, the highest position in the school system and the intermediary between it and the vice minister of education. In that position, he led the establishment of the Subsecretariat for Intercultural Dialogue, the supervising body that curbed the National Directorate's authority. Many people who had worked there, especially those who belong to the organization CONAIE, would characterize him as an enemy. Kowii cited the urbanized, upwardly mobile dimensions of professionals as "screw[ing]" the linguistic movement, even as he self-identifies as one.

He continued:

Había un dirigente comunista.	There was a communist leader.
"Ñukanchik derecho. Ñukanchik lucha. Ñukanchik autogestiones," creo que decía.	[In speeches,] I think he would say, "Our right. Our struggle. Our self-management."
De Kichwa solo decía ñukanchik *y nada más.*	In Kichwa, he would only say *ñukanchik* ("our") and nothing else, [since *derecha, lucha, autogestiones* are borrowed from Spanish].
Entonces, hablamos en español y escribimos en español, todos,	So, we all speak in Spanish and we write in Spanish, all of us,

desde la [educación intercultural] bilingüe hasta los políticos de Pachakutik y las organizaciones indígenas.

from "*la bilingüe*" [intercultural bilingual employees] to the politicians of Pachakutik and the Indigenous organizations.

I asked him when they did speak Kichwa.

Es que nuestro problema es que solo estamos con el discurso.	Our problem is that we only have the discourse.
Hasta hacemos levantamientos pero en la práctica no ejercemos,	We even do uprisings [and we may use it], but in practice we don't exercise it.
más bien las bases mantienen la lengua.	Better put, the bases maintain the language.
Los papás hablan con sus hijos en la lengua	Parents speak to their kids in the language
y los hijos hablan con sus novias	and the sons speak with their significant others.
pero aquí no cambia nada,	But here [in Quito] nothing changes.
es como dicen pura paja.	It's, as they say, pure nonsense.
Por etiqueta política, por marketing.	For political tagging, for marketing.
Entonces es un problema eso.	So that's a problem.
Todos los indígenas que se han civilizado en lo occidental	The Indigenous people have been civilized in what is the Western,
y nos hemos formado élites.	and we have been trained as elites.
Los profesionales de la dirigencia política hablan menos la lengua.	The professionals of the political leadership speak the language less.

His criticism centers on positions of authority and office work in Quito, where especially those on a national stage in the city tend to speak more Spanish. Kowii's critique echoes the contrast that Elena described between office employment and Kichwa use. Through geographic and socioeconomic mobility, in his words, "*nos hemos formado élites,*" claiming that Kichwa speakers have been educated to form an "elite" class. Key to his understanding of this change is a difference between talk about Kichwa in roles for which directors speak publicly for others, and routine, cross-event occurrences of speaking the language. According to his hierarchy, those at the top—politicians, educational directors, linguists, those of the "political leadership" whom he equates with "professionals"—tend not to speak Kichwa for daily communicative purposes while also realizing that Kichwa is politically helpful. Kichwa, he said, is a "discourse," a language used for official talk and as an emblem of Indigeneity but that is not commonly spoken. Most individuals who direct bilingual education are proficient in Kichwa; they just tend not to routinely speak it. When they do, they more often speak Unified Kichwa.

Kowii's example shows how difficult the official recognition of Indigenous languages is, in part, because of the systematic changes in language use that co-occur with office and city life. Many salaried professionals have lived in cities for years, too (he speaks about and from Quito), including directors in the national bilingual education offices. Though parts of his comments provide an exaggerated rhetorical effect (such as "Indigenous people have been civilized in what is the Western, and we have become elites"), his more measured statement, "With the professionals of the political leadership, the language is spoken less," fits with my own experiences in the school system. Further, his example of multilingualism shows how their work has required the use of words from Spanish, a challenge for speech-giving.

His comments emphasize racialized ("Western," "civilized"), classed ("elites"), and urbanized ("here") change in language shift. There is resonance between his and Elena's comments about professionals identifying "wherever they want." Likewise, Marta, a Kichwa speaker who worked in Indigenous education since the 1980s and who appears in the next chapter, but is now retired, echoed frustration with employment in the national coordinating offices of the school system and pinpointed professionalization as leading to racialized difference emerging from educational institutions and urban life. In an interview at her desk in the National Directorate offices, she tearfully lamented changes toward becoming *mestizos*, such as individualism, that she saw.[11]

El mestizo es individualista, ¿no?	The *mestizo* is individualist, no?
Queriendo ser más que los de abajo, digamos.	Wanting to be greater than those below [them], let's say.
Queriendo demostrar lo que sabe, lo que tiene, los títulos, cosas así.	Wanting to demonstrate what they know, what they have, degrees, things like that.
Dicen "soy magister, soy doctora."	They say I'm a master, I'm a doctor.
Entonces, ese es el pensamiento mestizo.	So that's *mestizo* thought.
Y en el pensamiento indígena, no cabe eso.	And in Indigenous thought, that doesn't fit.
En una comunidad, una persona netamente indígena,	In a community, a clearly Indigenous person,
los títulos no tiene por que resultar en ninguna parte.	the degrees have no reason to result in anything.
Si por el estudio, por las oportunidades que ha tenido—	If because of studying, because of the opportunities that they've had,
conoce más, sabe más,	they're familiar with more, they know more,
tiene que ser mucho más humilde que el resto....	they have to be much more humble than the rest....
y eso no hay aquí.	And that's not here [in DINEIB].

Por eso no se ha dado mucho avance en la educación bilingüe.	That's why intercultural bilingual education hasn't advanced a lot.
Los profesores no son capacitados, no tienen una formación real en otras palabras.	The teachers aren't trained, they don't have a real preparation, in other words.

Marta emphasized that studying has come with changes in authority and displays of knowledge. She described *mestizos* as more likely to seek degrees. According to her logic, schooling has brought about a racialized "individualist" perspective that emphasizes some superiority and hierarchy. In "communities," not urban centers, she noted, norms hold that one avoids self-promotion and that becoming more knowledgeable coincides with becoming humbler. She characterized a form of professionalization as "*mestizo*" and that the obtaining of advanced degrees presents a clear rupture with her description of Indigenous life philosophies. Master's and doctoral degrees come with claims to expertise and self-promotion, which contrasts with those who are "plainly" or "clearly" (*netamente*) Indigenous. She also said that teachers ultimately pay the price for office professionals that continue to receive degrees, since they have less training, and she attributed the main reason that bilingual education has not "advanced" to individualistic orientations. Like Elena, she positioned teachers as different from other "professionals."

As Marta continued, she emphasized how everyone changes but that her experiences with those who work in the national offices show a different kind of change from the cross-generational change that she has seen with her adult children:

Jamás una cultura es estática, es dinámica,	A culture is never static. It's dynamic,
siempre va cambiando, generando cosas,	it always continues changing, generating things,
pero también hay que seguir descartando las cosas negativas, ¿no?	but one also has to keep discarding the negative things, no?
En ese sentido, por ejemplo yo he dicho a mis hijos,	In that sense, for example, I've told my children,
está bien que por la comodidad hayan cambiado de ropa,	it's fine, for comfort, that they have changed clothes,
que nuestra ropa no es fácil encontrar,	Our clothing isn't easy to find,
no es fácil confeccionar.	it's not easy to make.
Pero sí, como ellos están afuera, yendo, viniendo,	But since they're [her children] living outside [of Ecuador], going, coming,
debe ser más fácil conseguir otra ropa.	it must be easier to get other clothes.
Pero ya el pensamiento y el corazón sigue siendo indígena.	But their thinking and their heart continue to be Indigenous.

Cross-generational shifts, she said, such as not wearing the clothes of one's community daily, are common and expected. Lest we think she is an example of how older generations may lament change, she emphasized that she is not alarmed by change, because "culture" "is dynamic." She located changes on two distinct levels, ones like clothing that ordinarily happen because culture is not static, and deeper ones of heart and mind, which run counter to cultural expectations.

Language shift occurs with "hearts and minds" kinds of change. As Kowii noted, a pattern of changing language use tends to accompany professionalization, evidenced by Kichwa being spoken less overall than Spanish in national offices. Elena emphasized that "bilingual is a letterhead." Implicit to her point is that those who coordinate the school system are not, in fact, speaking as much Kichwa. Schooling, from primary schools to professional employment, has accustomed many Kichwa adults to speaking Spanish. They move between state institutions with relative smoothness and are used to reading and producing written texts in Spanish.

Shift to Spanish is common among teachers, too, depending on where they live. In fact, scholars have noted that teachers across the school system routinely do not teach Kichwa or speak the language with their children (Haboud 2004, 73). Spanish is often the default language of communication. According to the accounts presented here, the scales of difference, however—traveling greater distances, earning more advanced degrees, moving more fluidly through state institutions—set professionals from the National Directorate apart from other Indigenous professionals like teachers.

Conclusion

Indigenous movements are led by a small but increasing number of people who have advanced degrees and work salaried office jobs. Schooling has been significant for Indigenous peoples now having access to state power and some economic stability. Higher education, in particular, has contributed to the preparation of Indigenous directors for emerging leadership roles and provided credentials for historically marginalized peoples to assume middle- and upper-middle-class jobs. Yet, colleagues describe those directors as marked—more "Western" or "*mestizo*"—than others who are not directors of Indigenous organizations. Popular discourse about Indigenous movements, including how Correa criticized bilingual education officials, has drawn from these observations, even as such differences are relational. As Josefina showed, her extensive schooling has not led to the same level of income as her artisan siblings, even if she earns more than most other nonprofessional laborers.

Language shift is intimately linked to such differences. Teachers have long attempted to restrict Kichwa-speaking in institutional settings, and this history affects today's status quos of institutional talk. Bilingual education directors do speak more Spanish than Kichwa, even as they promote the teaching of Indigenous languages. This change is evident in Carlos's case, since he learned Kichwa as a nondominant language and his abilities later became rusty in the office. Josefina was exceptional in her Kichwa use, and that she was older than others in the office, and living with her mother. Thus, speaking Kichwa daily in the office probably had much to do with her patterns of communication. Others question why those who use Kichwa for state politics do not do so outside of those activities.

But differences are not limited to language use or clothing or other markers of Indigeneity. Most people associated with the school system describe transformation through preparation and employment in educational institutions. However, labels like "professionals" erase the diversity that such categorizations encompass and, furthermore, mute the double binds that people in such roles live. As anthropologist Joanne Rappaport (2005) notes, many Indigenous intellectuals are simultaneously insiders and outsiders. They are often culturally "inside" gatherings for *pueblos* and nationalities, but their mobility and ideas about the world make them outsiders, too. Similarly, when in the spaces of modernist institutions, they are "insiders" who work there but also "outsiders," constantly marked in comparison to their *mestizo*-identifying colleagues. Such characterizations are relative, as those who run Indigenous movements and work in Ministry of Education offices tend to be more "insiders" in *mestizo*-linked spaces than those whom they represent. As to whether they are further "outsiders" among those whom they represent, other parts of this book demonstrate such differences.

With professionalization, degree-granting and job promotions predicate individual success, which many Kichwa speakers consider at odds with community norms for solidarity and humility. Many Kichwa speakers view "professionalization" as a means for overcoming social and economic marginalization, even as they lament how people may change. Ironically, despite remarkable advances in bilingual education, the conditions of professional trajectories and employment mean that professionals may not be best positioned to halt and reverse Kichwa language shift.

PART III
DAILY ACTIVITIES AS STATE AGENTS

5

Translating the Law to Kichwa

Intertextuality, Authorship, and Intelligibility from Textbooks to Legal Texts

At her cubicle in the Ministry of Education, Marta stared at the Kichwa translation of a teacher manual on her computer screen. The office was cold, and she was wrapped up in her deep green shawl while quietly reading out loud. Other employees had carried out the translation, and Marta had highlighted all the phrases in the Word document that she said were not understandable to readers. Nearly every line had highlighter marks. Now she was making changes, trying to make the written Kichwa more intelligible. "*Yachachikkunaman kipa rikuchina ashtawan sinchi*" (getting the teachers look at this later is really hard), she said to me. "*Como maestra, me gusta que el profesor comprenda qué es el mensaje*" (As a teacher [myself], I like that the teacher [who would receive the document] understands what the message is).[1]

That Marta was in the ministry and authoring documents in an Indigenous language shows how throughout the world state policies have begun to recognize and support languages they previously erased. This chapter examines, ethnographically, a major advance in the naming of Indigenous languages as "official": the translation of legal documents to languages rarely used in state-authorized texts. Since Ecuador's 2008 constitutional recognition of Kichwa, this designation has spurred state-sponsored Kichwa translations, such as the Constitution, several laws, and signage on government buildings, carried out by school system employees like Marta. Such changes can excite speakers as they see the public inscription of their languages, and there is potential to, literally, rewrite the state in a translation.

This chapter goes behind the scenes of these emerging translations to understand some key concerns of those translating. I argue that state-sponsored translations to Kichwa are closely intertwined with the writing practices of previously produced state documents, such as textbooks. Kichwa translators routinely seek to honor previously produced documents and their authors through continuing similar writing practices, such as those of the existing Kichwa version of the Constitution. However, as translators made some of the earliest attempts to translate state documents to Kichwa, they find it hard to avoid some maintenance of the status quos of state power. A major factor in this result was how language standardization affected the translation of the Spanish language Ley Orgánica de Educación Intercultural (Organic Law of Intercultural Education, hereafter "the Law") to Kichwa. Even as coordinators went to great lengths to ensure wide representation of linguistic differences among the translators, state-sponsored documents tend to prioritize some Kichwa speakers over others, such as those with educational credentials who support and understand standardized linguistic forms. As Marta showed, making a standardized Kichwa translation may even prevent teachers from reading a manual.

The translators' concerns about how to translate were even overtly constrained by state politics, too, which again made other Kichwa texts important. Heads of state can use criticisms of Indigenous language texts to exacerbate disagreements among directors and organizers. Translators were aware that President Rafael Correa's officials and supporters had previously amplified criticism about bilingual education employees who authored Kichwa textbooks that were hard to read, which made the sociopolitical context of translating the Law as fraught as the linguistic endeavor. This risk was an example of Correa's ongoing aggression toward his critics like members of the Indigenous organization CONAIE (Confederation of Indigenous Nationalities of Ecuador), to which many translators belonged. Heads of state can use criticisms of Indigenous language texts to exacerbate disagreements among directors and organizers.

While I routinely spent time with translators in the bilingual education coordinating offices as they carried out Kichwa translations, this chapter focuses on the 2012 national workshop that produced the translated text that was later edited and published as the Law. The translation workshop brought together policymakers, linguists, teachers, and others—all school system employees—to write the Kichwa version of the document. In the next section, I place assumptions from translation theory into conversation with anthropological theory and the work of the translators themselves. I then examine the translation of state documents to Indigenous languages, their connections to other state documents, like textbooks, and how national politics affects them. I show that there is a double bind in who is recognized, erased, or marginalized anew based on the task at hand and the large scale of readers who must be addressed in the authoring of the text.

About Translation and Standardization

Translation inherently involves intertextuality, one text's connections with other texts. Research on translation has shown the singular intertextual significance of the source text, the work that is being translated to another language (Cao 2007; Venuti 2008). In other words, scholars emphasize that translation involves primarily a form of replication of *that* text, such as how "the source-language text" "is replaced" by signifiers in the language of translation, the "target language" (Venuti 1994, 17; Bassnett 2013; Lefevere & Bassnett 1998; see also Gal 2015, 227). Indeed, as Marta told me that day in the office, she would sometimes read the Spanish version again, rewrite it for herself, and then rework the translation in Kichwa. However, for state documents with wider audiences than solely teachers, this ethnographic research revealed, somewhat differently, that the resulting Kichwa translation's relation to an array of other state documents written in Kichwa was ultimately as influential for translation as the source text, the Spanish version of the Law. Many translators emphasized the importance of what I call here cohesion—that Kichwa words and grammar are used similarly across the small number of existent state documents.

Concerns about cohesion limited challenges to language standardization and even sweeping change to state texts through translation. Such transformations have occurred elsewhere with the translation of constitutions to Indigenous languages. For lesser-spoken Indigenous languages than Kichwa, such as Nasa in Colombia, intellectuals reconceived of justice, authority, and the Colombian state itself as they translated the 1991 Constitution from Spanish to Nasa (Rappaport 2005, 5). They replaced those concepts with others grounded in a Nasa point of view. Nasa translators viewed the translation process as encouraging and contributing to future political struggle since they had rarely experienced state recognition (Oróstegui Durán 2008). However, in Ecuador rather than discussing, for example, political strategies or "radical interpretation[s]" (Povinelli 2001, 321) to redirect or contest state power—such as using open-endedness in the interpretation of meanings to transform the law (Joseph 1995) or even reinforcing the ambiguity of abstract words to provide a pathway for future legal claims (Handman 2017)—most Kichwa translators were singularly concerned with either maintaining the norms of Unified Kichwa or crafting an intelligible translation for readers. Though there have been several decades of significant state recognition for Kichwa (more than, say, for Nasa), there is less intelligibility in any one linguistic register, given the many regional differences across the language family.[2] Kichwa has a larger and more varied set of speakers. The role of language standardization in translation compounded this challenge instead of ameliorating it. This example, thus, shows how texts other than the source text can predominantly shape translation.

Additionally, Kichwa translators had to confront colonial dimensions of translation that were not just about moving from Spanish to a translation in Kichwa; they contended with the use (or avoidance of) Unified Kichwa words and grammar based on those of standardized Ecuadorian Spanish. Translation is often about comparing forms, references, and uses across languages as they cohere in texts (Hanks 2010, 158; Silverstein 2003b). This perspective decenters "a language" from translation and refocuses on signifiers and meanings and how they cohere or contrast as registers (Gal 2015) like "Unified Kichwa" or "Kichwañol." The use of registers, such as standardized ones, is key to understanding the very process of translation and who state-sponsored translations may prioritize, such as those who understand Unified Kichwa.

Indigenous linguists and education directors usually see an importance to coining words and elaborating technical registers, which has implications for authoring and translating texts. As this book has shown, the process of standardization often makes a register that is lexically "pure," such as by minimizing loanwords from other languages and inventing words in Indigenous languages (Guerrettaz 2015; Rodriguez 2016; Swinehart 2012). But making others aware of those words and encouraging their use is not easy. For example, in Venezuela, a missionary translated the national anthem to Warao, and state institutions and Warao teachers adopted this anthem for use. In so doing, the Warao people are illustrated as a part of the multicultural Venezuelan state for those who do not identify as Warao, and they appear united by using a shared register of the language that excludes words from Spanish. However, few Warao citizens knew the invented words in the anthem beyond memorization (Rodriguez 2016). Similarly in Ecuador, Unified Kichwa is a drastic change for most Kichwa speakers who fluidly borrow or transpose Spanish words and grammatical forms into everyday Kichwa speech. The calquing and inventing of words and grammar for standardization—which many translators see as important for making Kichwa a distinct language worthy of recognition and translation—is often hard to understand.

Many Kichwa translators sought what translation studies scholars call "domesticating translations" (Bassnett 2009; Venuti 1994), those that avoid looking for precise equivalents and instead rewrite texts based on how people would communicate in the language to which they are translating. For example, some expressed the importance of maintaining the "spirit" of the original text—trying to convey the gist of the statement without literally translating—and aimed to use nonstandard, intelligible registers. Yet, their task was also challenging because the Spanish content of the Law used various technical registers, such as legalese. Legal translation requires proficiency in other technical linguistic registers, such as legal and bureaucratic situations of language use (Cao 2007, 9), which includes even more terms unknown to everyday language speakers. Ideologies about legal communication tend toward precision and respect for legal process (Latour 2009; 198–99; Mertz 2007; Richland 2008, 79). Legal registers, too, are monologic, foregrounding the consistent use of standardized ways of communicating over others, simultaneously narrowing the voices and subject positions indexed in communication (Tomlinson 2017). This perspective further complicates the transcribing of the many, diverse colloquial forms of communication.

Furthermore, with translation of laws to Indigenous languages, translators must consider how law defines, prescribes, and even enforces societal ideals (Cao 2007, 13; Howard, Pedro, & Ricoy 2018) and, additionally, how law implicitly sets and draws from norms about how to write and speak. Language standardization involves "normalization," elaborating shared norms about how language use should occur (Chapter 3; Urla et al. 2017, 29; Faudree 2015b). The intertextuality of norms further adds to academic understandings of translation. Unified Kichwa was normatively used in other state-sponsored texts, and many translators wanted the translation to be written in a similar register to other texts like textbooks.

The translators' concerns for the consistency of Kichwa across state-sponsored texts took several forms. First, a major consideration for translators was a controversy over textbooks written in Unified Kichwa that were hard to read. Some translators wanted to avoid similar outcomes and so lobbied to not use the same standardized words to translate the Law, but others emphasized the importance of consistency across all texts. Second, since there are many forms and registers of Kichwa, translators had to consult a wide array of texts, such as dictionaries. The idea that words in their translated text should match Kichwa entries for the Spanish words in dictionaries, too, ultimately thwarted the efforts of translators who wanted to make the document as readable as possible (not necessitating the use of a dictionary). Sometimes even the "standard" varied across the texts, such as the word listed in a dictionary versus the one used in the translation of the Constitution, showing an immense challenge to linguistic normativity. Third, beyond lexicon, some translators emphasized the standardization of Kichwa *grammar* and using it consistently across multiple documents like the Constitution and textbooks. Grammatical rules influenced what could be written in the Law, yet they implicitly stipulated Kichwa's equivalency with standardized Ecuadorian Spanish. Some translators offered the alternative argument of altering previous norms to better intelligibility in the new documents. However, cohesion and its repetition of standardized forms prevailed.

Textbooks and Challenges of State Publications in Indigenous Languages

Some political challenges of translating the Law were similar to those found in the authorship of other state-sponsored Kichwa texts. Before turning to the workshop, I consider experiences with other prominent state texts, such as the Constitution and the *Kukayu* textbooks, to which the translators made references as they worked. More than five years before the translation workshop, bilingual education employees authored the *Kukayu* ("a light, portable snack" in Kichwa) textbooks for use in the school system and which teachers lamented for being difficult to read as written in Unified Kichwa. The following comments introduce this scenario.

Marlon worked as the subsecretary, the highest post in the school system, for a period of my research. He learned Highland Kichwa growing up from his grandparents and had long been an employee in the National Directorate. Seated at his cubicle, I asked him about written Kichwa. He cited the Constitution and the *Kukayu* readers as prominent examples of hard-to-read Kichwa.[3]

Si yo me pongo a leer la constitución, yo no he de poder.	"If I start to read the Constitution, I probably won't be able to.
Primero estamos acostumbrados a hacer [la lectura] en español....	First, we are accustomed to doing it in Spanish....
Si yo mismo me pongo a leer, con estas palabras,	If I start to read it myself, with these words,
hay muchos términos nuevos creados.	there are many new created terms.
Eso pasó con los Kukayus también.	That also happened with the *Kukayu*s.
Se crearon muchos términos	Many terms were created
y no se socializaron con los profesores.	and they were not socialized with teachers.
No sabía qué significaban...	I didn't know what they meant...
y por eso no se puede aplicar los textos."	and that's why one can't apply the textbooks."

Marlon described four important lessons for authorship, translation, and audiences who read state documents in Kichwa. First, most Kichwa speakers under the age of fifty are bilingual and more commonly read Spanish.[4] For the most part, even directors of the school system have undergone schooling in Spanish, making Kichwa somewhat of a secondary language for reading. Second, Marlon and others are especially accustomed to reading technical and legal work in Spanish, and the presence of neologisms in technical Kichwa affects readability. As the head of the school system, he even cited such words as barriers that prevented him from reading the Constitution, indicating the gravity of their use. Third, Marlon showed that these challenges exceeded legalese. The coining of new words makes even primary school textbooks hard to read. Fourth, Marlon made clear that he was not simply complaining that the *Kukayus* were difficult to understand but that the textbooks are so challenging to read they go unused in classrooms. Kichwa translators thus have a well-founded concern for making the emerging text intelligible for readers. At the conference, translators were concerned with questions of readability, especially in juxtaposition with the textbooks and other circulating texts.

On the one hand, the *Kukayus* are the most systematic texts the school system has elaborated, consisting of fifty-four textbooks from first to tenth grade for various subjects including mathematics, applied sciences and art, history and geography, Spanish, Kichwa, physical education, and others, depending on grade level (Figure 5.1). In general, the Kichwa and

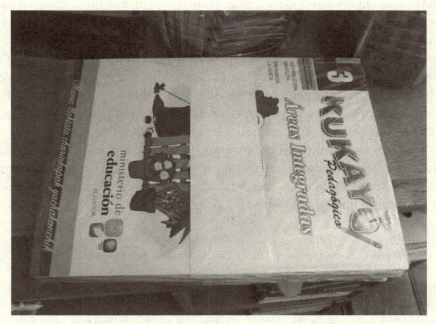

Figure 5.1 *Kukayu* textbooks were stored and still shrink-wrapped in the classroom featured in Chapter 7. Photo by author.

history-geography books are written in Kichwa and the others in Spanish. The books arose from initiatives led by several bilingual education regional directorates and attempted to unite curricula across the country's Highlands (Atupaña 2006). On the other hand, while the series is remarkable as a comprehensive set of textbooks, the *Kukayus* have become notorious for the challenge of producing written work that both serves national political and educational goals and is intelligible to an array of readers. The textbooks, moreover, became fodder for those aligned with President Correa to ridicule directors of the school system. Officials from his Ministry of Education had previously published criticisms of the *Kukayus* on their website for teaching students about Indigenous organizations and Pachakutik, an Indigenous movement that sponsors affiliated candidates for elected office like a political party, and for being hard for teachers to understand.

Within this context, bilingual education directors were under much pressure, as any materials they produced could become politicized to denigrate them. Two episodes of the television show *Ñukanchik Muskuy* ("Our Dream" in Kichwa) focused on the *Kukayus*, and one in particular highlights the political peril of authoring Kichwa texts. As a public television production, the program formed part of the state's intercultural programming. The channel that produced and aired it was widely agreed upon as promoting Correa's agenda. In the episode, a Kichwa journalist and host, Sami, invited three bilingual education directors, two of whom were also members of CONAIE, to appear in the studio. Plenty of Kichwa speakers supported Correa, and their voices tended to be showcased, such as how Sami served as the host. The episode foregrounded the disconnect of the directors from those whom they serve. The translators at the conference worked within this hostility, aware of the *Kukayus* controversy and probable repercussions from readers, colleagues, and members of the president's political party.

The show quickly turned confrontational when the host asked the guests to watch prerecorded clips inserted into the television broadcast and comment on them. The video cuts to a teacher from one school, where I have researched, while she flips through a *Kukayu* textbook.[5]

Estos textos hicieron,	They made these textbooks,
creo que se reunieron los supervisores, los pedagogos, los técnicos,	I think that the supervisors met, the pedagogic experts, the technicians,
Pero..., hay un Kichwa demasiado sofisticado.	But..., there is an extremely sophisticated Kichwa.
Hay palabras que no sabemos ni qué quieren decir.	There are words that we don't even know what they mean.

The video then shifts to the director of the school:

Es un idioma totalmente diferente,	It's a totally different language.
no tiene nada que ver con el hacer cotidiano de hablar.	It has nothing to do with the daily act of speaking.
Si los profesores no entendemos, los papás [tampoco], peor los niños.	If we teachers don't understand, the parents [either], the children worse.

The recording returns to the studio where the host Sami is seated with the uncomfortable looking directors. One guest's eyes dart around while another looks down at the floor. The camera zooms in on one guest's face as Sami asks: "*Compañera, ¿qué recomendación hace usted?*" (Colleague, what recommendation can you make?). The guest, Victoria, responds, her voice rising:

Dice que no entienden algunos vocabularios,	She [the teacher] says they do not understand some vocabulary.
yo creo que es deber y la obligación de los maestros también investigar.	I believe it is also the duty and obligation of teachers to investigate.
Ahora, si nosotros ponemos un Kichwa—un kichwañol—sería absurdo.	Now, if we used a Kichwa—a *kichawañol*—it would be absurd.
Lamentablemente el Kichwa ha perdido esa riqueza que ha tenido,	Unfortunately, Kichwa has lost that wealth that it has had,
que esos kukayus pedagógicos . . . han recogido,	that those pedagogic *kukayus* . . . have collected,
inclusive léxicos que existen en otras comunidades.	including lexicon that exists in other communities.

The teacher and director focused on unfamiliar words as a source of misunderstanding in the *Kukayus* and emphasized how the textbooks include Kichwa that seems like "a totally different language." Paired with her critique of "extremely sophisticated Kichwa"—a characterization of Unified Kichwa—the school director indicated that bilingual education authors are ignoring the wide range of people who "don't understand" the register. The teacher further distinguished herself from planners with "I think that the *supervisors* met, the *pedagogic experts*, the *technicians*," naming the more authoritative jobs of Kichwa speakers as those who are responsible for the textbooks.

In response, Victoria offered that one solution might be using a Kichwa register that includes many Spanish loanwords (*kichwañol*, which is somewhat pejorative), but that "it would be absurd," implying that such a textbook would not bolster learning Kichwa. Implicit in Victoria's comments is that state-sponsored Kichwa texts, such as the *Kukayus*, should illustrate lexically "pure" Kichwa. Authors do not wish to produce a Kichwa text replete with Spanish loanwords, as they see it as working against efforts to get speakers to use new Kichwa words and to make Kichwa equal to Spanish. Yet, if they continue to enact purist ideologies, they make bilingual education inaccessible to most people. Virginia emphasized that Kichwa "has lost that wealth that it had" and that the *Kukayus* "collected" words that were disappearing from use, so the teachers may not have been aware that some of the signifiers of the "totally different language" were older words that are less known. Though Victoria did not mention this possibility, printing versions of the books in several registers would require additional resources but could be another option.

Background on the Translation Conference

The participants at the workshop to translate the Law gathered in the mountainous province of Cotopaxi about an hour and a half south of Quito and were acutely aware of such challenges around state-sponsored Kichwa texts. The translators had all worked as state agents for years, either in the national planning offices, in regional offices, or as school-based educators. Most were members of Indigenous organizations, such as CONAIE. Most grew up speaking regional Kichwa registers from an early age and learned to speak Spanish from schooling-ages on. Their familiarity with Unified Kichwa varied, with a subset of the translators being proficient Unified Kichwa speakers and others having basic familiarity. All would consider themselves fluent in Kichwa and Spanish.

The organizers of the workshop, two women who were members of the Kichwa nationality and from the Central Highlands who now lived in Quito and worked in the National Directorate, followed common strategies for Indigenous authorship. Their careful planning sought to acknowledge the multiplicity of voices in a written text and to seek diversity in the translators' backgrounds to further inclusivity and reader intelligibility (Faudree 2015b). In other words, they sought to have a variety of perspectives about how and for whom the document should be written (by inviting few curriculum authors and linguists from the National Directorate offices; many regional office administrators, evaluators, pedagogists, and linguists; and schoolteachers) and by inviting two representatives from each Ecuadorian province where Kichwa speakers reside to have representation across Kichwa registers. All participants were invited to comment on whether the emerging translation was intelligible.

The organizers also carefully planned to have an array of Kichwa-language documents to reference in translation, such as the Constitution and all the dictionaries they could gather. Even the source text was multiple. The co-organizers had already worked together to draft a Kichwa translation of the Law themselves so the translators would have a Kichwa-language version and not just the Spanish-language version to reference. They also asked another National Directorate employee who was working as a translator in Ecuador's National Assembly to author and bring his own translated version of the Law so there would be more than one Kichwa-language translation available.

The translators assembled in a spacious, chilly room in a large building owned by the school system that was used for conferences. It doubled as a hostel and workspace for making school furniture. The workshop consisted of five days of meetings where attendees spent hours discussing the best ways to translate the Law. Translation principally happened in small groups of four to five people with each group responsible for a section of the Law. There were explanations and mini-work sessions at the beginning of the conference, and at the end, all translators collectively checked the translations drafted by each small group.

Cohesion across State Documents

While the *Kukayus* example shows how Unified Kichwa words and texts are linked to unintelligibility for readers, this example shows how concern about the recurrence of forms across major state documents (intertextual cohesion) was ever-present and shaped decisions about how to translate and write. The translators' efforts toward cohesion demonstrate citationality, a form of intertextuality in which signifiers and norms for interpretation are reproduced across distinct time-spaces (Nakassis 2012, 626). A citation continues a form and indexes prior uses by its recurrence (Bauman 2004). Translators' efforts to use the same words in various state documents show how citationality continues to connect new Kichwa texts with previous ones by repeating standardized words.

For example, on the last day of the conference, all twenty-five translators in the room were discussing each article of the law that had been translated in small groups.[6] Two Kichwa speakers representing their group led the session as others checked their translations. Participants asked whether some words in the translation were used in other state documents. Their predicament in this example rested on how to translate the frequently used word: article. One presenter asked, "*Kay mama pachapak kamachiypika imatak nisha nin* artículo?" (In this law, what does "article" mean to say? What is "article" called [in Kichwa]?). A forty-five-minute conversation ensued. Eight different possibilities were offered by participants: *Kapak* (significant power or royal), *niki* (order, ordinal), *yupay* (number), *kamachiy* (law), *nishka* (so-called), *kashka* (been, existing), *rimashka* (declared), and not listing any translation. After a couple of exchanges, a translator in the audience said that how Kichwa was written in the Constitution should be continued in the Law:

¿Si fuésemos a cambiar la Constitución...?	[What would happen] if we were to change the Constitution...?
Ahora de cualquier manera eso ya está.	Now either way that [word] is already there [in the Kichwa version of the Constitution].
Nosotros tenemos que dar valor pues,	Well, we have to give [it] value.
si no, ¿cuál sería el criterio de la ciudadanía?	If not, what would be the evaluation of the populace?
¡Que nosotros mismos no valemos!	That we don't [even] value the [Kichwa version of the Constitution] ourselves!

As one of few state proclamations written in Kichwa, translating "article" differently in the law from how it is written in the Constitution risked disrupting the cohesion of official documents. They consider readers, here "the populace," as lamenting changes in the consistency of word use. In fact, a noticeable change in terminology across texts could be so perilous as to show that the translators "don't value" their own work. Changes across major state documents may not just invalidate the documents, but also their work as Kichwa translators altogether. They risk being perceived as flippant or as not respecting previous efforts.

Another strategy for maintaining cohesion was to use words found easily in common dictionaries. The elaboration of dictionaries involves processes of standardization to choose and organize words. However, even standardized words vary across texts. As the group continued to discuss how to translate "article," they collectively decided on *niki* (also used in the Constitution) as the most appropriate option when translator Pedro interjected to emphasize the role of dictionaries for readers.

El asunto es que no todos están con ese mismo criterio,	The matter is that not everyone has that same criteria [for the word]
por eso yo tengo la idea	and that's why I have the idea
de, más bien, poner lo que está ya establecido en el diccionario,	that it's better to put what already is established in the dictionary,
en cualquier diccionario.	in whatever dictionary.
Me imagino que [el diccionario] debe tener rigurosidad aprobada por muchos cientistas, lingüistas todo eso, ¿no?	I imagine that [the dictionary] must have rigor approved by many scientists, linguists, all of that, no?

Porque si nosotros nomás inventamos [las palabras]—	Because if we just invent [the words],
claro que nosotros vamos a entender entre nosotros,	of course we're going to understand among one another,
pero ¿qué tal si alguien coge ese libro y consulta en [el] diccionario?	but what happens if someone takes that book and consults the dictionary?
No va a entender absolutamente nada pues.	Well, they're going to understand absolutely nothing.
Ahí en el artículo [el diccionario] pone tres opciones:	There, under article, [the dictionary] gives three options.
Dice nishka, kashka y rimashka,	It says *nishka*, *kashka*, and *rimashka*.
cualquiera de las tres opciones que puede ser.	It could be whichever of the three options.

Pedro offered two reasons why following the dictionaries was important. First, dictionaries were written before the translation efforts, and they imply authority. Kichwa dictionaries are a collaborative work whose authors follow a "rigor[ous]" protocol; therefore, using dictionaries to help guide the possibilities of word selections implies rigor in their own work. Pedro emphasized that since "not everyone has the same criteria," choosing one of the words listed in the dictionary would alleviate misunderstandings, since they have undergone some standardization. Second, access to reference sources like the commonest dictionaries is important given the disagreements around unintelligible publications like the *Kukayus*. Following his perspective, if a reader can find the word in the dictionary, they can learn it. Pedro, further, spoke out against a possibility in which readers would find words so rarely used that they are not even in a dictionary.

Yet, his comments also indicate how reference shifts across texts. *Niki*, for example, conveys order, not the literal translation of "article" found in a dictionary. Its reference necessitates additional context beyond what many dictionaries provide. Pedro also worked somewhat against consensus and inclusion when he invoked authority and expertise by emphasizing that dictionaries are approved by "scientists" and "linguists." Though Pedro (and others) viewed dictionaries as important documents for clarifying the translation, many Kichwa dictionaries include more Unified Kichwa neologisms than other words used in everyday talk. However, as cases elsewhere have shown, Indigenous language readers often prefer finding words in dictionaries that are not neologisms, such as words from different regional registers (Rhodes et al. 2018). Similarly in Ecuador, Pedro's focus on rigor also bolstered standardization in contrast with how many others across the school system use Kichwa and seek to learn older words falling out of use or words used in other regions, even as the dictionary listing for *article* differed from the Constitution.

As Pedro's comments show, standardization involves aligning with authority. At this conference in his smaller translation group, he often positioned himself as more in favor of many aspects of standardization than other group members. He was born and grew up in a Highland province with many Kichwa professionals and had studied more than others at the workshop, who were mostly regional-level planners or teachers. His stated views about science at the workshop closely reflected those I heard among national planners who write major texts in Kichwa. Pedro's comments show how translation involved making decisions about which and whose forms of knowledge would manifest in state documents.

There were other approaches at the workshop, but they did not prevail. Even one organizer of the conference, Marta, emphasized writing a document that readers could understand. She described this importance in the vignette that opened this chapter, and at the workshop she offered an alternative philosophy of intertextuality to cohesion as she sought to make an understandable translation:

Yo creo que la idea principal era mejorar lo que ya existe.	I think that the main idea [of the workshop] was to improve what already exists.
Para eso teníamos las dos propuestas,	In order to do so, we have the two proposals
más la original que está en castellano,	plus the original that's in Spanish.
entonces nosotros teníamos el trabajito de revisar viendo las tres cosas [propuestas] y sacar una que sea comprensible....	So we've had the small job of revising while looking at those three things and making a draft that is intelligible....
Entonces ahora, si vamos a discutir lo que ya está en la Constitución,	So now if we're going to argue about what's already in the Constitution,
si no puedo tocarlo o voy a modificarlo,	if I can't touch it or modify it
o no tiene significado,	or it doesn't make sense,
¿adónde vamos a llegar?	where are we going to arrive?

Marta noted that a primary goal was "to revise," including the use of the two translations of the law the co-organizers and one other translator had carried out and brought with them to the workshop ("the main idea [of the workshop] was to better what already exists"). Counter to other participants' emphasis on cohesion and standardization, Marta offered an alternative form of intertextuality than cohesion in which state-authorized texts are linked to one another but that bettering them still upholds and improves that connection. Marta viewed translations of state texts as connected for improvement. Reader intelligibility was a major part of how Marta and her co-organizer demonstrated this perspective on intertextuality in planning the workshop, since she ensured the translators had other Kichwa translations to reference. Nevertheless, though other translators sought a different lexeme than did Pedro, their preference, *niki*, still supported a recurring way of writing across state documents. The final published translation of the Law included *niki* for "article," showing cohesion as the prevailing act of intertextuality.[7]

Grammatical Intertextuality for Standardizing Kichwa

In other conversations with me, Marta sharply criticized Unified Kichwa and many of the National Directorate's policies, a tendency that was reflected in how she managed the conference by encouraging a range of perspectives about Kichwa use. Nonetheless, standardization and cohesion prevailed even in decisions about grammar. Marta was nearing the end of a long career working in bilingual education, having been responsible for efforts like authoring children's books and national literacy advocacy. Before her employment in the Ministry of Education, she had worked for the prominent bilingual education Project (see Chapter 2) that had emphasized the use of local registers of Kichwa for authoring children's books and not Unified Kichwa. This employment experience likely figured into her distrust of language standardization. But more translators at the workshop supported cohesion and upholding norms. Early during the workshop on February 1, 2012, Marta and her co-organizer held a session to discuss translation strategies. About twenty-five people gathered in the meeting room with tables and rolling chairs.

She and her co-organizer invited Washington, a *mestizo*-identifying linguist and educator who worked as a mid-level coordinator in one of the school system's Central Highland regional offices, to lead a session on translation strategies. He was the only non-Indigenous-identifying person who spoke Kichwa (other than me) at the conference. Facing the large, sun-filled room, he spoke from a whiteboard with marker in hand. Participants frequently answered questions or interjected, making the session especially dialogic. One of Washington's explanations, as well as the dialogue that ensued, shows several lessons for how translation involves standardization across texts: first, how Unified Kichwa's grammar is modeled on Standardized Ecuadorian Spanish; second, how standardization may replace more common Kichwa norms and the philosophies tied to them, alienating the speech of people who are less versed in linguistics and "rigor"; and third, that Kichwa writing has syntactical and grammatical norms that reflect ideologies about writing in Spanish. These ideas are repeated across texts, including the *Kukayus*. In the following exchange, Washington instructed how to write translations and based written Kichwa on norms for standardizing Spanish:

Vamos a hacer dos oraciones en español y en Kichwa para ver cómo funcionan los adjuntos.	We're going to do two sentences in Spanish and Kichwa to see how dependent clauses work.
Es el análisis sintáctico.	It's syntactic analysis.
Ahora la corriente es hacer oraciones bien grandes [en español], ¿no?	Now it's common [in Spanish] to make long sentences, no?
Pero, en Kichwa esta misma oración vamos a ver que, como el verbo va al último, opera al revés.	But in Kichwa, this same sentence, we're going to see how the verb goes last. It works reversed [from Spanish].
Entonces, hagamos una.	So, let's do one.

He uttered and wrote the following sentence in Spanish:

El profesor enseña español a los alumnos en la escuela.
The teacher teaches Spanish to the students at school.

He proceeded to correct elicitations from the audience, coming up with the following comparable sentence in Kichwa which he wrote on the board for analysis.

Example 1
Yachachik[ka]   yachana wasipi yachakukkunaman **español shimita**[mi] yachachin.
Teacher[topic]   in school   to students   **Spanish**[affirmation] teach.
"The teacher teaches Spanish to students at school."

As he demonstrated in his writing, phrase-by-phrase, he made Kichwa syntax "reversed" yet parallel to a normative way of writing Spanish. The accusative case marker (in bold, here functioning as a direct object) is closest to the verb, followed by indirect objects, and so forth, in what he described as an inverted mirror of standardizing word order in Spanish. In other words, each marker occupies a similar slot and distance from the verb across the two languages but from right to left in Kichwa instead of Spanish's left to right. Like Spanish, Kichwa has long sentences that can be made more equivalent in form. He noted that in Kichwa "the verb goes last," which is common to the Quechua language family and one difference from Spanish (Adelaar 2004, 207).

This norm for writing and simultaneously standardizing Kichwa grammar based largely on Spanish led to participants reading the translation aloud as they considered it. A translator in the audience suddenly interjected, saying, in Spanish, "*No está bien estructurado eso en Kichwa*" (That's not well structured in Kichwa). He then dictated two possibilities that ordered sentences in contrasting ways:

Example 2
Yachachikka **mishu shimita**[mi] yachana wasipi <u>yachakukkuna</u>man *yachachin*.
The teacher ***mestizo* language**[affirmation] in the school to the students *teaches*.

Example 3
Yachachikka **español shimita**[mi] <u>yachakukkuna</u>wan yachana wasipi *yachachin*.
The teacher **Spanish language**[affirmation] with the students in the school *teaches*.

In the second two examples, the translator from the audience moved the direct object (in bold) two slots away from the verb (in italics) toward the beginning of the sentence, and it no longer exhibited the description of reverse parallel of Spanish's word order. The participant used case markers in a similar fashion to the moderator but disputed the syntactic slot in example (2).[8] The dissenting participant's example (2) also shows a change in the use of *mishu* (*mestizo* language or Spanish). The participant offered a lexically "purer" sentence than the facilitator, though *mishu* is likely more common in the region where he is from and is pejorative in some contexts.

In examining the phrases that function as indirect objects in the examples, which are underlined, example (3) further illuminates how Unified Kichwa is based on grammar from Spanish. In addition to a change in word order, the translator used *-wan* ("with") for students (an instrumental case marker) instead of the facilitator's *-man* ("to") students (an allative case marker). This change is significant for two reasons. First, the facilitator's use of *to* is a translation from the personal *a* in Spanish, where the preposition *to* should precede animate direct objects. On the contrary, *-wan* ("with") exhibits less grammatical calquing from Spanish. In other words, the dissenting translator contested the example as wrong and provided a grammatical counterexample (3) that is less calqued from Spanish.

Second, by using instrumental case (*-wan* "with") in example 3, the dissenting translator identified the noun to which the case marker is attached as the instrument or means through which the doer (the subject, here "teacher") carries out the action. In the Quechua language family, this grammatical construction can also render the noun it marks as an important doer, in addition to the subject—the causee (Adelaar 2004, 214)—which means that the translator's use of this case may attribute greater importance to students as instruments of and contributors to the goal of teaching.[9] In contrast, the facilitator's use of "to" (-*man*, allative case) in example 1 is inconsistent with its use for nonhuman subjects in the Quechua language family (Adelaar 2004, 214) and its specifying movement toward places (Howard 2014, 62). In addition to potentially replacing Kichwa philosophies that manifest in grammatical forms, examples 1 and 2 perhaps even extend Latin cases to Kichwa. With Latin, the marking of the direct object with accusative case may have originally indicated the goal of a movement before becoming a wider marker of direct objects.[10] This extension would be reflected in the broader use of *-man* in Kichwa, too.

At that moment, Marta noted that all dissent should be considered. A few audience members sparred with Washington, but he invoked other texts and "rules" to assert that Unified Kichwa forms based on standardized Spanish were the correct ones.

Washington: 1 *Aquí la estructura es la que se utiliza en todas las traducciones.*
Here the structure is the one used in all the translations.

Another participant: 2 *No todo un siempre.*
Not always.

Original dissenter: 3 *No todo un siempre.*
Not always.

Washington: 4 *Tiene que ser así.*
It has to be like that.

5 *En español, va el complemento directo luego del verbo.*
In Spanish the direct object goes after the verb.

6 *Sí, luego va el complemento directo y es una regla, incluso.*
Yes, the direct object goes afterward and is even a rule.

7 *El indirecto debe estar detrás del complemento directo.*
The indirect [object] should be after the direct object.

8 *Usted cree que no está bien eso, pero esa es la regla. . . .*
You think that it's not right, but that is the rule. . . .

9 *En los* Kukayus *hemos hecho. . . . Esa es la forma cómo se utiliza.*
In the *Kukayus* we've used them, that's the form that is used.

10 *Verá, compañero. Es algo también que no podemos negar,*
Look, colleague, it's something that we can't deny.

11 *en español puede perder el año en la universidad*
In Spanish, you can fail the year at the university.

12 *cuando está estudiando literatura en español. ¿Por qué?*
When you're studying literature in Spanish. Why?

13 *Porque las personas hablan bonito, pero pónganse a escribir,*
Because people speak pretty but sit down to write,

14 *a estructurar observando las reglas de la sintaxis.*
to structure while observing the rules of syntax.

15 *Ya para la escritura tienen que observar ciertas reglas, pues.*
Well, for writing people have to observe certain rules.

16 *Lo mismo en el Kichwa, también tenemos esas reglas.*
The same [happens] in Kichwa. We also have those rules.

17 *Hablamos con los dialectos.*
We speak with dialects.

18 *Ya para escribir hay un Kichwa unificado.*
Now for writing, there's a Unified Kichwa.

As Washington guided the discussion and assumed the role of expert, he based his argument for standardization on cohesion. For example, as he described how to translate in more general terms, he noted that the "structure" he proscribes is used in "all translations" (line 1), even though participants disagreed with him (lines 2–3). "Structure" entails standardization, and he invoked totality and authority to present Kichwa as uniformly written. He further referenced the *Kukayu* texts as following a fixed Unified Kichwa grammatical order (line 9). The previous section made clear the controversial nature of the *Kukayus* because of their use of Unified Kichwa. "That's the form that is used" justifies using it again because it has already been used in standardization efforts. Intertextual practices figure centrally into legal language use and are essential for how legal documents invoke and construct authority (Goodman et al. 2014, 460), such as by referencing legal precedent. This point extends, implicitly, to cohesion across Kichwa texts.

Washington also transposed standardized Ecuadorian Spanish onto Kichwa's grammatical forms as he evaluated Kichwa syntactic order for writing by describing how Kichwa should be modeled on Spanish's rules, proscriptions understood by few. Many speak well in Spanish, he said, but when they must write, they may even not pass their university courses. Washington also presented standardized Spanish language norms as analogous for Kichwa by citing Spanish literature classes in universities as a reason translators should write using Unified Kichwa (lines 12–18). While laws and other official documents are made possible by linguistic recognition, they risk remaining unintelligible for readers, offering another example of authoritative authors who write in hard-to-understand ways, and reproducing ideologies about normativity from Spanish in Kichwa. While some translators agreed with Washington, others expressed concern for how standardization will link new state documents to prior ones that are hard for Kichwa speakers to comprehend.

Defining Knowledge in Translation: Whose Ideas Manifest?

The above paragraphs show how language ideologies and forms of intertextuality emerged and concretized. As evident in Pedro's emphasis on dictionaries invoking "rigor approved by scientists [and] linguists," the choosing of which Kichwa forms to use while translating also presupposed and enacted authority. Who becomes an authority for Kichwa calls attention to whose and which linguistic forms, and the understandings of the world that they draw from, ultimately manifest in state documents. The roles and positionings that emerge among translators as they translate help to better understand whose voices are emphasized in state-sponsored tasks.

In other conversations with me in his job at a regional planning office in a Northern Highland province, Pedro had contested parts of Unified Kichwa, such as the alphabet (Limerick 2018). Yet, at this conference in his smaller translation group, he often positioned himself as more in favor of many aspects of standardization than were other group members, for example, Sisa. Sisa held a teaching degree, between a high school diploma and a bachelor's degree, and lived in an Amazonian town not far from where she grew up. She worked as a teacher at a bilingual school there. Throughout the workshop, she mostly spoke Spanish (as did Pedro), though her Spanish demonstrated a greater degree of influence from Kichwa, which she otherwise spoke daily.

In the following example, Pedro extended his support of rigor to defining what constitutes "academic" in our small translation group. He was comparatively more credentialed than the three other group members, more responsible for national planning for the school system, and was from a Central Highlands province. Members of the group tried to translate the following line to Kichwa from Chapter 7, Article 18, line E of the law:

Cumplir con los deberes que deriven de su participación en formas asociativas para la prestación de servicios no académicos relacionados con el quehacer educativo	Fulfilling duties that derive from their participation in associative groups for the rendering of non-academic services related to the educational task

The phrase is one bullet point of a list of multiple responsibilities and obligations that the Law specifies that members of an educational community should carry out. This line defines how people like parents should be involved in school activities that are not strictly academic, such as selling food to raise money. Since there was no preexisting register of Kichwa that has close equivalents for numerous words in this clause, the article was especially difficult to translate. It was nearly impossible to write a Kichwa version of the phrase that was both comprehensible and did not borrow words from Spanish.

This challenge meant that there were many possibilities for translation, and translators disagreed on how to translate "non-academic services" in particular. Should they use *yachay* (knowledge) or *llamkay* (work)? Could they use *kamay* (authority or administration)? Or could they better describe "non-academic services" as *amawta* (scientific) or *amawtay* (science)? Like much of the Law, the translation of this article was challenging because bureaucratic and somewhat abstract terms are less commonly used in Quechua; speakers tend to focus on how specific people act in a particular way on an occasion (Adelaar 2004, 234). Their conversation also shows that beyond straightforward equivalencies, translation depended on the translator's definition of science and knowledge—what is "not academic"?—concepts that are related to Kichwa standardization. Contrastive words could index differing ways of understanding Indigeneity and schooling. In the following transcript, the original talk in Spanish is italicized and the talk in Kichwa is not italicized.

1 Pedro:	*¿Cómo que a nosotros en la [educación] bilingüe dicen* yachak *para dar clases?* How is it that they say that we in bilingual [education] are *yachaks* (shamans or, literally, knowledgeable person) for teaching classes?
2 Other participant:	Yachak *es médico.* *Yachak* is doctor.
3 Sisa:	Kamay *es administrador,* kamaychik *es las autoridades.* *Kamay* is administrator, and *kamaychik* is authorities.
4 Pedro:	*Chuta, aquí no dice eso.* Shoot, here it doesn't say that.
5 Other participant:	*Dice "presta servicios."* It says "provide services."
6 Sisa:	*Este diccionario dice—* This dictionary says—
7 Other participant:	Yachana wasikunapa llamkaykunata intintina. To understand schoolwork. [reading a translation]
8 Pedro:	Shinapash, amawta yachachikkunapika [*sic*]— But, [*sic*]in teachers of science (using the word *amawta*)—
9 Other participant:	—yachaykunapika— (correcting) in [scientific] knowledge

10 Pedro: *Para dar los servicios no académicos dice. Ahora eso es ya—*
In order to provide non-academic services, it says. Now that is already—

11 Sisa: *Al contrario [porque son servicios académicos].*
The opposite [because they're academic services].

12 Pedro: Amawta *viene de sabios científicos.*
Amawta comes from wise scientists.

13 Other participant: *Conocimiento científico.*
[Correcting:] scientific knowledge.

14 Pedro: *Conocimientos, sabiduría, es* amawtay.
Knowledge, wisdom, that's *amawtay*.

15 Nicholas: *¿En las comunidades dicen así también?*
In the communities do they say it like that too?

16 Pedro: *Sí—*
Yes—

17 Sisa: *Sí dicen* amawta *científicos los Kichwas.*
Yes, Kichwas do say *amawta* to talk about scientists.

18 Pedro: Amawta nishka.
Amawta is said.

19 Sisa: *Pero los abuelos, tayta abuelos eran científicos, algo natural.*
But grandparents, grandfathers were scientific, something natural.

Es que no son preparados como nosotros así estudiando muy bien,
The thing is that they aren't trained like us, studying really well,

pero fueron científicos de la naturaleza.
But they were scientists of nature.

Por ejemplo, en medicina natural saben más que uno, los abuelos.
For example, in natural medicine, our grandfathers know more than one [we] knows.

20 Other participant: *Y los productos. Estudiaban la naturaleza.*
And products. They studied nature.

21 Sisa: *Por ejemplo mis abuelos saben más que nosotros—*
For example, my grandparents know more than we do—

nosotros que somos preparados no sé, pero, no conocemos.
we who are educated, I don't know, but we're not familiar with it.

Sí, son científicos.
Yes, they are scientific.

22 Pedro: *Yo diría que antes a falta de la educación, a falta de letras—*
I would say that in years past, the absence of education, the absence of writing—

23 Sisa: *Todo eso.*
All of that.

24 Pedro: *y el entorno, por necesidad reutilizaron*
And the environment, because of necessity they reused

y se dieron cuenta [de] que eso hacía bien,
and they realized that that helped,

pero eso no me permite ... calificar la rigurosidad científica para decir amawta.
but that does not allow me to grade its scientific rigor to say *amawta*.

¿Por dónde amawtay?
Near the meaning of *amawtay*?

25 Sisa: *Son sabios, pues.*
Well, they're wise.

Both Sisa and Pedro agreed that *amawta* is a possibility for describing the "academic" part of "academic services." However, this consideration led them to discuss more contextually dependent aspects of the word's reference. Pedro noted that *amawta* is "rigorous" (line 24), associated with hypothesis testing as leading to more legitimate knowledge. This emphasis seemed to be influenced by the definition of "science" in Spanish. He contrasted this process with recycling as a primary focus of ancestral knowledge (line 24) and equated the development of recycling as more of an adaptation than the rigor implied by *amawtay*. In constraining what *amawtay* could include, Pedro more closely aligned himself with Indigenous people who have studied in schools and Western notions of science. For him, "academic services" could be translated using *amawtay*, since they needed to describe schooling. The word was relatively straightforward in delineating activities that were not necessarily connected to studying or schools.

On the contrary, Sisa began by offering *kamachiy* (authority) as an option for translating "academic services." For her, *amawtay* included a wider definition of knowledge, one that is beyond what is learned in classrooms and in which many people can be "wise" (line 25). Thus, she saw "non-academic" as hard to neatly delineate with *amawta*, since people outside of schools know and do things that should be considered within the word's reference. Some difference in perspective surely has to do with her life. Where she lives, for example, while shamans do not have credentials, they are frequently consulted on an array of matters, including health problems. She emphasized her grandparents' knowledge as a more inclusive definition of *amawta*. Sisa's comments reveal ambivalence toward schooling in defining knowledge, for example "my grandparents know more than we do—we who are educated," and "it's clear that they aren't trained like us, studying really well, but they were scientific in regard to nature."

Sisa did not disavow the importance of schooling. In fact, she positioned herself as similarly credentialed as Pedro and others by using "us," people who have studied, unlike her ancestors (line 19's "It's clear that they aren't trained like us, studying really well"). Even as Sisa aligned herself with schooling, however, she expressed concern about its limits and whether *scientific* goes beyond schools and the philosophies that they promote. Her response, "well, they [her ancestors] are wise," illustrated that her definition of *amawta* included a wider range of scientific people and ideas. The choice of a Kichwa word for *knowledge*, thus, shows assumptions about whose views are indexed in a translation and how they understand what it means to be Kichwa. This is one of many challenges that translators had to consider. The Kichwa version of the Law ultimately translated this idea as *amawta yachaykuna* (scientific knowledge), showing that *amawta* became the official translation.[11] As Chapter 2 shows, state modernization efforts have long supported the norms of people who have studied, more like Pedro. These are identities that standardization tends to signify (see Chapter 3). Rewriting official documents through Kichwa translation raises questions of which ways of seeing the world are concretized in the translation and in state documents more generally.

Conclusion

The official recognition of Indigenous languages, and its results like translations of laws, comes with questions of what constitutes Kichwa. Studying how laws are translated to Kichwa shows that translators seek to make a text that is situated in relation to an array of previous texts beyond the source, the original-language law. Bruno Latour (2007) similarly conveys this expansive sense of interconnectivity when he writes that a law is helpfully understood as a text linked to other texts made and enacted by networks of people and objects. In this Ecuadorian case, his point extends to translation. Legal translation to Kichwa involves consideration of cohesion across many kinds of state documents, conventions, and conversations.

This array of intertextual connections also brings various groups of people together for translation, some physically present and some anticipated as readers. As anthropologist Paja Faudree (2015a) notes, authorship in Indigenous languages foregrounds a central question: who is reading? Decisions about how to write involve considering who will read the document, including the words that they will understand. At the same time, the normalization inherent to law-making, including the norms established in language standardization, risks excluding many Indigenous-language speakers while prioritizing those who can read a standardized register. Widely shared ideas about what constitutes understandable Kichwa—ideally a register that facilitates the state's citizens to take up, appreciate, and use the documents being produced—are in tension with state norms for standardizing Indigenous languages and the persons and ideas foregrounded by them.

Other nation-states have seen alternative pathways to inclusion for Indigenous language translation that follow how legal translation scholar Deborah Cao (2007) describes source-language legal texts as routinely functioning differently from target language texts. While the former may carry more legal force, the latter may serve important communicative purposes for understanding what laws are and how they relate to different ways of understanding the world.

For instance, in translating Spanish-language legal acts to Quechua in Peru, translators positioned the authors and readers of the Quechua version as a collective "we," shifting away from the third person verbs of the Spanish document to rewrite how Quechua speakers relate to the law and other state institutions. Translators, furthermore, used Spanish words for concepts that do not correspond to Quechua conceptions of governance, such as using Spanish's *ley* (law) or *derecho* (right) (Howard, Andrade, & Ricoy 2018). Such borrowing modeled which ideas were foreign by using Spanish to refer to them. Translators also acknowledged the mutual unintelligibility of Quechua linguistic registers across the large nation-state by authoring versions in respective regional registers, such as Chanka and Ancash Quechua. In contrast, in the Ecuadorian case, the instructive or even decolonizing potential of translation was limited by cohesive intertextuality and language standardization. Norms in Ecuador about Kichwa writing tend to involve avoiding lexical borrowings from Spanish.

Translating this law thus shows how decision makers for translating become authorities and what they write ultimately becomes part of a small body of texts that represent the language they reclaim. Despite gains in recognition, translators of a law to Kichwa had to deal with the discourses and registers of state documents that are saturated with bureaucratic ideas and technical Spanish terms, which inevitably foreground some speakers of Kichwa over others. Such challenges exist in other contexts of language planning, but the politics of making a language official compounds those challenges. How Kichwa is modeled becomes, simultaneously, a metonym for the people who communicate in that language, despite numerous register differences, and also representative of the state for which translators work. Those doing translation encounter double binds that saturate the process, and mis-steps can be used against them and their social movements in national politics.

In other parts of the world, a shift away from the legal use of colonial languages has yielded court spaces in which litigants can invoke local senses of justice in their use of another language, such as the systematic application of Cantonese in courtrooms in Hong Kong (Ng 2009). In this early scenario in Ecuador, recognition has yielded the translation of select legal documents but not yet systematic legal use of Kichwa. All judges who would interpret the law speak Spanish. Lawyers, similarly, are Spanish speakers, even if they also speak Kichwa. In this context, translation is less about making a major document that would challenge the preexisting Spanish language Law.

When understood within a recent history of state documents that have been critiqued for a lack of readability for Kichwa speakers, we find recognition politics upholding predominant norms and registers that reproduce forms of the status quo, a challenge for Indigenous state agents and, especially, translators. Some of the disagreements seen in this chapter, such as the one between Pedro and Sisa, demonstrate that the ideas of cohesion and normativity tend to place the spotlight on Kichwa as understood by professionals like linguists, those closer to the central state apparatus. This implicit priority poses a challenge for the rewriting of the state through alternative forms of communication and ways of understanding the world, including those that may be linked to nonstandardized Kichwa.

6

Speaking for a State

How and Whom to Greet?

Introduction

Can Indigenous language use transform public speaking in state-sponsored events? This chapter examines how greetings are one of the primary ways that speakers showcase or make visible their languages and forms of Indigeneity for others. Greetings have now become central to state-authorized talk and indicate promise and peril in speaking Indigenous languages on behalf of state institutions.

Throughout the world, Indigenous language speakers commonly use curtailed ways of speaking like greetings to demonstrate speakers' presence while carrying out other functions. For example, Native-identifying Californians use Elem greetings to invoke Indigeneity despite no longer being fluent in their languages. Such greetings can also establish intertextual links to their ancestors for Indigenous audiences and frame ensuing talk in English as from a Native perspective (Ahlers 2006; 2017, 47). Aboriginal Australians also use introductory genres of public speeches like welcoming to remind audiences of injustices, of their current acceptance, and of land entitlements, even as they do so in English (Merlan 2014, 302). I build on research to show that, even though Indigenous language greetings indicate a simplification of linguistic diversity, there is vast complexity to their use.

Directors of the school system routinely use standardized Kichwa greetings during public speaking events, which brings the language family into state-sponsored communication and marks the Ecuadorian state as intercultural. Such forms of talk increase awareness of the presence of Indigenous language speakers and remind of their significant advances in establishing a bilingual school system. Furthermore, adding Kichwa use to conversational openings upholds the parameters of institutional talk by maintaining conventions of respect and politeness for those who do not understand. Indeed, greetings carry out interactional recognition, or acknowledge interlocutors (Searle

Recognizing Indigenous Languages. Nicholas Limerick, Oxford University Press. © Oxford University Press 2023.
DOI: 10.1093/oso/9780197559178.003.0007

& Vanderveken 1985; Duranti 1992; Hillewaert 2016), though in this case they also prioritize listeners who are not proficient in Kichwa. Standardized greetings, instead of consisting of "traditional" speech styles, curtail Kichwa and make it analogous to Spanish as used in institutional settings. Standardized Kichwa greetings are, thus, widely disliked by other Kichwa speakers for how they simultaneously entextualize, or foreground, Unified Kichwa from other ways of speaking Kichwa. Such greetings have become emblematic of a state-sponsored register of Kichwa, and Kichwa-speaking parents and teachers may associate Unified Kichwa with the state-authorized citizens who use it.

By foregrounding Unified Kichwa over other ways of speaking and enregistering a particular speech style for use in the school system, greetings carry out state recognition in public address. This claim contrasts with how scholars have seen greetings as inconsequential or as small talk that builds social relationships (Malinowski 1923; Bach & Harnish 1979) but of little importance in terms of referential content (commonly referred-to-meanings) (Searle 1969). I show here that the referential content of greetings is important because their equivalency with Spanish makes such greetings more amenable for use in Spanish-dominant public speaking. In this case, the similarity of the Unified Kichwa greeting to its Spanish counterpart makes Kichwa familiar to non-Indigenous-identifying others but awkward and foreign sounding to Kichwa audiences. While progressive considering decades of state repression, such ways of speaking are simultaneously divisive for those who understand Kichwa.

Unified Kichwa openings consist of lexicosyntactic hybrids, known as calques. They are Kichwa words but translated from Spanish grammar, reference, and use instead of more local ways of speaking. Moreover, their use tends to occur with extensive Spanish speech, further prioritizing Spanish-speaking addressees. Bilingual education directors thus risk angering Kichwa-speaking listeners and constraining a movement to reclaim a language to curtailed speech acts. However, they encounter a double bind because more extensive Kichwa speech may not demonstrate a commensurate form of Kichwa for those who self-identify as *mestizo* and may even lead to anxiety or censure from ministry higher-ups.

For example, Juan, a high-ranking planner in bilingual education, lamented how even in his role in the Ministry of Education, he seldom uses Kichwa beyond the act of greeting. Late one evening while seated at his kitchen table, Juan, typically unflappable, was frustrated after dealing with conflicting expectations from Spanish-speaking bosses, bilingual peers, and a range of teachers. His red poncho had accrued the wrinkles of a day's work at the office. As Juan explained to me:[1]

Entonces, ¿cuándo hemos hablado Kichwa?	So, when have we spoken Kichwa?
En un evento.	In an event.
¿Y qué es lo que hablamos?	And what is it that we say?
Simple y llanamente un par de saludos.	Plainly and simply a pair of greetings.
Y así es imposible fortalecer y desarrollar la lengua.	And like that it is impossible to strengthen and develop the language.

As Juan implied, the goal of "strengthen[ing]" Indigenous languages in bilingual education was limited by how he and his colleagues used Kichwa as employees in state offices, even as their jobs focused on getting people to speak Kichwa. As Juan lamented about coordinating in the National Directorate, he and his colleagues tended to speak mainly Spanish for several reasons beyond their control. First, all senior officials speak Spanish but not all speak Kichwa, making communication in Spanish more expedient and, ironically, inclusive. Second, those who do speak Kichwa grew up speaking Spanish in schools and now live primarily in the capital city, Quito, where Spanish is predominantly spoken. Most routinely speak Spanish more than Kichwa, as Chapter 4 showed. Third, Kichwa does not currently have the technical vocabulary needed to carry out job requirements like budget making, personnel management, and textbook authorship. Directors must invent words to describe many of these activities or borrow them from Spanish. Though Indigenous languages are experiencing an era of linguistic prominence, language planning must contend with historical alterity and racialized domination that shape the patterns of and possibilities for language use and reclamation.

Most relevantly, however, Juan's comments show how Ecuador's case of language shift has implications for state politics. On the one hand, greetings have become key speech acts for bringing Indigenous language use to state spaces and events from which it was formerly restricted. On the other hand, not only is "plainly and simply a pair of greetings" less significant in comparison to how directors speak Spanish, but moreover, according to Juan, his and others' use of greetings has made "strengthening" Kichwa "impossible." For instance, one of the most common greetings in this context is *alli puncha mashikuna* (good morning, colleagues). While it uses Kichwa words, the expression is a translation of a Spanish greeting common to office life (*buenos días compañeros*).

This chapter presents an ethnographic story of how such greetings are used and how they indicate a larger predicament of language shift, state recognition, and intercultural citizenship for Kichwa speakers. Here, I build on research on greetings by analyzing standardized greeting use in Ecuador, tracing the ideologies they uphold and the double binds they depend upon and entail. The use of standardized greetings can alienate others who might comprise a social movement to encourage Kichwa use. Greeting use is perhaps the most emblematic case of how institutional constraints affect Kichwa and Indigenous state agents in ways that I have described throughout this book.

Using Greetings for Commensuration

Participation in state recognition tends to imply following certain terms of engagement (Rappaport 2005; Povinelli 2001) that encourage those of immense social difference to demonstrate commensurate traits that others can then view as equivalent (Carruthers 2017; Kockelman 2016). Multilingual talk has become key to a politics of commensuration. In this case, greetings demonstrate that Indigenous peoples are represented in the state apparatus and often signify that the speaker will soon speak Spanish. Unified Kichwa greetings set openings apart from more widely used forms of Kichwa and make Kichwa commensurate with Spanish in two ways. First, they consist of formulaic phrases from Spanish calqued into Kichwa.

Alli puncha   *mashi-kuna*
Good morning (Spanish calque)   Colleague/friend-PLURAL (Unified or Imbabura Kichwa)

This greeting reproduces the Spanish *Buenos días* in standardized Kichwa (*Alli puncha*) followed by the named addressees (colleague + plural marker) in Unified Kichwa (*buenos días compañeros*). The syncretism—in this case demonstrated by two languages with texts that are equivalent in form and reference—makes Kichwa analogous with Spanish, which is spoken soon thereafter. Such greetings are easily translated back to Spanish for non-Kichwa speakers. Second, Unified Kichwa greetings continue and point back to prior events of language use. Social participant roles (e.g., state representative) and genres (e.g., introductory openings) are based on routine speech in Spanish-dominant podium speeches, simultaneously leading other Kichwa speakers to associate Unified Kichwa forms with communication by state-authorized Indigenous persons like professionals who are now in charge of the school system from office spaces in the city.

As an example of what calques replace, one day I was at a bilingual school conversing with teachers Ruth and Jorge, who described more common greetings. After lamenting the use of Unified Kichwa by national directors,

Speaking for a State 159

Ruth began a conversation about greetings. "*Para mi es muy frío, muy insípido*" (For me [Unified Kichwa is] very cold, very insipid), she said in Spanish.[2] She continued:

1 Ruth   *No podemos decir,* "Alli puncha *tía María*"
            We can't say, "*Alli puncha*, Aunt Maria,"[3]

2   *cuando saludamos.*
            when we greet.

3   *Decimos así conversando*:
            We say it conversing,

4   Imanalla kawsapanki, *tía?*
            "*Imanalla kawsapanki*, Aunt?" (How do you [affectionately] live?)

5   *En cambio si se dice* "alli puncha"
            On the other hand, if one says "*alli puncha,*"

6   *eso es frío.*
            that is cold.

7   *Mi tía siempre dice*
            My aunt always says,

8   *buenos días de dioooooo mijiiiita*
            "Good morning of Go:::::d, my little dau::::ghter,

9   *¿Cóooomo te ha iiiido?*
            ho::::w has it go:::::ne for you?"

10   *Así saludamos.*
            That's how we greet.

11   *En cambio si yo le digo:*
            On the other hand, if I say to her,

12   alli puncha *tía,*
            "*Alli puncha*, Aunt," [flattened intonation]

13   *entonces*
            then [voicing aunt],

14   *¿¡Qué estás diciendo?!*
            "What are you saying?!" (laughing)

15 Jorge   *En las comunidades*
            In the communities,

16   *el saludo es*
            the greeting is—

17 Ruth   *Muy amable.*
            Very amiable.

18 Jorge   *Sí, por ejemplo yo tengo una tía que es ya mayorcita,*
            Yes, for example, I have an aunt that is now older.

19   *desde lejos saluda,*
        From far away she greets,

20   *pero no con la boca nomás,*
        but not only with spoken words.

21   *sino saca el sombrerito.*
        Rather, she takes off her hat.

22   *Imanallatak kawsakupankichik?*
        "*Imanallatak kawsakupankichik?*" [How are you all [politely] living?]

23   *Tiyakunkichikchu?*
        "*Tiyakunkichikchu?*" [Are there people there?]

Ruth and Jorge showed that there are more elaborated and common forms of greeting in their communities and claim that they would never use the unified greetings. Instead, they blend Spanish's *Buenos días* into a dialogue of other greetings in a local variety of Kichwa (lines 4–9). Such linguistic blending, however, would deny Indigenous state agents from illustrating a pure, equivalent language as they speak. The transcript also shows the greetings more common to Kichwa speakers from Jorge's region of birth, such as "*Imanallatak kawsakupankichik?*" or "*Tiyakunkichikchu?*" These examples demonstrate Kichwa as an agglutinative language with various particles adding up to make lengthy words, frustrating grammatical and semantic parallelism with Spanish. An entire sentence can be expressed in just one word, as the second example shows. These examples of common greetings are also more difficult to translate to Spanish.

A common property of greetings is their relative predictability in form and content (Duranti 1997). Here, inter-linguistic norms increasingly affect the form and content of greetings in institutional talk. Whom, then, do Unified Kichwa greetings successfully acknowledge through their use? Based on Ruth and Jorge's description, the answer is not primarily them. Unified Kichwa greetings simultaneously foreground racialized others who identify as *mestizo* and who can follow the pragmatics of Indigenous language use. These greetings are primarily simplifications targeting outsiders (Ferguson 1981). Their use indexes difference among co-present audience members even as the talk occurs in Kichwa. Such simplification set apart some forms of speaking from less equivalent ones and also makes standardized Kichwa the most seen and heard way of communicating in state-sponsored events. The directionality of translation across languages matters in terms of who adapts to whom, engendering strong feelings from other Kichwa speakers and even a sense of loss.[4]

Furthermore, common ways of speaking other varieties of Kichwa, such as Jorge's example of hat-waving across the mountain (line 21), would be harder to make sense of while speaking in an auditorium. In Kichwa, rises and falls in intonation accomplish politeness and form bonds with listeners, as Ruth demonstrated in lines 8–9. Yet, such contours would be strange while uttering a brief standardized greeting, as evidenced in Ruth's jocular flattening of her voice with *alli puncha*. Standardized Kichwa greetings thus transform disparate reference and communal norms—ruralized ones like hat-waving across the mountains—into commensurate slots in Spanish speech-giving, but they simultaneously sound cold (line 6), laughable (line 14), or confusing (line 14) to other Kichwa speakers. The example shows how greetings depict unusual ways of speaking as representative of Kichwa speakers who are more peripheral to the state apparatus.

"Having a Language"

Research has shown how people adopt state discourses by repeating the words of state officials and documents, such as "terms of recognition" (Appadurai 2007), "lexicon" (Krupa & Nugent 2015, 7), "vernacular" (Scott 1998, 323), and a "common language or way of talking about social relationships" (Roseberry 1994, 361). Social movements may use such words to frame claims for legal advancement (Johnston & Noakes 2005; Sieder & Witchell 2001). As I show in this section, historically marginalized peoples may not only need to describe an emblematic form of an Indigenous language for recognition but also demonstrate, and hence make, a modernist version of it (see also Urla 2012). In other words, speakers of Indigenous languages adopt the words of the state—as anthropological theory foregrounds—but also use, bilingually, languages to demonstrate state recognition.[5]

The First Meeting of the Andean Pueblos and Nationalities for *Sumak Kawsay* in 2011, a summit sponsored by various state agencies and situated within the President Correa's intercultural agenda, shows the importance of making Kichwa commensurate for recognition. Located in the cavernous auditorium of the Casa de la Cultura Ecuatoriana (Ecuadorian Culture Center) in Quito, representatives from Bolivia, Guatemala, and Ecuador gathered to discuss *sumak kawsay* ("good living"), a model of economic development (Figure 6.1). Kichwa leaders routinely decried that a phrase that refers to an Andean philosophy for interspecies harmony and balance now describes a development project in Spanish (*buen vivir*).[6] The audience from Ecuador included numerous members of Indigenous nationalities, Montubios (coastal

Figure 6.1 The inaugural event of the Meeting. Photo by author.

mestizos from the countryside), and Afro-Ecuadorians. State agents were speaking to, for, and about cultural difference.

A theme that emerged at the event was that Spanish-speaking marginalized peoples lacked moment-to-moment acknowledgment in the speeches of state agents. For example, a *mestiza*-identifying Spanish-speaking official began by thanking groups from Ecuador and other nation-states who made the journey when she was suddenly interrupted by yells from the audience about an omission. She corrected, "*Y por supuesto el pueblo Montubio está presente*" (And, of course, the Montubio *pueblo* is present!), acknowledging those who demanded not to be forgotten. As the event continued, audience members were invited to take the microphone to comment. A Montubia woman criticized the individuals running the event, highlighting the difficulty of gaining here-and-now nation-state support:

1 *Nosotros creemos en la necesidad de visibilizar los íconos*
We believe in the necessity of making visible the icons

2 *de la historia de los pueblos montubios,*
of the history of the Montubio pueblos,

3 *así como estaban diciendo antes los compañeros afro.*
as the Afro [Ecuadorian] comrades were saying....

4 *También nosotros, compañeros, somos excluidos*
We also, comrades, are excluded,

5 *y también hemos sido invisibilizados,*
and we have also been made invisible.

6 *nosotros estamos en la constitución.*
[But] we are in the constitution.

7 *Tenemos derechos*
We have rights,

8 *y creemos que se deben respetar esos derechos*
and we think that those rights should be respected,

9 *o si no nosotros mismos los vamos a hacer respetar,*
or if not, we are going to make them be respected.

10 *porque en este mismo evento, compañeros,*
Because in this very event, colleagues,

11 *ha venido la ministra de cultura*
the Minister of Culture has come.

12 *y sin embargo nunca nombró a los montubios en su exposición.*
However, she never named the Montubios in her exposition.[7]

I spent the event sitting in the audience next to Gloria Yungaicela, a Kichwa woman and one of the highest-ranking officials at the National Directorate (see also Chapter 3). At that moment, Gloria looked at me and shook her head, saying quietly in Spanish, "*Es difícil para ellos, es que no tienen una lengua*" (It's hard for them. It's that they don't have a language).

Gloria and other Indigenous state agents have come to understand that languages are prime emblems for invoking and enacting recognition. Others don't "have an [Indigenous] language," she noted, in a description similar to the bilingual requirement inscribed in the founding of the national coordinating offices and to notions of universal ownership in modernist ideals (see Chapter 2).[8] Successful state recognition in Ecuador is not cast from constitutional citation alone, as the Montubia woman mentioned in her rebuke. Though the woman noted that her community had visible "icons" for recognition, Gloria acknowledged a distinct language as the one that the Montubios lacked if they were to count for the state. Hearing the frustration of other marginalized *pueblos* for being ignored at the event, Gloria's answer, as one of the most senior Indigenous state agents, was that they lacked a comparable, showcase-able version of Kichwa.

Gloria and others have seen the necessities of "having a language" for bilingual education in promoting and enregistering the modernist (and nationalist) view of Kichwa. Away from the noise of the auditorium the following week, I asked Gloria about her comment.[9] "*Nosotros hemos tenido un poco de análisis*" (We've done a little bit of analysis), she responded.

Por ejemplo, en la educación intercultural bilingüe la Dineib es para pueblos y nacionalidades indígenas porque está caracterizada por la lengua y la cultura,	For example, in intercultural bilingual education the National Directorate is for Indigenous *pueblos* and nationalities because it is characterized by language and culture.
entonces en ese contexto, tienen que tener una cultura, tienen que tener una lengua, para poder dar atención.	So, in that context, they have to have a culture, they have to have a language, in order to be attended to.
Entonces, en ese caso para que tengan también acceso a todo.	In that case [I meant] so that they also have access to everything.

Gloria delineated groups as "we," Indigenous peoples who gain cultural and linguistic recognition, and "they," who do not "have a language" and "a culture." "They" will struggle since they have no recognizably distinct language. In other words, they are marginalized anew. By describing Kichwa this way, Gloria also muted widespread ideologies about linguistic difference within the language family. In the early days of research for this project when I told people in the office that I was interested in how they spoke Kichwa, they would frequently laugh, "Which Kichwa?" I soon gathered that for people from various parts of Ecuador, finding a common way of speaking and understanding depended upon years of practice speaking across varieties and sometimes necessitated use of Spanish (see also Chapter 3).

Modernist ideologies about Kichwa also mask the blending of Spanish into Kichwa that occurs throughout Ecuador. Gloria's casual Kichwa talk often freely borrowed from Spanish. During the *Sumak Kawsay* event she dealt with a steady stream of calls and visitors, and a large percentage of her interactions occurred in Kichwa that drew freely from Spanish. For example, a young man whom she had taught as a public schoolteacher came by to ask in Kichwa if there was a phone booth nearby. "*Tiyashka*," or "Turns out there is," she responded in Kichwa. She then handed him money, saying, in Spanish, "*veinticinco centavos*" (twenty-five cents). Such blending is different from the more standardized Kichwa she would use for speaking to larger audiences as a national state agent. Anthropologist Paul Kroskrity (2010, 197; 2018) notes that a key tenet of theorizing language ideologies is that they are multiple because of the "divergent perspectives . . . of group membership" based on "the meaningful social divisions . . . within sociocultural groups." "Having a language" indicates that such views are not only reflective of social difference, but a strategy in its management. Interculturality involves offering and building on the recognition of Indigenous languages. Greetings remind of this recognition and make state recognition hearable as a distinct language. As the next section shows, Unified Kichwa and limited use also forestalls negative reactions from others, including bosses, indicating another way they are comparatively state-authorized.

Maintaining Order

The use of greetings indicates and manifests the uncomfortable relationship between people located further to the state's periphery, emblems (like "a language"), and the state apparatus and its employees. Directors tend to use commensurate, and as this section shows, curtailed forms of speaking since extensive and incommensurate Kichwa speech can provoke frustration among non-Kichwa-speaking bosses and other audience members. In an era of increased acceptance and tolerance, how one speaks Indigenous languages can determine "safe," instead of "dangerous," forms of difference (Lomawaima & McCarty 2002). Speakers of marginalized languages in public spaces routinely risk their language use will be seen as threatening, in part, because others do not understand them (Hill 1998), and commensurate forms of Kichwa aid in managing the reactions of others.

In this case, greetings also fit Kichwa use to public speaking conventions. As conversation analysts have long argued, "openings" function to maintain orderliness in how they follow conventions and build rapport (Schegloff & Sacks 1973, 290). In this example, the recurrence of standardized greetings in openings functions to make Kichwa recognizable and, hence, nonthreatening for non-Kichwa speaking bosses, who make decisions about their employment. Extensive speech in Kichwa is sidelined, and instead a quick utterance that invokes Indigeneity is confined to the beginning of the speech before the more substantial content is presented in Spanish. The abbreviated use of greetings that others can interpret as similar to speech in Spanish functions to draw equivalencies between the two languages.

Marlon Muenala, a senior director of the school system, recounted the limits of speaking Kichwa at events.[10] In a public ceremony for the national directing office's anniversary, his boss, a non-Kichwa-speaking *mestizo*-identifying vice minister of education, was present. Marlon, Gloria, and the vice minister each had speaking roles and were seated on stage. A newspaper article had recently criticized the Correa administration for the persecution of Indigenous organizations and, according to Marlon, the vice minister had asked to personally review the content of his and Gloria's speeches for any possible response. They both acquiesced and sent speeches with Kichwa listed solely as openings and closings. Gloria, however, went off script (see Chapter 3). Marlon recounted, his voice rising: "*En el evento mismo, ella casi habló más en Kichwa que en español*" (In the event itself, she almost spoke more in Kichwa than in Spanish!) As the vice minister became increasingly dismayed, he asked Marlon, "*¡¿Que está diciendo?!*" (What is she saying?!) Bosses can reproach speakers and, with enough discontent, remove them from directing roles. If they do not have tenure in the office, they risk being ousted from national employment.

Marlon's speech followed Gloria's and responded to the vice minister's admonishment. His address began with *alli puncha tukuylla* (good morning, all), in Kichwa. He addressed "*wawakuna*" (children), "*yachachikkuna*" (teachers), and "*apukkuna*" (leaders) and then switched to Spanish.

1 *Ya pues mashi Doctor*
  Well okay, *mashi* Doctor

2 *Vice-Ministro de Educación*
  Vice Minister of Education.

3 *Cómo me gustaría seguir hablando*
  How I'd like to keep speaking

4 *en el idioma materno que es el Kichwa*
  in the mother tongue that is Kichwa

5 *pero no va a llegar ese mensaje a todos.*
  but that message is not going to reach everyone.

6 *Por eso,*
  That's why

7 *y con respeto a todos,*
  and with respect to everyone,

8 *haré uso del idioma castellano,*
  I will make use of the Spanish language,

9 *que es un proceso de interculturalidad.*
  which is a process of interculturality.

All Ecuadorian citizens, Marlon suggests, including Spanish speakers and the vice minister, need to understand the message. This model of interculturality involves *not* making the majority feel excluded or uneasy through extensive talk in Indigenous languages, though Marlon would "love to keep speaking in the mother tongue." His speech was tailored to non-Kichwa speakers—in this case, mainly self-identifying *mestizos*—and hailed them as addressees. An especially important member of "everyone" (line 7) was the vice minister, who five minutes earlier had become upset over Gloria's extensive Kichwa use. Hence, Marlon spoke Kichwa briefly and then switched to Spanish with a phrase that signals he finished something (line 1 "well okay") and addressed the vice minister as he began to speak Spanish.

As research on codeswitching has shown, people can speak in comparatively marginalized languages to increase feelings of solidarity for listeners who know those languages while making those who do not understand feel distant (Woolard 2005). Such speech can be strategic, such as when Rapa Nui–speaking political leaders, who more routinely spoke Spanish, used only Rapa Nui in a visit with Chilean senators to bolster their difference from their Spanish-speaking audiences (Makihara 2008). In this case, Marlon limited his Kichwa use to a standardized greeting to mark that difference was present but compartmentalized, commensurate, and, therefore, in his view, "respect[ful]."

Compartmentalization or lexical purism does not always constitute modernist or state-authorized ideologies. In other Indigenous language families, for example, speakers routinely carry out ceremonial and even everyday speech by wholly separating each language. For the Arizona Tewa, speakers describe their use of language separation like maintaining the separation of colors of corn in farming through distinct small fields (Kroskrity 2009, 44). They associate a lexically pure form of their language with a purer Indigenous identity (Kroskrity 2000; 2009; 2018). However, compartmentalizing a lexically pure variety of Kichwa and then switching to standard Spanish is a dramatic change for most Kichwa speakers, who routinely blend Spanish words into everyday Kichwa speech. Directors' use of purist and compartmentalized Kichwa, as shown with languages elsewhere (Das 2016; Irvine & Gal 2000; Tomlinson 2017), elides remarkably diverse ways of communicating in Kichwa, as the educators lamented. In the aftermath of the vice minister's concern, Marlon's show of "respect" for all audience members returns the speech to the nonthreatening use of Spanish.

Kichwa, Audiences, and Images of Citizenship

Anthropologists have shown how speakers of Indigenous languages use genres to reproduce or transform traditions. For example, speakers use storytelling to carry out many actions relevant for public speaking, such as establishing ceremonial authority (Bauman 2004; Falconi & Graber 2019). State agents as public speakers can utilize the genre of openings with Kichwa greetings in combination with self-descriptions in Spanish, such as Indigenous *pueblos* in harmonious coexistence in the nation-state, to depict *interculturalidad* and its commensurate cultural and linguistic difference.

For example, in 2011, the Ministry of Education and other government agencies sponsored an *"encuentro intercultural"* (intercultural meeting) with two Canadian First Nations teachers. Attendees filtered into the conference room of a Quito hotel dressed in their finest ponchos, hats, and embroidered shirts. Representatives from the Canadian Embassy and the two Canadian guests were seated prominently to the left of two bilingual education officials and one *mestiza*-identifying representative from the Ministry of Education. Other guests, mainly directors from Ecuador's regional bilingual education planning offices, all of whom were members of Indigenous nationalities, were seated at onlooking tables. A closer look at Esteban Chuqui's speech (the highest-ranked director of the school system at that time) shows how greetings demonstrate "the Kichwa language" with talk that does intercultural recognition. He spoke Kichwa for longer than other speakers at the event, yet he followed norms for compartmentalizing it to an opening.

1 *Mashikuna, shinaka alli shamushka kapaychik.*
Friends, so please be welcomed.

2 *Yupaychanchik*
We are grateful

3 *ñukanchik kayashkaman shamushkamanta,*
for you all having come to our called meeting,

4 *tukuy mashikuna.*
all of you, friends.

5 *Shinallatak Canadamanta shamuk runakuna*
The people who have come from Canada,

6 *ñukanchik napayta chaskipaychik.*
please receive our greeting.

After uttering those thirteen seconds of Kichwa, he paused. He then began to speak in Spanish, re-greeting non-Kichwa speaking guests in a three-minute speech:

7 *Estimados representantes de la embajada de Canadá,*
Esteemed representatives of the Embassy of Canada,

8 *representantes del Ministerio de Educación,*
representatives of the Ministry of Education,

9 *compañeros directores,*
comrade directors [masc.],

10 *directoras de la educación intercultural bilingüe*
directors [fem.] of intercultural bilingual education

11 *y también de las nacionalidades.*
and also of the nationalities.

12 *Para nosotros este es un momento muy importante,*
For us, this is a very important moment

13 *porque aparte de seguir trabajando en nuestros pueblos,*
because apart from continuing to work in our pueblos,

14 *en nuestras nacionalidades, en nuestro país,*
in our nationalities, in our country,

15 *nosotros ahora vamos a abrir las puertas.*
we are now going to open the doors.

16 *Estamos abriendo las puertas a otros países del mundo,*
We are opening the doors to other countries of the world

17 *justamente para hacer lo que la constitución de la República nuestra manifiesta,*
just to do what the constitution of our republic manifests,

18 *que somos un país plurinacional*
that we are a plurinational country,

19 *que somos un país intercultural*
that we are an intercultural country,

20 *... [con] estos 23 años de experiencia de trabajo realizado en nuestros pueblos.*
.... [with] these twenty-three years of work experience carried out in our pueblos.

21 *Ahora no solamente nuestra responsabilidad recae*
Now our responsibility not only returns

22 *en las comunidades y pueblos indígenas*
to the Indigenous communities and pueblos,

23 *sino también vamos a trabajar con los pueblos indígenas,*
but also we are going to work with the Indigenous pueblos,

24 *afro-ecuatorianos, montubios y mestizos del Ecuador.*
Afro-Ecuadorians, Montubios, and *mestizos* of Ecuador.

25 *Vamos todos a juntarnos*
We are all going to band together

26 *para que lleguemos a lo que la constitución nos manda, a vivir en plenitud.*
to arrive at what the Constitution has sent us, to live at the peak.

27 *Tenemos que colaborar entre todos.*
We have to collaborate among everyone.

28 *Tenemos que valorar los conocimientos,*
We have to appreciate the knowledges,

29 *las bondades que tienen cada una de las culturas en nuestro Ecuador*
the goodness that each one of the cultures in our Ecuador has,

30 *y en diferentes países del mundo.*
and in different countries of the world. . . .

31 *Muchas gracias, bienvenidos, bienvenidas, a todos ustedes*
Many thanks, welcome [masc. and fem.] to all of you

32 *a este país multidiverso, plurilingüe.*
to this multidiverse, plurilingual country.

With his speech forms, including his use of greetings, Esteban made Kichwa and Kichwa speakers commensurate with Spanish and *mestizos* in several ways. First, he produced a here-and-now image of state recognition that "We [Ecuadorians] are opening the doors . . . to do what our constitution of the republic manifests" and "to live at the peak," "do[ing]" such constitutional-"liv[ing]" through his presence and speech. He named different groups in Spanish—such as the previously neglected Montubios—doing further momentary "official" recognition as an example of "what the Constitution has sent us." He thus paid closer attention to the here-and-now acknowledgment of all marginalized peoples than the state agent at the *Sumak Kawsay* event. These words also use the modernist characterizations of state documents to depict others, such as with the bounded "goodness that each one of the cultures has." He further mentioned interculturality and plurinationalism (lines 18–19), two designations listed together in the 2008 Constitution that he in turn cited (line 26).

Second, beyond adopting the state's terms for Indigenous emblems and peoples, Esteban's speech in sequentially ordered co-occurring languages put intercultural recognition into practice. While the languages reflect equivalency, they were not given equal time. Kichwa was confined to the genre of "opening," limiting its use within the parameters of speech-giving in Spanish. Since most of his talk about state recognition occurred in Spanish, Esteban showed which language has more communicative import. Also, his bilingual speech forms demonstrated the modernist ideologies of *interculturalidad* that hold cultures as equivalent and clearly bounded in lexical bilingualism. For example, he maintained Kichwa and Spanish as separate and used Kichwa calques, as with *alli shamushka kapaychik* "please be welcomed," and *napayta chaskipaychik* "please receive a greeting." "To send a greeting" is a common phrase in office Spanish and even the word "greeting" *napay* sounds strange to many other Kichwa speakers. His juxtaposition of Kichwa and Spanish co-occurred with his descriptions of Ecuador as a nation-state and, thus, represents a "plurilingual country" (line 32), one with the cooperation of Indigenous *pueblos*.

Third, Esteban invoked Indigeneity through the differences in whom he greeted across languages, further showing how he used bilingual communication to speak on behalf of the state. In Kichwa, he greeted Indigenous peoples from both Ecuador and Canada, then switched to Spanish to greet international outsiders (Canadian Embassy employees), Ministry of Education employees more generally, and then other affiliated colleagues (lines 7–11). Thus, he named and prioritized listening audiences differently, foregrounding Indigenous audiences in Kichwa and associating them with that language. In Spanish, understood by all present, his use of "we" referred to all Ecuadorians who "continue to work in our pueblos . . . and our country" (lines 13–14), including non-Indigenous peoples who "band together" to "arrive at what the Constitution has sent us" (line 25). The "we" in Spanish is inclusive of everyone—*mestizos,* Montubios, all Indigenous peoples (line 24)—while the Kichwa "we" includes solely Indigenous peoples. His speech in Spanish allowed him to describe the intercultural state.

Contesting Greetings

Predominant ways of presenting information are often challenged in interaction (Carr 2009; Goffman 1974; Silverstein & Urban 1996a; 1996b), and such is the case with Kichwa standardized greetings. The following example shows a "disruption" (Goffman 1974, 350), a breach of expectations for unfolding communication so severe that it interrupts other participants' involvement. After Esteban spoke, the floor was opened up for discussion. Esteban prompted the Ecuadorian Indigenous audience members in Spanish to mention *"de qué nacionalidad son y cuál idioma hablan"* (which nationality you belong to and what language you speak). Another Kichwa-speaking director clarified (again, in Spanish): give *"un saludo en su lengua"* (a greeting in your language). Each participant began by speaking Kichwa or another Indigenous language, usually their name, where they were from, and a greeting for those running the event. Speakers then switched to Spanish to ask a question. The carefully delineated openings with greetings were repeated by person after person, thus showcasing such speaking styles as representative of Kichwa and state-authorized persons—as perceptible for Kichwa-speaking listeners—and the importance of Indigenous languages to the intercultural state for *mestizo*-identifying addressees. The English-speaking Canadian guests watched attentively, even though there was no translation to English for the Kichwa segments but instead only for Spanish.

Then there was a rupture of convention by a regional director named David. As he was called on to speak, David began to talk in Kichwa using the convention of greeting, ("*Yupaychani mashi, mashikunawan tukuykunaman shuk alli puncha nishpami napayta chayachini*"; Thank you, colleague, with the colleagues I'm making arrive a greeting to everyone of saying "good morning"), but he did not then switch to Spanish. As he passed twenty seconds of speaking a Kichwa that blended ways of speaking Unified Kichwa and Imbabura Kichwa, other Kichwa speakers in the room began to look around at one another. David offered that he and his peers in Ecuador had gotten "further ahead" with state recognition than the Canadians. He wanted to know if the visitors had other examples that would help his Ecuadorian colleagues. In the meantime, other Kichwa speakers fidgeted. As David neared the two-minute mark of speaking in Kichwa, Esteban waved his hand at me. He whispered in Spanish, "*¡Anda a coger el micrófono y traduce! ¡El man ya está hablando mucho tiempo!*" (Go over to take the microphone and translate! The man is speaking for a long time). The paid interpreters only spoke Spanish and English. Kichwa was no longer curtailed, nonthreatening, and commensurate but, rather, provocative.

In the end, David spoke for over three minutes in Kichwa except for a few Spanish words, such as "Canada." His extensive talk still made other Kichwa-speaking officials uncomfortable as a clear violation of the norms of state speech. When I later spoke with David, he said that the school system was "weakening" Kichwa, in particular, with "greetings" (affirming Juan's earlier point that greetings made it "impossible" to "strengthen" Kichwa). He wanted to "obligate" other directors to make Kichwa more important. His reference to the need for obligation conveys his frustration with the routines of how state agents like himself speak Kichwa. Paradoxically, extensive Kichwa-speaking in a language reclamation movement becomes a subversive act. David's reaction shows how Kichwa speakers question whether intercultural talk prioritizes them and their understandings of how Kichwa is used.

Conclusion

Anthropologists Michael Silverstein and Greg Urban (1996b, 11) propose that institutional politics involve "a struggle to entextualize authoritatively," that is, to offer and increase the adoption of some pre-supposable texts over others. State planners are especially consequential spokespeople for marking difference, promoting interculturality through select and commensurate Kichwa use, and getting others to adopt the format. For Kichwa-speaking state agents, others' recognition and reuse of curtailed, commensurate, and modernist expressions depict and signify state power as inclusive of Indigeneity, bringing the presence of Indigenous languages and their speakers to formerly restricted spaces. Recognition depends not just upon legal precedent as written into "official" documents but also on metalinguistic labor in Kichwa use to gain awareness for Indigenous languages.

Yet, what does institutional success look like? Standardized Kichwa greetings have become pervasive forms of public speaking, but they also function to demonstrate an ideology that their language is pure and commensurate with Spanish. This sort of language ideology marginalizes many people anew: oppressed groups who do not "have a language," state agents who speak in Kichwa more than is sanctioned, and Kichwa speakers who speak other varieties or blend their language with Spanish. Interculturality is inclusive even as the onus continues to be on Kichwa speakers to change. Indigenous language use becomes as much about Kichwa speakers acknowledging non-Indigenous-identifying audiences as about the Ecuadorian state acknowledging Kichwa speakers, yielding a double bind in how to be inclusive while demonstrating difference.

While intercultural politics elevates *some* historically oppressed peoples into positions of power (Jackson 2019), as the Montubio counterexample showed, ongoing work in such positions depends upon the nuances and repercussions of discursive struggle and comes with double binds. The use of Unified Kichwa also favors those Kichwa speakers conversant in that register, especially speakers who live in cities, have studied, and are conversant in the routines of institutional speech (see Chapter 3).

Furthermore, each time a director uses Kichwa to speak for the state, the pattern of solely greeting in Kichwa becomes more routine. For Kichwa-speaking, this routinization has double-edged implications: Kichwa is heard and recognition is reinscribed, yet the context of acceptable use is further constrained and concretized, yielding a problem for those who direct Indigenous movements. Ecuador's Indigenous organizations encounter challenges around unification and getting their diverse membership base to mobilize, leading scholars to ask: "Is the cultural project of the Indigenous movement now in crisis?" (Martínez Novo 2014b, 209). The politics of greetings in intercultural talk manifests such division, including in how teachers and other policymakers vehemently disagree with the use of standardized greetings as representative of Kichwa.

7
Modeling Intercultural Citizenship through Language Instruction

Introduction

How does Kichwa language instruction in schools extend and contest intercultural policies and politics? And, what are some benefits and consequences? As the previous chapter shows, contemporary language politics intersects with intercultural-citizenship initiatives to promote the use of commensurate greetings as conversational openings for more extensive talk in Spanish. This chapter extends my analysis of state-authorized Kichwa use in two ways. First, teachers can strategically encourage the use of greetings alongside other signifiers, such as forms of dress and songs, in projecting students as intercultural citizens. Second, somewhat differently from the case of those who direct the school system, students and their parents are some of the most marginalized citizens of the capital city. Teachers' use of greetings and other markers of intercultural citizenship shifts how students may be construed—away from the foremost markers of inequality. Teaching students to sing songs across languages, for example, and coaching them in the kinds of clothes to wear, aid the commensurability of Kichwa with Ecuadorian office Spanish and emergent bilingual students with racialized others (like *mestizos*) as Ecuadorian citizens.

I further suggest that, following many teachers' perspectives, Kichwa language instruction implies a double bind. On the one hand, teaching Kichwa in classrooms helps speakers have more pride for Kichwa, increases the language's legitimacy in the eyes of many, and supports the advances made by advocates within state offices. As I explained earlier, the arrival of Kichwa to instruction has also provided jobs for many speakers of the language family. On the other hand, there are several challenges. For example, educators may teach students to become part of the larger state intercultural project by adopting specific ways of speaking Kichwa that many disagree with. The use of Unified Kichwa is also different from how students' parents and other family members speak the language. Herein lies a double bind: teachers may see that more local ways of speaking, or even talk entirely in Kichwa, risks closing off public spaces and social mobility to students. The teaching of select Unified Kichwa forms helps to socialize students into the intercultural dimensions of Kichwa language politics. Yet, this socialization is double edged because its focus on equivalence masks the real structural inequality that students experience and may marginalize anew other ways of speaking Kichwa.

In this chapter, I focus on one school where I researched, as this school closely followed the larger intercultural goals of the school system. I place together ethnographic examples from a field trip, the market where the school is located, and educators' and students' upbringings to show what intercultural language instruction looks and sounds like and how such ways of speaking are different from common Kichwa-language practices. Elena, the teacher featured in this chapter, describes her own life growing up with her parents who spoke mainly Kichwa with Spanish mixed in, and she foregrounded their marginalized backgrounds in comparison to the school system's directors who have higher education degrees. Teaching select Kichwa greetings is especially striking because the students often incorrectly use the greetings, indexing their lack of familiarity with Unified Kichwa forms. Yet, for the school's immediate needs, it is less important whether students use "correct" and "incorrect" Kichwa, but rather that they successfully project themselves as intercultural citizens primarily in curtailed and commensurate Kichwa use.

A Field Trip

On a sunny morning in June 2011, second-grade teacher Elena was leading a line of about thirty students who were paired up and holding hands. We were entering the president of Ecuador's offices in Quito, where she had arranged a tour. As we passed through metal detectors, the children yelled, chased each other, and generally acted boisterous. Elena largely ignored them. But as we began to ascend the stairs to start the tour, Elena turned to the Spanish-speaking guards.

"*Yupaychani!*" (I am grateful!), she boomed in Kichwa. Her exaggerated volume cued the students to repeat what she had said.

"*Yupaychani!*" the kids yelled, in semi-unison.

"*¿Qué significa eso?*" (What does that mean?) asked the staid guard in Spanish.

"*Es 'gracias' en Kichwa*" (It's "thank you" in Kichwa), Elena replied.

She then spoke to the children in Spanish, telling them to continue up the stairs. The kids repeated *yupaychani* several more times for office staff members as we started the tour. We then passed into a large room where a guide said that President Rafael Correa would be dining that day. Two stoic men, wearing suits and carrying walkie-talkies, stared at the kids. On their way out of the room, two boys stopped: "*Kayakama!*" (See you tomorrow!), they yelled in Kichwa at the security detail. The men's eyebrows rose, and Elena let out a deep laugh. "*Kayakama?!*" she said. "*¡Ustedes no vienen mañana!*" (You all aren't coming back tomorrow!). Then, as we were leaving the building, two other boys waved goodbye to another guard: "*Alli puncha!*" (Good morning!), they said, to which the guard formed a slight smile.

We then left the presidential offices and went to a nearby museum. A young tour guide, a *mestiza*-identifying, Spanish-speaking woman dressed in slacks and a collared shirt, greeted the students with a cheerful *buenos días* (good morning). Immediately, she pointed at the girls who were wearing black skirts and golden necklaces, "*Qué lindas!*" (How pretty!) she said. "*¿Son los uniformes de la escuela?*" (Are these the school's uniforms?). "*¡Así se visten!*" (That's how they dress!) exclaimed Elena. "*Son indígenas*" (They are Indigenous), she further explained. The woman nodded with a smile. Elena then asked the students in Spanish to line up, and they formed ordered rows.

"*Ahora vamos a cantar*" (Now we're going to sing), Elena said as she began a song in Spanish that starts with the phrase "*Buenos días*" (Good morning). The students joined in enthusiastically. When they finished the song, without Elena's prompting, they immediately began to sing it again, this time in Kichwa. The same rises and falls in pitch occurred as they sang in Kichwa. After they ended the song, Elena began to sing a comparable song in English, and the students joined in. When they finished, the guide clapped, "*Me encanta!*" (I love it!) she said enthusiastically.

This ethnographic example illustrates not just a field trip from an intercultural bilingual school, but also how interculturality involves a form of Indigeneity evoked, principally, through curtailed forms of Kichwa that are literal translations from Spanish. During the field trip, when students greeted the guards, their Kichwa consisted of calques from Spanish that the previous chapter showed are common in Unified Kichwa but not in other registers. *Alli puncha*, for example, is "good morning," translated from the widely used Spanish greeting of *buenos días*. Many Kichwa speakers consider this greeting "strange" or "cold."

Similarly, *yupaychani* (root *yupa* plus suffixes *-y-cha-ni*), the first person, singular, present-tense conjugation of the Kichwa verb *yupaychana* "to be grateful," demonstrates a use similar to *gracias*, as Elena told the guard. Though *yupaychani*'s grammatical forms are not calqued from Spanish, the word is used similarly. Instead of *yupaychani*, the children's parents would more likely say *pagui*, an abbreviated and borrowed version of the Spanish phrase "*Dios le pague*" (may God repay you) assimilated to Kichwa's vowel system. *Yupaychani* is a word the students had likely only heard in Elena's classroom as she taught them how to say "thank you." This verb is more common to Northern Highland Kichwa in the province of Imbabura and is used less in varieties of Kichwa in Central Highland Ecuador, from where the students' parents had migrated to the capital of Quito.

At first glance, a straightforward explanation for Elena's instruction would be that, like many teachers around the world, she viewed a standardized register as the "best" or most correct way to speak. This example of language use outside the school's walls, however, helps unpack how Kichwa is taught as part of a larger-scale political project. The field trip shows that students learn to use Unified Kichwa greetings for outsiders who do not speak Kichwa and for whom they can demonstrate intercultural citizenship. In an age in which Kichwa is recognized in the constitution and non-Kichwa-speaking citizens are aware of the language's existence, *how* one depicts Indigenous identities becomes key to promoting the school system and its schools. Elena's teaching considered the metapragmatic effects of multilingual speech for Spanish-speaking others. In other words, how students learned to speak in Kichwa had more to do with the characterizations about what such forms would accomplish as they project students as certain types of citizens identifiable to Spanish-speaking addressees.

Key to this point is that the students did not speak "correctly" in Kichwa on the field trip. Residents of Ecuador almost exclusively say *buenos días* at the beginning of an encounter in the early hours of the day. The students, however, yelled *alli puncha* as they were leaving, violating norms for the phrase's use. Such misfires occurred more than once, as Elena also corrected their use with *kayakama* (see you tomorrow), a calque in form, reference, and use from the widely used phrase *hasta mañana* in Spanish, when she told them that they were not actually returning the next day.[1]

Using short, formulaic Kichwa phrases evokes and offers an Indigenous identity for listeners who do not understand Kichwa, but Kichwa-speaking listeners would note that the students are misfiring. Philosopher of language J. L. Austin (1962, 16) describes a misfire as a kind of mishap that arises from the botched utterance of words, as when one member of a marrying party misspeaks "I do" in a ceremony and the marriage is not fulfilled. As Throop and Duranti (2015, 1056) point out, in formal and public settings, speech-act misfires and nonlinguistic signifiers can direct the attention of onlookers and, in the process, manage observers' reactions to them.

In other words, misfiring depends on who is listening. Many Kichwa speakers would be puzzled to hear the students use these linguistic forms as they were uttered. But the students' misfires are nonetheless successful because the audience can be further divided into those who understand Kichwa and those who do not, the latter being addressees oblivious to acts of misfiring because they react to Kichwa use within the parameters of communication in Spanish. The listening practices of others who are racialized differently continue to affect bilingual education (Flores & Rosa 2015), this case in how heritage language instruction occurs. In hearing just a couple of words in Kichwa, Spanish speakers have a general idea of what students may be saying through genre expectations and because the students speak Kichwa in accordance with familiar norms for Spanish. And if the audience does not understand, they can ask and quickly be told, as did the first guard above. For these addressees, the students made Kichwa equivalent to Spanish.

The example above also shows how intercultural citizenship foregrounds and exceeds commensurate greetings and goodbyes. Becoming intercultural citizens involves a coherence of forms, such as by singing the same song successively in three languages. In the moment of singing, the students' words begin to resemble and presuppose one another across the three languages with the aid of similar musical patterns. Those intonations help listeners interpret that the words of the songs are similar, which presupposes that the languages and the speakers are, too, distinct but equivalent. In other words, through such speech, the speakers themselves become commensurate. In the last section of this chapter, I analyze the reaction of a visiting Ministry of Education official to unpack this claim.

Nonlinguistic forms contribute to commensuration, too (Throop & Duranti 2015). The students' regionally marked dress, for example, facilitated commensurate processes of differentiation, as Elena made clear when she emphasized to the tour director that such forms of dress are common to the students and explained them as "Indigenous." Similar songs across languages, greetings, and ways of dress co-occur in the self-presentation of Kichwa speakers as examples of intercultural citizenship. Such presentations elicit comments like "I love it" from onlookers. This observation shows how the study of poetics, or the coherence of signifiers in context, is essential for analyzing intercultural citizenship, which I further consider in the next section.[2]

These presentations offer a somewhat divergent image from the challenging circumstances of the lives of many students, whose parents typically have little experience with schooling. Most are bilingual in Kichwa and Spanish, but many understand and speak Kichwa better even as the students may not be able to communicate in the language family. A subset of parents is unable to read or sign their names, and almost all had recently moved to the capital city. They speak Kichwa in ways that are not parallel with the references and uses of office Spanish and often mix Spanish into local varieties of Kichwa. Many mothers remain afoot throughout the day selling fruit wherever someone will buy it. Fathers may work in construction. These are some of the signifiers likely to hinder students' movement across public or institutional spaces, a claim I further unpack in this chapter through an ethnographic portrayal of the market right outside the school's gates. Teachers are especially skilled at presenting intercultural citizenship identities for others, and students mirror such language use as they demonstrate intercultural citizenship identities.

Multilingualism and Becoming Intercultural Citizens

The field trip shows how state designations have increasingly recognized certain forms of equality, and how those forms are used in everyday activities like schooling while invoking and continuing forms of recognition. As political scientist Wendy Brown (2008) shows, such ways of speaking and acting normalize institutionally sanctioned identities and render deviant forms as more marginal. These actions like greetings and songs are markers of citizenship, which implies relationships, practices, and identities surrounding membership and belonging, especially in relation to the state (Ahmad Dar & Ahmad Najar 2018; García-Sánchez 2014; Sørensen 2008). Scholars have defined citizenship as membership in publics that exist beyond the colonial logics of the state, as well, such as local philosophies of mutual recognition and support (Simpson 2007; Levinson 2011). National policies define and regulate citizenship and provide insight into how state actors envision and enforce community, belonging, and inclusion (Khan 2019; Lowenheim & Gazit 2009; Schissel 2019). Schools are "premier sites" of citizenship (Paz 2019, 78). Teachers can instruct students on how to become model citizens or help them understand how they may be excluded from those ideals.

This case in Ecuador echoes how teachers elsewhere invoke, continue, or thwart state policy and citizenship identities in teaching students to become certain kinds of civic participants across subjects of instruction.[3] This chapter examines how languages are taught in schools, how specific ways of speaking and writing are linked to certain kinds of persons, and, further, the relationships between classroom instruction and the broader contexts of multilingual communication and state policy. My linguistic anthropological analysis unpacks these connections to the students' actions, demonstrating how the linguistic forms used by the children parallel the modeling of identities in other state offices; how the forms draw from and depict intercultural identities; and how the students are situated within historical trajectories of who does and does not count as a citizen.

Since citizenship is presupposed and done in language use (Stroud 2019, 18), how people become aware of citizenship involves the *communication of citizenship* within schools and beyond them (Paz 2019). In this case, a poetics of resemblance—across languages and across Indigenous and *mestizo* identities—especially shapes how students are perceived. Key to how students exhibit citizenship identities is how their linguistic and nonlinguistic signs mirror and signal other signs or other aspects of context (Parmentier 1997; Silverstein 1981). Singing three songs demonstrates equivalency in language use. The greetings are analogous across languages, which showcases the languages as comparable, too. Such displays cohere to resemble or index other levels of context for onlookers, such as the identities of the speakers themselves.[4] However, if democratic citizenship includes, abstractly, a premise of equality for all, such presentations elide differing relationships between the state and children or adolescents whose life circumstances are vastly unequal.[5]

The opening example shows how intercultural citizenship requires metacultural and metalinguistic labor on the part of teachers and students to carry out relatively unusual ways of speaking Kichwa that indicate intercultural actions and identities. The language use of teachers and students and its implications for citizenship demonstrates two points seen throughout this book. First, citizenship efforts are intertwined with, more specifically, emergent speech forms and registers instead of simply entire languages. Second, there is a paradox of intercultural teaching: while teachers who teach Kichwa in this way work against the history of exclusion, they simultaneously reconfigure Kichwa to extend state-sanctioned language use and identities. It is through this point of entry—how language-ideological processes unfold in interaction—that this chapter analyzes the everyday politics of multilingual instruction in a nation-state whose politics and policies prioritize the recognition of markers of intercultural citizenship, including standardized language use.

Making a "Goldmine"

When I visited intercultural bilingual schools in Quito during this research, most taught Kichwa infrequently and, if at all, in a similar fashion to Elena's classroom, with limited instruction restricted mainly to vocabulary words. This finding is shared by the school system's own research, which found "low application" of Indigenous languages in schools throughout the country.[6] I add here that a key part of how Kichwa is taught often involves abbreviated, standardized Kichwa, for example, vocabulary words like greetings, days of the week, and numbers. In Elena's classroom, students copied lists of numbers from the board (such as *shuk* "one," *ishkay* "two," etc.) and memorized songs and dialogues (Figure 7.1), which made Kichwa instruction exceptional given that intercultural bilingual schools often do not teach Kichwa.

Similar to examples of Indigenous languages elsewhere in the world, in Ecuador teachers and administrators have found the transition to classroom instruction difficult. My experience is that teachers did not have the necessary support for Kichwa instruction in situations of language shift. In other words, there was not much guidance for how to craft classroom instruction and pedagogy for young people who increasingly cannot speak or, sometimes, understand Kichwa. National curriculum materials are written in Unified Kichwa but, with language shift, Kichwa is now a nondominant or second language for most students. With urban migration, most students at Elena's school, despite having parents who speak Kichwa at home, were unable to converse in Kichwa beyond the limited vocabulary items learned in class. They would not be able to learn Kichwa in a classroom without specialized pedagogies for translanguaging or heritage language instruction. That teachers do not emphasize Kichwa proficiency is part of this larger-scale challenge seen throughout the school system and in Indigenous education elsewhere.

The challenge is also an intercultural one. Elena often glossed over the referents or definitions of words students were learning. Her emphasis on Kichwa is best described by the phrase "making visible" used in a national policy document that cites Kichwa's guarantee in the Constitution and the Organic Law of Intercultural Education and calls for the presence of Ecuador's pueblos and nationalities: "*visualicemos la presencia de los pueblos y nacionalidades del Ecuador*" (let's make visible the presence of Ecuador's *pueblos* and nationalities).[7] In practice, making visible tends to mean the use of different but commensurate forms, including linguistic ones. Elena did this well, and she was considered a model Kichwa teacher at

Figure 7.1 A poster of Ecuador's national hymn translated to Kichwa, along with the names of months in Kichwa peeking out from behind. These are the kinds of songs and vocabulary words that are more common to classrooms, which are less commonly known by those who speak Kichwa daily. Photo by author.

the school. The school director often sent visitors to her classroom to view exemplary identity-based schooling. Her school was one of the most favored by those in the National Directorate because of such use of culturally relevant pedagogy. Elena had been an important part of the school's efforts as a committed teacher who covered more material in Kichwa than many others.

Intercultural notions of Kichwa indicate a point in a longer trajectory of vast change. Given the racialized and discriminatory history of state policy, most professionals in the school system have seen for themselves the change in Kichwa from completely oppressed to valued and intercultural. Teachers who have worked in the school system for years know that even if they dislike Unified Kichwa, it gains support from others, significantly donors and volunteers. Roberto, the school's director, remarked on such forms of teaching as a transformation of Kichwa from total marginalization to intercultural acceptance. Roberto's uncle was the first Kichwa-speaking teacher in the large central Ecuadorian province of Chimborazo, located several hours from the capital. When his family moved to Quito, Roberto, inspired by his uncle, founded the school.

On June 11, 2012, I was seated in the computer lab and asked Roberto if he had wanted the teachers to teach in Kichwa when he established the school twenty-five years ago. He paused and shook his head.

En el inicio fue muy grave.	In the beginning it was very serious.
No querían saber nada de Kichwa los mismos indígenas.	They didn't want to know anything about Kichwa, the very Indigenous people.
Hasta a nosotros han pegado, hasta nos han insultado,	They've beaten even us [the teachers]. They've even insulted us.
"Escuela de indio, que mi hijo no tiene que hablar Kichwa.	"Indian school, [I want] my child to not have to speak in Kichwa.
Tiene que hablar español."	They must speak Spanish."
Pucha, un sacrificio para nosotros para crear esto.	Shoot, [it was] a sacrifice for us to create this.
Hoy en la actualidad casi no tenemos ningún problema de eso.	[But] today, in these times, we hardly have any problem with that.

As Roberto explained, teaching Kichwa at school has never been easy and was often impossible. Earlier in his career, Kichwa yielded so much embarrassment that even Kichwa-speaking parents forcefully attempted to prohibit teachers from speaking the language to their children. Kichwa speakers' use of any marker linked to Indigeneity could yield problems from interlocutors. He noted that today is systemically different. Parents no longer object. As he went on to say, Kichwa use is not just acceptable but economically useful. During that same interview, I asked Roberto whether promoting the children's Kichwa heritage helped the school.

Claro. Nosotros conseguimos contactos, con fundaciones, con ONGs.	Sure. We get contacts with foundations, with NGOs.
Entonces ahí conseguimos becas, regalos, útiles escolares.	So there we get scholarships, gifts, school supplies.

Hay mucha gente que no tiene esa posibilidad de comprarle un esfero.	There are a lot of people [at the school] who don't have the possibility *of buying a pen.*
Entonces nosotros también apoyamos por ese lado.	So we also support them that way.

The children's presentation of select forms of difference linked to Indigeneity can, in demonstrating culturally and linguistically relevant schooling, increase scholarships or gifts for students who have few resources. I asked Roberto whether donations are better when students show donors that they are Indigenous. He nodded vigorously, his voice rising with conviction.

Exacto, ¡así es!	Exactly, that's it!
Alguien le llamaba esta escuela "la mina de oro."	Someone once called this school "the gold mine."
Todas las fundaciones quieren trabajar aquí. ¿Por qué?	All of the foundations want to work here. Why?
Porque aquí están concentrados los niños que necesitan.	Because here there is a concentration of children who need [the help].
Para ellos, es más fácil justificar el trabajo que ellos están realizando.	For them [NGOs], it's easier to justify the work that they're doing
Usted sabe que cualquier financiamiento de exterior	You know that whatever financing from other countries
aquí tienen que ellos rendir cuentas....	they have to account for it here....
Entonces para ellos es más fácil presentar— estas son gentes que necesitan.	So, for them it's easier to present—these are people in need.

The process of becoming "a gold mine" relies on offering potential donors and observers an example of people in "need," which Roberto equated with "Indigenous" in answering my question. He emphasized that a significant number of foundations ("all") try to work at the school because they can better "justify" their work. "It's easier to present" such people with markers of Indigeneity. His use of the verb "present" focuses on the onlooker. It parallels the national policy document about Kichwa "making visible." How the students act is instrumental to achieving interpersonal recognition and motivating funding, and notions of Indigeneity are important for exhibiting certain kinds of classed differences ("people in need"). In Quito and throughout Ecuador more generally, teachers and parents are accustomed to linking Kichwa identities to formal instruction in schools. Indeed, Roberto had been a member of the school system for long enough that he knows most of the individuals who work in the National Directorate and has seen how they present themselves as Kichwa speakers. He has attended countless events where directors promote the system, including by using the greetings students spoke on the field trip. Similarly, Elena can instruct students to present linguistic and cultural forms for others in ways that support the school's mission.

Teaching Indigenous Languages and Urban Inequality

The following ethnographic examples indicate how and why Elena and the students use commensurate and abbreviated ways of speaking and reduce linguistic variation and competing interpretations of Kichwa. On June 22, 2011, I was reheating the previous night's soup for breakfast with twelve-year-old Jenifer, the youngest daughter of the Kichwa-speaking family with whom I lived. Jenifer attended Roberto's school, though her family resided in a working-class neighborhood in a different part of the city. While their financial situation was slightly more stable than those of many families at the school (see Chapter 1), the children's Kichwa proficiency levels followed a similar generational pattern to other students: Jenifer's older sister speaks a regional variety of Kichwa extensively with her parents and, especially, older relatives, one that mixes in words from Spanish; her older brother, the second child, understands much Kichwa but struggles to speak it; and Jenifer, as the youngest child who moved to the city as a toddler, would emphasize that she cannot speak or understand Kichwa. Jenifer's situation is similar to that of her peers insofar as many of them struggle to speak extensively in Kichwa, in part because they largely speak Spanish on a daily basis. At school, when I spoke to groups of students in Kichwa, they would often say that they did not speak Kichwa or point to another student who they said knew more than they did. In general, that student would then, in turn, deny their classmates' assertion. As with other Indigenous languages, long-standing shame for speaking Kichwa complicates efforts to understand proficiency. Indeed, other students would commonly refute their peers' denials, noting that the student "was embarrassed." Embarrassment and shame for speaking Indigenous languages has been widely documented in the Andes and elsewhere (Hornberger 1988; Hornberger & King 2001). But, in general, though the students would speak with greetings and songs, most of them, like Jenifer, could not speak extensively in Kichwa. They also tended to be especially embarrassed by nonstandardized ways of speaking Kichwa, such as how their parents speak. Their reactions to everyday Kichwa speech vis-à-vis their routine use of Kichwa at school indicate that greetings and songs are less stigmatized.

The school's location in a market—where many of the children's parents work—is linked to the most marginalized forms of Indigeneity. That day's conversation with Jenifer illuminates some aspects of urban inequality that students (and onlookers) might associate with Kichwa and its speakers. On that Saturday morning, I was asking Jenifer about how she liked school. She told me that she enjoyed the school, the teachers, and her friends, but that there was just one thing that she hated: the location. "*¡Es muy feo!*" (It's so ugly!) she said, in Spanish. "*Botan frutas en la calle. La gente se orina. No me gusta*" (Fruit gets thrown in the street. People pee. I don't like it). The entrance to the school is located off the main street of one of the busiest markets in Quito. Walking down the path of the market, one hears blaring vehicle horns and people yelling in Spanish, "*¡Choclos! ¡Frejol! ¡Aguacate!*" (Corn! Beans! Avocado!). Exhaust wafts up from the busy road where the market ends. According to vendors' accounts, thieves frequent the area. In just such spaces, many of the students' parents, grandparents, aunts, and uncles sell fruits and vegetables at tables. Most of the women working in the market wear regionally marked hats and skirts, and most men wear jeans and T-shirts. In the stone streets, smashed fruit, urine, and animal excrement rot in the blazing morning sun.

In the market, adults chat in Kichwa and Spanish, mixing the languages together. "*A ver, paganamunta o mana paganamunta, rikushun,*" one student's mom commented as she sold fruit, looking at me while a customer was deliberating on prices.

A ver	***pag**anamunta*	*o*	*mana*	***pag**anamunta*	*rikushun*
Let's see	pay-because	or	not	pay-because	see-first person plural future

"Let's see, to pay or not to pay, we'll see."

Like many Kichwa speakers, the mother took words from Spanish (in bold) and fitted them into Kichwa grammatical categories, using the Spanish verb *pagar* as a verb root and adding the Kichwa ablative-case marker. She also used the Spanish conjunction *o* (or). She further illustrated her use of nonstandard Kichwa through the case marker *-munta*. In Unified Kichwa and in the Northern Highland Ecuador, individuals frequently say /manta/, but in central Ecuador, [a] often changes to [u] in case suffixes (Muysken 1977). Speakers of Central Highland varieties of Kichwa, such as the children's parents, routinely mix Spanish forms into Kichwa, linguistic forms common just outside of the school's fence. In Central Andean Ecuador, one

Kichwa speaker might greet a neighbor with a quick *buenos días* in Spanish before asking a single-word question in Kichwa such as *tiyakunkichikchu?* (roughly: is anyone here?, as seen in Chapter 6). Such linguistic forms are common just outside of the school's fence, but students are not taught to employ these ways of speaking.

An interview with Elena helps unpack the contrastive identities that intersect with language use. Elena, too, has parents who cannot read and write alphabetically, who make their living as vendors (in their case, ambulatory ones), and who speak mostly in Kichwa mixed with lexemes from Spanish. This familiarity contributes to her teaching practices in Kichwa. On May 31, 2012, Elena compared her parents to the parents of her students. The communicative practices of parents were a part of those connections.

Elena:

Antes en la comunidad, ellos no tenían terreno.	Before, in the community, they [my parents] did not have land.
No tenían plata. Eran pobres.	They didn't have money. They were poor people.
Mis papás han sido inmigrantes como ahora los papás de los niños.	My parents have been immigrants, like now the parents of the kids.
Ellos han nacido aquí muchos. Mis papás eran así....	Many of them [the students] have been born here. My parents were like that....
Mis papás primero vendían cuadros.	My parents first would sell paintings.
Allá mismo compraban y revendían,	There [in another city] they would buy and then resell,
así como aquí compran frutas y revenden.	much like here they [the parents of the students] buy fruits and resell them.
Los dos son analfabetos. No saben leer. Mi papá suma, todo eso,	They're both illiterate. They don't know how to read. My dad can add, all of that,
pero no sabe leer. Mi mamá ve las horas.	but he doesn't know how to read. My mom can tell time.
No sabe leer, pero sabe donde es las horas.	She doesn't know how to read, but she knows where the hour is.
Sí, tenemos un relojcito en casa.	Yes, we have a little clock at home.
Ella sabe por donde es, si son las 3, ya va a ser las 5.	She knows where the [hand] is, if it's three o'clock, that it's almost five o'clock.
Ella sabe. Ella no estudió, ni sabe que es escuela ella.	She knows. She never studied. She doesn't even know what school is.
Ni mi papa.	Neither does my father.

Nicholas:

¿Ellos hablaban Kichwa?	Did they speak Kichwa?

Elena:

Kichwa. Kichwa. Y algunas palabras en castellano.	Kichwa. Kichwa. And some words in Spanish.
Con nosotros cuando éramos niños hablaban en Kichwa y en castellano.	With us, when we were kids, in Kichwa and in Spanish.
Así como los padres de ellos.	Like their [the students'] parents.

Elena described the economically precarious life experienced by her parents and parallels this life with those of her students' parents. When I asked her about her parents' Kichwa-speaking, she portrayed their speech patterns as largely Kichwa-based, mentioning Kichwa twice for emphasis. And their Kichwa speech was certainly not Unified Kichwa; it blended in words from Spanish. "Poor people," she said, those who speak in such a way, are her parents and the parents of her students. Elena said that her own parents, like those of the students, are "illiterate" "immigrants" who, without land, are forced to buy and resell goods to make a living. Indeed, the students' parents, many of whom work just outside the school selling fruit, serve as a reminder of other Indigenous identities that could also be promoted by speaking in and teaching regional and lexically blended registers of Kichwa in Quito. While calques and songs are more acceptable, regional varieties of Kichwa that blend in Spanish continue to be disparaged and less accepted in public spaces, such as on field trips or with visitors (like potential funders) to the school. Elena's mom, she acknowledges, can tell time but cannot read and write, indicating how not attending school is associated with a more challenging life.

Misfires and Modeling, Again

Two years after the vignette that opens this chapter, Elena had a new group of students. Frequently, as I entered the classroom that year, Elena coached the children to say "*Alli puncha, mashi.*" The children would usually only get this partially correct. If I said "*Buenos días*" when I entered, they would often respond, "*Alli puncha, mashikuna,*" correctly associating *alli puncha* with the interactional context of greeting while showing their unfamiliarity with the grammatical norms of Unified Kichwa, pluralizing *mashi* using the suffix -*kuna* (Figure 7.2). "*Solo es mashi*" (It's just *mashi*), Elena would comment in

Figure 7.2 Calqued greetings as signage in the classroom with parallel Kichwa and Spanish translations. Photo by author.

Spanish. This example shows how students clearly understood how to deploy Unified Kichwa greetings for others, invoking Indigenous identities through language use. As I show below, in some contexts, those greetings invoke intercultural citizenship, too. Yet, the students misfired grammatically by using a plural marker when addressing just one person, calling attention to their unfamiliarity with the routine use of those words.

Elena prepared students to respond to classroom visitors in similar ways. Another school day shows how such linguistic forms are key for intercultural citizenship identities. On May 28, 2012, as the children were sitting at their desks wearing crimson school uniforms, Elena announced that in a week, representatives from the Ministry of Education (not the National Directorate of Intercultural Bilingual Education) were going to observe the class. "*Niñas, vengan con* anaku" (Girls, come with an *anaku*), she requested, asking them to wear skirts common to their region of birth. She made the request in Spanish, similar to how she would speak with them when no visitors were present, with the Kichwa word describing an article of clothing. The officials would evaluate her teaching of a civics class, she said, so she practiced a class on the history of the Ecuadorian flag. That she planned to teach a civics class that referenced Indigeneity and demonstrated abbreviated Kichwa use indicates how the lesson integrated Indigenous identities into participation in the Ecuadorian state. She clearly saw Kichwa as signifying their citizenship positions. Yet how she taught the students to use Kichwa clarifies which form of Indigenous citizenship she sought to showcase: an intercultural one.

On the following Monday, while Elena was preparing for the presentation, I took the kids to the cafeteria for their morning porridge. Afterward, as the children went to the playground, I sat outside and chatted with parents. There were about thirty women, mostly mothers, who had arrived to discuss the school with the Ministry of Education officials. They were all wearing regionally marked clothes from the province of Chimborazo. Some were sitting on stairs, and others were sitting on the large rails leading up to the entrance of the building (Figure 7.3). Several women were breast-feeding infants, as they spoke Kichwa with loanwords from Spanish. Throughout the day, the parents and teachers spoke Kichwa in a similar fashion.

Later, when Elena ran a session during which the parents evaluated the school for the Ministry officials, she translated nearly all dialogue and explanations from Spanish to Kichwa, using some words from Spanish when necessary. Even between one another, the teachers spoke less-standardized Kichwa that day as they filled out self-evaluations in front of the guests. During

Figure 7.3 Parents and their children waiting to be called into the school. Photo by author.

the visit, I heard more Kichwa, in general—and nonstandardized Kichwa, in particular—being spoken by the teachers to one another than I had ever heard at the school. But when it came time to teach the students in her class for the Spanish-speaking visitor, Elena continued to coach the students to speak with select Kichwa forms and to alternate between languages. When Elena mentioned that the guests were about to arrive, the room suddenly got quiet. A woman with curly red hair, accompanied by Roberto, opened the door, and Elena immediately began to speak.

Elena (in Spanish):

1 *Director, Señora delegada del Ministerio de Educación, compañero maestro,*
Director, Madam Delegate from the Ministry of Education, colleague teacher,

2 *compañero Nicolás, mis queridos niños,*
colleague Nicholas, my dear children,

3 *esta mañana vamos a trabajar,*
this morning we are going to work,

4 *y yo quisiera que saludemos a nuestros compañeros que están aquí*
and I would like for us to greet our colleagues who are here

5 *en Kichwa, castellano, e inglés.*
in Kichwa, Spanish, and English.

Seamlessly, with not even a half-second's lag time, the students responded. "*Alli puncha, mashikuna!*" screamed the kids, in Kichwa, automatically and enthusiastically. But Elena decided that this word was less appropriate for the current audience and corrected them, speaking in Kichwa, thus masking the correction for non-Kichwa speakers. "*Yachachikkuna. Yachachikkuna!*" (Teachers. Teachers!), she said, using a word from standardized Kichwa that they probably did not know. "*Ya-cha-chik-kuna,*" repeated the kids, syllable by syllable. "*¿En castellano?*" (In Spanish?), said Elena. "*Buenos días, profesores!*" (Good morning, teachers!), they yelled in Spanish, but only some students added the word "*profesores*" to the end. "*¿Y en inglés?*" (And in English?), she asked. "Good morning, teacher!" responded the students. It is likely that their use of the singular form of the noun shows that these are memorized phrases. Of the greetings in the three languages, I believe that they only had full referential knowledge of the Spanish one, suggesting that the image of commensurate multilingualism is more important than linguistic proficiency, which is further evidenced below. Students correctly associated *alli puncha* with the interactional context of greeting, even as Elena decided that "teachers" would be a more appropriate form of address in this situation.

Immediately, Elena thanked them, "*Yupaychani, wawakuna*" (I thank you, children), she said in Kichwa. But the children misunderstood and instead of replying, "You're welcome" or recognizing Elena's acknowledgment that the lesson was over, they continued the repetition drill. "*Yu-pay-chani, wa-wa-kuna*," they began to yell in unison. Elena flinched, putting her palms up to try to indicate that they should not thank themselves. After she squirmed, she told them in nonstandardized Kichwa that they had misfired: "*Imamanta? Upallachiy.*" (Why? Be quiet.) However, the guest, unaware of the misfires, beamed and nodded in approval. The director did not smile. Elena then told them in Spanish about a game they were going to play for the lesson, and the remainder of the class continued in Spanish.

Later that day on the playground, I asked a group of three kids from the class what *alli puncha* meant. They paused, "*No sé*" (I don't know), said one in Spanish. No one else answered. On a different day, a student came up to me on the playground with a question, "*¿Mashi es tu nombre en Kichwa?*" (Is *mashi* your name in Kichwa?), he asked in Spanish, demonstrating that he did not know the referent of the standardized-Kichwa word, which his parents were unlikely to use. Tracing how students model speech—how they compartmentalize Kichwa from Spanish, abbreviate it, and demonstrate it as one of three equivalent languages—shows how they are more familiar with how select standardized phrases function for listeners and how non-Kichwa-speaking onlookers perceive them, than with the referential meanings of words. Such displays happened repeatedly over the years of students' passing through Elena's (and others') classrooms, as the example at the presidential offices from two years earlier demonstrated.

In the lesson, there are several ways in which multilingual instruction demonstrates intercultural citizenship, some more straightforward than others. First, Elena and the students showed, primarily through their language use, that the school is part of the state's intercultural bilingual school system and that being Ecuadorian can include being Indigenous. Indeed, Elena began a civics class about the Ecuadorian flag with Kichwa use. Additionally, the students curtailed their use of Kichwa, signifying how some people may perceive the use of Kichwa as "threatening" if they do not comprehend it, as described by safety zone theory regarding Indigenous languages (Lomawaima & McCarty 2014), but here in extensive use. In other words, extensive Kichwa can exclude those who do not understand.

Moreover, the students used words from standardized Kichwa, making their Kichwa use commensurate to office Spanish. For this ethnographic example, how the students spoke Kichwa presented the language family as similar to Spanish and English, paralleling the citizenship identities they projected. We can count the number of languages that students spoke based on similar grammatical form, reference, and use in alternating greetings in Kichwa, Spanish, and English. The interaction in which forms are quickly recited comparably across more than one language abbreviates Kichwa use and makes it like Spanish while sounding somewhat strange to most Kichwa speakers. Kichwa is not an Indo-European language and has significant differences from Spanish in grammar and semantics, in addition to consisting of various registers that are not always mutually understandable even within Ecuador. Despite these differences, Kichwa was presented as analogous to standardized Ecuadorian Spanish.

For the girl students, the poetics of intercultural identities also involved wearing forms of dress that represent Indigeneity, as Elena made clear when she told them to come to school wearing *anakus* (the boy students typically wear black pants with their uniforms, which do not necessarily signify Indigenous identities). The process foregrounds standardized and acceptable Indigenous identities rather than radical or classed difference. Ultimately, these ways of presenting collectively model the commensurability of the speakers for Spanish-speaking others, linking such speech with the speaker and "making visible" state-authorized and equivalent forms of Indigeneity.

In order to more fully comprehend how bilingual education became indicative of citizenship identities, I consider how others understood the students' demonstration. The evaluator from the Ministry of Education's reaction confirmed how students modeled intercultural citizenship through strategic Kichwa use. She self-identified as *mestiza* and was a director of a non-EIB school in Quito who was working part time for the Ministry of Education in school evaluation. Her situation was unusual in that she had attended a well-known non-EIB public high school that offered Kichwa classes. Her experience was that learning Kichwa was quite different from learning Indo-European languages, and she later said that she could never speak more than Kichwa greetings. As she put it, "*pero difícil el Kichwa*" (But Kichwa [is] hard). "*¡Los cuatro o cinco años estudié Kichwa! Es difícil el Kichwa. Más difícil que el alemán*" (For four or five years I studied Kichwa! It's hard, Kichwa. Harder than German). Her answer conveyed how linguistically different Kichwa is from Spanish and, based on her language learning experiences, not easily learned in a classroom.

I asked her why she wanted to study Kichwa, and her response confirmed how the students' language use demonstrated intercultural citizenship:[8]

Yo me sentía como persona	I felt that as a person,
que era una obligación en mi país saber dos idiomas.	it was an obligation in my country to speak two languages.
Eso es. Era mi obligación.	That's it. It was my obligation.

Todos tenemos que saber tres idiomas.	We all have to know three languages.
Tenemos que hablar español.	We have to speak Spanish.
Tenemos que hablar Kichwa.	We have to speak Kichwa.
Y tenemos que hablar inglés.	And we have to speak English.
Como aquí en la escuela.	Like here in the school.

Her answer thus offered a depiction of contemporary citizenship identities in Ecuador. As the students "here in the school" demonstrated, an "obligation" for people "in my country"—Ecuadorian citizens—is to speak "three languages": Spanish, Kichwa, and English. In other words, she understood that the students' language use, demonstrating the three languages as distinct but equivalent, modeled this ideology in their presentation. She mentioned schooling as a key institution for fulfilling national civic expectations, similar to what anthropological theory suggests. Demonstrating the use of three languages shows one's belonging to the intercultural nation-state. It shows a more inclusive form of and responsibilities for citizenship, including Indigenous languages and their speakers in defining national belonging. Her positioning of citizenship even goes a step further in suggesting that those who do not identify as Indigenous should also learn Kichwa, linking the Indigenous language to citizenship for all in the country. Yet, it extends an ideology about languages as additive—as important but singular, discrete things (Bartlett & García 2011), which also makes the languages equivalent. This ideology erases the vast register difference across the Kichwa language family within Ecuador and complements the students' abbreviated and commensurate ways of using Kichwa. From the standpoint of language instruction, whether students are conversant in Kichwa is another question entirely.

Conclusion

Kichwa is taught largely as greetings and songs in classrooms through which we come to understand how teaching students to speak Kichwa in particular and constrained ways generates intercultural citizenship identities. As students model state-sanctioned language ideologies in their behavior, multilingual speech reveals commensurate languages and, in turn, speakers. Such teaching strategies both illustrate and promote Indigenous identities that are increasingly prioritized by national state policy. In Ecuador, linguistic and nonlinguistic signs and the poetics of their cohesion depict members of Indigenous *pueblos* and nationalities as intercultural citizens for non-Kichwa speakers.

The instructed ways of speaking Kichwa show increased acceptance for and knowledge about Indigenous languages. Kichwa is now taught in classrooms, and *mestiza*-identifying visitors encourage certain forms of use and even attempt to learn the language themselves. Bilingual education benefits from state-sponsored interculturality that, while significantly more inclusive than previous citizenship models, still reflects predominant notions of citizenship. The acquisition of the benefits of *interculturalidad* simultaneously suppresses other Indigenous persons, especially lower-classed dimensions of citizenship less commonly included in schooling initiatives, such as how Elena described her own parents.

In such circumstances, teachers encounter a double bind: do they uphold the larger state project of intercultural bilingual education, which includes ways of speaking Kichwa that many of them disagree with and which may further divide students from their parents? Or should they teach more local ways of speaking, potentially risking breaking with *interculturalidad* and risking that spaces and social mobility will be closed off to students? Would teaching the latter potentially decrease the school's ability to garner excitement, volunteers, and funding, or might it concern those who plan for the school system?

Kichwa that is commensurate with Spanish socializes students into the intercultural dimensions of Kichwa language politics. Yet, the focus on equivalence also shifts away from the structural inequality that they experience. Students and their families are some of the most disenfranchised citizens of Ecuador. Through learning certain ways to demonstrate Indigeneity, students can be made, if temporarily, into intercultural, multilingual citizens. However, those forms continue to curtail Kichwa and make its forms, references, and uses similar to standardized office Spanish. The modeling of modernist language ideologies is an emergent form of Indigenous language use, even as it consists of misfires for many who understand Kichwa.

Conclusions

Since its establishment in 1988, the intercultural bilingual school system in Ecuador has been one of the most prominent examples of Indigenous education in Central and South America. For more than thirty years, members of Ecuador's *pueblos* and nationalities have worked from state institutions in coordinating the school system and in teaching. This book has shown the ways in which state agents, institutions, and policies invoke and establish *interculturalidad* and reinscribe it in linguistic and educational politics, ultimately affecting how Indigenous languages are spoken. A politics of interculturality is premised on affirming the equality—and the equivalency—of the linguistic and cultural practices of members of Indigenous *pueblos* and nationalities with other Ecuadorians.

State recognition has increased Kichwa's prominence and use, contributed to an infrastructure of schools to serve more diverse students, and provided substantial professional employment for Indigenous language speakers. Kichwa and some of its speakers are more accepted than ever, and even the Constitution has been translated to Kichwa. Just several decades ago, teaching Kichwa in schools at all was nearly impossible, let alone speaking the language family as a state agent in the Ministry of Education. Yet, there are double binds. By coordinating the school system from national state offices, Indigenous education comes with more reach and authority. However, the desired outcome of educational autonomy is subjected to regulation by other state agents, and the norms of authoritative institutions have been hard to transform. The goal of national curriculum development also means that, inevitably, multiple ways of communicating will not be appropriately represented in any one set of materials. Furthermore, much of state recognition and use has centered on Unified Kichwa. Its words and expressions often parallel those of standardized Ecuadorian Spanish used in offices, which allows employees to carry out their jobs while offering a different version of Kichwa from how many use and identify with their language. A politics of recognition, moreover, supports Indigenous "professionals" while simultaneously putting them in problematic positions. For example, there are constraints on when and how state representatives can expectably speak and write.

The norms of state institutions influence those who pass through them, including communicative practices. The case sheds light on a question that social theory has long considered: how do colonial ideologies, practices, and hierarchies "shape" activities like planning and teaching? By using the verb *shape*, authors tend to indicate more than an influence and, instead, the coloring of the very ways that people see the world.[1] For example, political scientist Benedict Anderson (2006 [1983], 65) argues that (comparatively white) governing agents who were born in the colonies established the "shape of imagined community," transplanting forms of nationalism to newer contexts through technologies like newspapers. Similarly, Anthropologist Marisol de la Cadena (2005, 282) describes the significance of race for modern institutions in Peru and how a "privileged social group" can "impose its image on those it deems inferior." She emphasizes how schools were integral to this process through their use of "literacy, language, [and] clothing" to "shape Indigenous life" (277). Indeed, a longer tradition of scholars has shown how technologies and institutions tend toward the reproduction of sameness, a form of *shaping* (e.g., Baudrillard 1994; Benjamin 2010).

This case has also shown the relevance of the verb *shape*'s use for colonial and modernist institutions, such as those of the state. This book's analysis details, specifically, how practices and forms of power are reproduced, altered, or contested. Inevitably, there is governmentality in daily state-authorized communication. The application of the conceptual tools and methods of linguistic anthropology to understand bilingual education in Ecuador has also shown that forms—*shapes*, as a noun—are extremely important, including in sound waves and alphabets. In terms of language shift to Unified Kichwa, *shaping* is especially about calquing—a sort of translation of standardized registers across languages—in linguistic forms, meanings, uses, and ideologies. As Jacqueline Urla and her colleagues (2017) argue for Basque, these reproductions from colonial languages are not totalizing per se. Instead, such similarities recur in a gradient but systematic and analogous fashion. Such influences and translations take many shapes, such as standardized greetings and the order and content of textbooks. Those signifiers and ideologies about them prioritize racialized, classed, and urbanized identities closer to the state's Spanish-speaking center, which contributes to divisions among members who participate in organizing.

I now turn to compare Ecuador's bilingual education and recognition of Kichwa with examples elsewhere. In so doing, I review some of the double binds considered throughout this book. I also consider workarounds. Following calls to avoid analysis without activism (as cited in Hale 2006, 113), or to avoid the lack of political urgency that, paradoxically, often proliferates the work of academics who write under decolonial studies (as cited in Rivera Cusicanqui 2019, 109), I reflect on what implications the book has for current efforts to confront state power and for Indigenous language recognition and teaching. I do so by comparing examples of the contestation of state institutions and management throughout the Americas. I also consider and take inspiration from Indigenous language teaching and bilingual education in Mexico and Peru, more specifically. I end with a brief epilogue with updates to the school system in Ecuador.

What Is It Like to Be an Upper-Level State Agent?

Many of the double binds in this book manifest for those who become employed as national state agents. In Ecuador, bilingual education coordinators continue to be "outsiders" in state offices. Yet, like the predicaments of Indigenous intellectuals more generally (Rappaport 2005), Indigenous state agents tend to be more accepted as national citizens than those whom they represent. They end up in the difficult situation of addressing the expectations of many audiences and publics. Since members of Indigenous *pueblos* and nationalities in Ecuador work alongside one another to coordinate an entire school system, their challenges differ from the struggles of Indigenous-identifying state officials elsewhere, such as how similar employees in other nation-states may feel ignored, undervalued, or experiencing constant racism (Lahn 2018; Lahn & Ganter 2018).

In academic writing, there has been a tendency to portray such employees as undergoing "cooptation" (critiqued and used by Radcliffe and Webb 2015) or "domestication" (Hale 2004; McNeish 2008) in describing how state offices change and restrict the actions of Indigenous employees. These characterizations have also been common to political science analyses of social movements whose actors become employed in state bureaucracies (Ranta 2018, 127). My research does not support these characterizations. I agree that activism and research must better understand the ways in which state agents and institutions attempt to govern and restrict political organizing, including by offering employment to members of social movements. Yet, in Ecuador, I have shown how double binds are common for state agents; a major challenge has involved the conflicting expectations of those to whom they communicate. Routinely, they find no ideal option. The situation is more nuanced and complex than how words like "cooptation" and "domestication" portray.

This brings me to a second point about how to better understand and listen to those in positions of eminent power: ethnographic analysis offers a crucial tool for unpacking the ways through which state policy and politics play out daily (Aydarova 2019; Castagno & McCarty 2017; Ranta 2018). Though spaces of policymaking are challenging to gain permission for participant observation, interviews are inadequate for documenting the subtle forms of contestation and negotiation necessary for maintaining roles as state agents. For example, interviewees may find it difficult to fully express the contours of a double bind, as Bateson notes that double binds can be somewhat hard to describe in full for those who are in them. This ethnographic research shows how Kichwa state agents are often savvy—extremely bright and skilled—in making themselves and their cultural emblems commensurate for non-Indigenous state agents and others, even if they end up in difficult situations with few good responses. These strategies are hard to systematically describe in interviews.

Additionally, the literature's focus on how Indigenous state agents must offer "proposals"—less combative, carefully reviewed and regulated, rational documents—over "protest" foregrounds another point for discussion (Hale 2004, 19). Radcliffe and Webb (2015, 251) describe a shift in office hiring criteria for Mapuche-identifying employees in the case of the Chilean Ministry of Education. Previously, in Chile, applicants needed affiliation with a social movement to gain employment. In Ecuador, in the early years of the school system, employees across the school system similarly needed to be associated with and even sponsored by an Indigenous organization if they were to gain employment. Today, however, candidates in both contexts must formally apply for and compete among various applicants to be evaluated primarily based on their educational credentials and work experience.

Yet, as other authors have noted, these changes merit further attention. In Ecuador, many policymakers hired in the late 1980s and the 1990s—based on their affiliation with Indigenous organizations, as Chapter 2 shows—are still employed or have retired after decades of work. They have had tenure and have influenced office discussions, which means "protest" and political organizing have not disappeared. As Chapter 4 shows, directors of Indigenous movements, including those outside of state spaces, are now routinely degree-holding professionals. While schooling systematically affects the dynamics of Indigenous movements, those in state offices still believe in or belong to the organizations of struggle, even if being a public servant prevents them from wearing lanyards with Ministry of Education identification cards to protests. Nearly everyone in the National Directorate offices belonged to a major Indigenous organization.

CONAIE-affiliated employees were sidelined in major policy decisions during the Correa years, but those same employees publicly and even scathingly critiqued Correa and other employees associated with his administration (Montaluisa 2011).

Can Double Binds Be Loosened? Rejection, Organization, and Communication

How can Indigenous state agents work against or break double binds? Anthropologist Jessica Cattelino (2010) draws on Gregory Bateson's work and notes that "escape" from a double bind "may be impossible" and that people caught in double binds "cannot control the terms of their own representation" (252). One possibility she describes, however, is refusal to engage with the parameters of the state.[2] Her example indicates wholesale, systematic refusal, perhaps similar to the Zapatistas in Chiapas, Mexico, who pursued "autonomous municipalities" in the late 1990s, long before seeking their recognition by national state policymakers (Speed 2005). These municipalities, which also have organizational institutions that focus on social programs like education, now coexist with state-affiliated municipalities, sometimes sharing geographic borders (Mora 2017). Their example has become one of the best-known in the world for how to organize self-determination vis-à-vis the encroachment of state institutions.

Indeed, after several decades of studying multiculturalism, research has shown how a politics of recognition has largely stalled and even failed in concessions, resulting in the need for "radical refusal" that seeks self-determination and local organizing (Hale & Mullings 2020; Simpson 2014). This strategy presents a challenge in Ecuador, however, for those already directing and managing bilingual education. This book has shown how, in establishing a parallel educational organization within the state, bilingual education in Ecuador became both a paradigm for gaining Indigenous rights and at the same time was largely modeled on the main school system. The project was never a separatist one and, over time, the school system became further subjected to regulation by higher-up, non-Indigenous-identifying state agents, too.

One lesson from research elsewhere for this Ecuadorian case is that refusal-based strategies do "coexist and comingle" with rights-based strategies (Hale & Mullings 2020, 58). Along these lines, in Ecuador, perhaps one strategy could be for actors who are more peripheral to state politics to seek to repurpose state-sponsored categories and forms of institutional organization. For instance, anthropologist Rudi Colloredo Mansfield (2009) shows how, in Highland Ecuador, many residents adopted the state's bureaucratic categories for the organization of provinces and production units. They began to use such categories to organize themselves for political protest to confront neoliberal policies, and they have successfully done so for decades. While the national state's categories (like the term *comuna* examined in Colloredo Mansfield's work) may pervade local ideas of political formation, those forms can be harnessed for change, too, by the same people who take them up.

Might it be possible to repurpose former president Correa's use of the term "decentralization"? Correa's regime strategically used "decentralization" to expand centralized state control; the decentralizing aspect was that some additional bureaucratic tasks and decisions were delegated to planning offices outside of the capital, even as his administration officials altered regional and local office organizational structures. A more participatory form of "decentralization" could yield increased influence of teachers and political organizations for cooperation and collaboration. There are even some preexisting models that could be given increased importance. Throughout Ecuador, for example, historical Indigenous schooling "*redes*" (networks) do not coincide with state-imposed districts and zones. Most school directors and teachers, geographically located nearby one another, have forged long-term working relationships. Similar networks have aided teacher union-organizing elsewhere, such as in Central America (Stephen 2013) and Bolivia (Gustafson 2009). Such efforts could also make pedagogies that are more locally relevant and that move beyond "national" as the expected scale of curriculum.

Another change could be for Indigenous movements to seek employment for those who are not "professionals" to make decisions, mentor, and discuss policy implications at the national level. This change could potentially adapt governing models of how decisions are made in small towns and decenter some of the individualist and modernist tendencies that others have critiqued as common in the coordination of the school system. Coordinators would not have to look far for examples; Indigenous schools have long experimented with bringing such citizens into their walls.

For example, Elizabeth Sumida Huaman (2020) shows how a recurring component of Indigenous education is the inclusion of elders who teach about the significance of place or other more institutionally effaced forms of knowledge. Sometimes an exceptional student who has lived extensively with grandparents can even take a more central role in instruction while still a student or as an alumnus (Sumida Huaman 2020, 273; De Korne 2021). A more horizontal form of planning could seek to make similar changes at the national level. Such members of Indigenous *pueblos* and nationalities are already integral to many Kichwa speakers' lives, as Sisa showed in Chapter 5 with her discussion of expertise, elders, and shamans. They could help to dismantle predominant institutional visions such as of "accountability," calling attention to its hierarchy and epistemological grounding in a lack of trust or inspiration (Hetherington 2011).

Can Stage Agents Challenge Language Standardization?

With the pairing of the processes of language standardization and linguistic recognition, how can Indigenous state agents work against double binds in communication? Scholars have long detailed how, in various parts of the world, there is an inherent paradox to standardization (Gal 2006; Woolard 2018). Activists and planners often work to forge a variety with an agreed-upon set of forms and rules. This process attempts to make versions of Indigenous languages that are readily used for policy and planning. It also helps historically oppressed languages to be used in academic settings and facilitates the production of educational materials for citizens throughout the nation-state. Yet, in the process of crafting a national variety, most speakers feel the efforts are reductive and that their ways of communicating are being ignored.

The specifics of Unified Kichwa use show how double binds saturate acts of self-presentation and communication, too. Language standardization is indicative of the many ways in which planners occupy impossible positions: their language use is inevitably influenced by the needs and expectations of state communication, such as translating laws or giving speeches in Kichwa in bureaucratic or technical Spanish-dominant spaces; speaking to a national audience that will include listeners who speak different registers or do not speak Kichwa at all; and regulation and supervision by higher-ups. Some words and actions ultimately seem foreign to those who are supposed to be prioritized in address—such as working-class Kichwa speakers from across rural and urban Ecuador—which yields ire and a lack of support for the project. Unified Kichwa is also based more closely on some regional varieties (such as from Northern and Central Highland Ecuador) than others.

Perhaps one step toward multiplicity could be the outlining of several different registers of recognition, including those from more state-peripheral areas. Early efforts in Peru in the 1970s concentrated on six official varieties of Quechua (King & Hornberger 2006) and have since seen translations in multiple registers or dialects (Howard et al. 2018). Certainly, other hierarchies would be reinforced, but perhaps the scale of difference would be less and could lay the groundwork for dialogue across smaller differences. This work could build on decentralization, too. Jacqueline Urla's research has described a shift over time along these lines in the Basque language revitalization movement in Spain. While there was an early rigidity for using only a pure standard, the movement later tended toward the use of standardized and nonstandardized vernacular forms. This shift was most apparent in community-based media projects, suggesting that in addition to ideological critique, decentralization may be an organizational feature that can facilitate state-sponsored communication for nonstandardized Kichwa listeners.

Borrowing from Bateson, Cattelino (2010, 253) also suggests that state limitations may provoke "creativity," where double binds force unusual practices and realignments that could pave the way for different futures. Silvia Rivera Cusicanqui (2018, 55) offers a similar observation based on Aymara perspectives that call for "the recognition of this 'duality' [in double binds] and the ability to live it creatively."[3] Perhaps one option could be reimagining written texts. For example, what might a nonwritten form of the Constitution sound or feel like? Such efforts would also circumvent many of the challenges related to writing in Kichwa at all, as seen in Chapters 4 and 6.

As seen in Chapter 4, Gloria's example of offsetting would constitute a form of "creative" expression. Though Gloria risked reprimand from the vice minister by speaking at length in Kichwa, she ruptured the pattern of delimited use of Kichwa in state authorized talk. Her ways of speaking employed but also contradicted Unified Kichwa. While she used a small number of calques and standardized Kichwa, she offset that use by minimizing systematic calques—those based on forms, reference, and use of Spanish (such as not using *alli puncha*)—and by using contrastive forms (such as marking respect with the suffix -*pa* inconsistently) that modeled a plethora of registers. This change still evoked reproachment from a higher-up, but it has potential for challenging the expectations for Kichwa public speaking, especially as bilingual education directors aim to get people speaking and excited about Kichwa. Mitigated rejection of standardized forms could make a difference.

In terms of daily office politics, despite the influence of standardized linguistic forms, many people employed in the school system—including many planners themselves—critiqued and lamented Unified Kichwa (Limerick 2020). These reactions show the multiplicity of orientations to ways of communicating across the school system's institutions. Even if that multiplicity has largely not been able to influence policy, pervasive criticisms were voiced in office spaces and will inevitably continue in future discussions.

Can Schools Be Used to Stop Shift from Indigenous Languages?

Scholars have long asked a question that points to a double bind seen in this book: can schools be used to help young people communicate in Indigenous languages? Schooling is where children spend much of their time and is the primary institution of state-sponsored initiatives for bilingual education. Yet, until recent decades, teachers largely tried to stamp out Indigenous language use and exclude or assimilate speakers of these languages, so schools are challenging to repurpose.[4] This book has shown how, in Ecuador, the policy of a national Indigenous school system has long emphasized schools for teaching Indigenous languages and for making culturally relevant pedagogy. Yet, three decades after its commencement, many have lamented that the school system does not teach Indigenous languages in most schools and that most "bilingual" schools are similar to the schools of the primary school system.

Clearly, Kichwa signage in classrooms at all models that Kichwa now belongs in institutional spaces. In the school about which I write here, there were posters and signs that covered the classroom walls with Kichwa vocabulary words, and I saw similar displays in the various schools that I visited that did teach some Kichwa. However, as Chapter 7 shows, another concern is a double bind in the *register* of instruction in how Indigenous languages are taught, if they are taught. The classroom described here shows how students learned standardized Kichwa vocabulary words and songs that are commensurate with Spanish and more oriented toward presenting them as intercultural citizens. Students may not become fluent in Kichwa, but such presentations are more straightforward to teach and help the school gain much needed funds and volunteers.

Recent bilingual education research provides helpful pedagogical examples for how schools can overcome shift to colonial languages that could apply to cases in Ecuador. Teaching in Kichwa with the support of current research on second or nondominant language pedagogies would clearly be one way to increase fluency. Such pedagogies also push back against how students are embarrassed to speak Kichwa because it is stigmatized or because they are embarrassed that they are not proficient. One pedagogy along these lines elsewhere has been to make schools sites of immersion in Indigenous language use and instruction (May 2013; McCarty et al. 2021). Research has shown, furthermore, that increasing the use of translanguaging in the classroom is an important epistemological and instructional shift for comparatively suppressed languages. Recognizing and allowing for a space where multiple norms and registers across languages are used and explained (Wyman 2009; García 2009) can help bring different ways of speaking into the classroom and avoid marginalizing anew how students' families communicate.

These changes would require significant labor and change in Ecuador that go beyond a simple shift, though. They imply systematically reworking pedagogy and instruction to better support teaching Kichwa as a nondominant or heritage language family, which will be challenging to make in part because it has not existed. I think this is possible at a smaller level of scale—perhaps tailoring curricula for small regions or cities—and have been working with teachers to elaborate and pilot such a pedagogy. Another factor to consider would be the recruitment and support of more teachers who are comfortable with and excited about teaching Indigenous languages, and who speak registers similar to how students and their parents communicate. Such efforts, furthermore, would necessitate additional large-scale shifts in language ideologies in regard to how people see Kichwa—to be excited to speak and learn the language family—and also to foreground localized registers. Some of the former *has* occurred with intercultural recognition, as parents rarely protest that Kichwa is taught (see Chapter 7). But not protesting the teaching of Kichwa and becoming excited about teaching it are two different epistemologies.

This last challenge brings us back to this book's Introduction, in which linguist and planner Alberto Conejo said that, despite his and his colleagues' long-standing focus on getting Kichwa to be taught in schools, students still see and hear Kichwa as stigmatized outside of classroom spaces, which ultimately makes it challenging for schools to be singular institutions of change. As research has shown, this predicament points to improvements beyond the classroom (Messing 2009), though classrooms can be used to discuss how students see how each language has benefits and importance (Lee 2009).

Paralleling the aforementioned efforts to work against double binds in policymaking, the rethinking of who is involved in schooling and how they are involved could be one way to "reject" the forms of organization and norms of instruction in schools. Mexico offers some schooling examples that could be helpful. That nation-state has long had a national directorate devoted to Indigenous education, with the first one established in 1921, albeit with assimilationist goals (Citarella 1990, 15). Most scholars regard the establishment of the 1978 General Directorate of Indigenous Education as a major step for institutional forms of Indigenous schooling in Mexico (Citarella 1990, 37). Yet, for decades Indigenous schooling occurred in Spanish, and even the arrival of intercultural bilingual education in the 1990s did not lead to more culturally and linguistically relevant curriculum (Hamel 2008, 318–19). In this sense, national Indigenous education in Mexico has seen similar challenges and, organizationally, has been more problematic than in Ecuador in its history of directly assimilationist efforts.

But there are other smaller-scale stories. Applied linguist Lois Meyer (2018) emphasizes that the region of Oaxaca has seen more promising efforts than in other Mexican states. She foregrounds a coalition within the powerful teachers' union—more than a thousand Indigenous teachers working in rural parts of the state—as major agents of change. Their coalition was inspired and energized by the Zapatista movement in the neighboring Mexican state of Chiapas (Meyer 2018, 385). In 2001, they renounced their own previous practices, including state-authorized educational models that had not aptly served students, such as teaching in Spanish. They called for community organizations to generate broader and more equitable participation in schooling.

The initiatives that followed show the significance not just of small-scale Indigenous language initiatives but, also, extending and reworking school organization to involve other community members more directly. For instance, a committee translated writings about New Zealand Maori language nests to Spanish and circulated them to teachers. In 2008, a small Mixtec *pueblo* began these efforts, involving village authorities to investigate how a language nest might work. Eventually, community members chose guides or elders who would agree to speak to babies and young children in their languages, altering the students' linguistic repertoires *before* they arrived to school. Some aspects were different from New Zealand, such as the fact that guides were unpaid and their work aligned with their agricultural responsibilities, but they borrowed from the Maori example (Meyer 2018, 392). Since Ecuador's bilingual school system already stresses the involvement of parents, building on that historical focus with instructional and conversational involvement for parents could be a major route toward using linguistic recognition and reclamation to transform teaching practices.

Another effort to offer a credential to teachers in Mexico would seem to be problematic, given the tendencies of credentials to promote institutional expertise. But the credential taught teachers how to do ethnographic research, to document linguistic and cultural practices, and to apply those findings to reworking curriculum (Meyer 2018, 390), thus changing common roles and epistemologies in teaching. In other words, the courses emphasized how to listen, observe, and make small-scale pedagogy that reflected those observations. Both examples show how schools could still work to reclaim and teach Indigenous languages but that they must draw from different forms of participation and roles from those historically emphasized in schools.

Can Expertise Become Multiple and Multidirectional?

Another double bind in assuming roles as state agents is the linking of certain ideas and ways of communicating with authority. This book has shown how establishing expertise involves not just inhabiting a role of authority but also locating others in roles of laity, since one's expertise necessarily involves others who are unaware (Carr 2010, 22). In Ecuador, planners, teachers, and parents may lament "know-it-alls" (see Chapter 4) and the continuation of Kichwa policy that they see as positioning their ways of speaking as wrong, which leads to immense resentment toward the school system and those who direct it. Much bilingual education expertise in Kichwa depends upon modernist ideologies that stand in contrast with the experiences of most everybody else.

The case of Peru offers insights that could shift the landscape of expertise in schooling and language planning and, potentially, alleviate some of the double binds. Virginia Zavala's (2019) description of bilingual education in Peru details a similar divide between expert discourses that promote pure Quechua and others. However, Zavala notes that actors further to the periphery of state institutions and cities are having a significant effect on the revalorization of Quechua. There are similarities with the case of Ecuador, which may provide alternative pathways for encouraging Kichwa use.

Bilingual education planning in Peru has depended upon "experts," whom Zavala (2019, 63) describes as people who grew up in Quechua-speaking rural *pueblos*, were taught by linguists and educators, and who now live in cities. Unlike Ecuador, however, there has not, historically, been a comparable national bilingual education office and employees have been more dispersed, working in lower-level bilingual education offices, universities, or for NGOs. The centralized offices were instead the High Academy of the Quechua Language, which has overseen language planning, regulation, and maintenance for Quechua. As language policy scholar Serafín Coronel-Molina (2015, 78) details, in 1990, just two years after DINEIB was established in Ecuador, Peruvian Law No. 25260 recognized the Academy with some similarities to the National Directorate's legal recognition: "as a public, decentralized institution of the educational sector ... with administrative and academic autonomy" that would be overseen by the Ministry of Education. However, most of the Peruvian Academy's establishment did not transpire, as the right-wing Alberto Fujimori was elected president and funding quickly waned. Furthermore, over the years, the Academy fluctuated in number—sometimes having just two members—and early in its establishment did not necessarily include Quechua-identifying citizens (Coronel-Molina 2015). As the national center has had less influence, hip-hop artists with messages of political struggle and resistance, such as Renata Flores who has also translated and performed Michael Jackson's music in Quechua, offer examples of young people who introduce entirely different projects from that of bilingual education.[5] Zavala sees these examples as more promising for the future of Quechua-language reclamation in Peru.

In Ecuador, there are similarly exciting and complementary activities. For example, the hip-hop group Los Nin performs and records in Spanish and Kichwa and has drawn crowds to concerts for more than a decade. They have offered direct political appeals to reprioritize Kichwa registers and philosophies, and these days there are multiple other Kichwa hip-hop artists who have emerged, too.[6] Another example is Kichwa.net, an organization and website founded by Sacha Rosero Lema, an Otavalan who has lived in Spain and became proficient in Kichwa after childhood. The website has a wide array of materials to learn Kichwa as a nondominant language—an approach largely absent in the school system—and routinely offers classes and events in that region. The materials combine many of the resources that intercultural bilingual education offers, too—dictionaries, grammar lists, textbooks—in a widely accessible and user-friendly format.

Radio is another medium that has long provided ways to disseminate local Kichwa registers and to provide entertainment and information by and for those who live in more rural areas. Initiatives for teaching and valuing Kichwa have taken off in this medium (Ennis 2019), including with an online radio show produced and disseminated from New York.[7] Projects more peripheral to state offices do not just offer alternatives to bilingual education but may be exciting, ultimately shape the discourses of what should be planned for in state institutions, and change the larger Kichwa landscape in a way that complements and benefits the school system.

More recently, Peru has more closely followed the Ecuadorian examples and, in 2011, established the General Directorate of Alternative Education, Intercultural Bilingual Education, and Alternative Services in Rural Areas (DIGEIBIRA) that would carry out linguistic and educational policy. The state office would set national policy, including standardizing Indigenous languages, developing curricula in them, and providing professional training, even if budget cuts have not led to much fruition (Kvietok-Dueñas 2019, 57–58). Yet, the office developed three larger-scale models for teaching Indigenous languages based on varying needs of learners that could be helpful in Ecuador, including plans for rural areas with "monolingual" Quechua-speakers, for rural areas with language shift, and for urban areas with language shift. These plans have expressed support for "heritage language" instruction and acknowledge more dynamic forms of multilingual communication than state-authorized ideologies tend to entail (Kvietok-Dueñas 2019, 58–59). Perhaps, at the national level and given decades of exchanges across the nation-states, this case could serve as justification and a model for planning changes to bilingual education in Ecuador.

Epilogue

In 2017, Ecuador elected a new president, Lenín Moreno, who replaced the term-limited Correa. Moreno had served as Correa's vice president during his first term and belonged to Correa's (now former) political party Alianza País. Moreno publicly broke with Correa on multiple issues (in addition to allowing corruption charges against Correa's second-term vice president, who went to prison), leading to an open feud. At the early stages of his presidency, Moreno attempted to shift Correa's more combative and restrictive policies toward social movements and the press to be more tolerant. Citing state debt, he also undid several economic restrictions and taxes that Correa enacted, showing a turn to more common yet detrimental neoliberal multicultural policies (see Becker & Riofrancos 2018).

As Chapter 2 argues, the president has a major effect on education rights. While Correa funded the intercultural bilingual school system well, he attempted to control it. Moreno promised funding for the school system, and he met with CONAIE leaders within the first six months of his presidency. His ascent had CONAIE members and other Indigenous directors meeting to plan and discuss how bilingual education could be "returned" to them.[8] The Ministry of Education also announced the production of new textbooks in Indigenous languages, maintenance for schools, and preparation for more than 8,000 teachers.[9] Moreno even described Correa's closing of rural single-teacher schools an "error" while lamenting their replacement with the Millennial Schools that involved lengthy commutes for students.[10] CONAIE also sought the restitution of the major Indigenous university, Amawtay Wasi, which Correa's administration had closed under the pretext of a low score from the higher education accreditation institution, and the university has since been reopened.[11]

On July 6, 2018, Moreno continued to elevate the status of the school system within the Ministry of Education. He signed Presidential Decree 445 that raised the status of the coordinating office of the school system from "Undersecretariat" (*Subsecretaría*) to "Secretariat" (*Secretaría*), with the new head of this office having a title that would be equivalent to the other vice ministers of the Ministry and not reporting to one of them, as had occurred when I was carrying out research. This book has shown how *intercultural* has tended to translate much of the Spanish-speaking world of institutions into Kichwa while leaving fundamental ideologies and practices unchanged. However, observers have emphasized this decree as *plurinational* in its efforts to profoundly transform society.[12] In addition to avoiding another level of regulatory supervision within the Ministry's organizational structure, the decree also proclaimed the Secretariat an "affiliated entity" (*entidad adscrita*) to the Ministry of Education that would have "administrative, technical, pedagogic, operative, and financial independence," all the while carrying over the personnel and materials to be under the care of the new office (Article 1). Yet, the decree also stipulated that the minister of education would name the head of the office (Article 3), which continued to directly subject the school system to the head of those offices and the presidential governing regime.

As Moreno's administration ceded regulation of bilingual education, they also continued to cut social programs and the education budget. In October 2019, Ecuador was again thrust into the international spotlight. For nearly two weeks, a multitude of protesters in Quito demanded that Moreno repeal decree number 883, which proclaimed the elimination of gas subsidies. The decree would raise the cost of many products from food to transportation. Bus fares in Quito alone were scheduled to increase by 60 percent. Moreno had accepted a loan from the International Monetary Fund, which forced Ecuador into austerity measures that would devastate many Ecuadorians, especially the poorest ones.

Ecuador's Indigenous organizations were suddenly united against the measures. Though they have manifested significant divisions over the past fifteen years, Indigenous mobilizers demanded a policy reversal as they filled the capital from near and far, including distant parts of the highlands and the Amazon. Moreno fled to the coastal city of Guayaquil and temporarily moved the capital there. The protests attempted to close off roads into and within Quito and other smaller cities throughout Ecuador. As tensions escalated, police violence contributed to the deaths of at least eleven people, with thousands of others injured and still others imprisoned.[13] In Quito, universities turned into zones of aid for the protestors, with hundreds of volunteers working around the clock to provide food and medical care despite enduring tear gas attacks from the police. On October 14, 2019, in a meeting with representatives of Indigenous organizations and *pueblos*, as well as government officials, Moreno repealed the decree, and protests subsided. Indigenous organizations continued to demand the ouster of cabinet members who bore authority over police brutality, as well as the release of imprisoned protesters. Years later, some of the most prominent institutional decision makers who oversaw the state-sponsored violence of the protests saw few repercussions and even appointments in US universities.[14] Furthermore, though the protests yielded some temporary economic reprieve, many of Moreno's austerity measures remained in place. For example, as Ecuador suffered "excess deaths" early in the COVID-19 pandemic and became one of the world's deadliest places, the Moreno administration continued to prioritize payments to debtors and cut public health funding (Rayner 2021). The economic depression that emerged exacerbated inequality and made living conditions even more perilous.

As Moreno's unpopular administration continued, the employees of the now Secretariat of Intercultural Bilingual Education worked with CONAIE and others to elaborate changes for an updated version of the Organic Law of Intercultural Education (LOEI, as described in Chapter 5) that would aim to further codify and expand upon Moreno's bilingual education presidential decree.[15] The Ecuadorian Assembly approved the updated LOEI on March 9, 2021, and Moreno signed the text into law a few weeks later.[16] One noteworthy legal description was the establishment of a Plurinational Council to propose strategic planning and evaluation to the National Education Authority, presumably the minister. The Council would include a member of each nationality, an Afroecuadorian, and Montubio, as well as directors and an authority of the Ministry (Articles 84–85).

On the one hand, this designation yields a more plural process of decision-making that before was often left to the subsecretary and director of the school system, and it includes more nationalities as equals in the decision-making process. This seems to have contributed to members of other nationalities than Kichwa assuming more responsibility for the administration of the school system. On the other hand, the designation appeared to shift authority away from those who have historically coordinated the school system from the offices, including many of the Kichwa speakers who worked so closely over the years to plan for and implement the daily policies.

Some other major changes in the updated Law included another name change for the school system to the Sistema de Educación Intercultural Bilingüe y Etnoeducación (Intercultural Bilingual Education and Ethnoeducation System), and which stipulates a director of ethno-education and defines ethno-education and its focus for and by Afro-Ecuadorians and Montubios (Article 92.1). The system thus indicates a recognition and advance for those populations, built on the struggle of people like the Montubia audience member in Chapter 6 who implored that the state agent recognize her people. The updates also include "*soberanía epistémica*" (epistemic sovereignty) for the school system's curriculum (Article 92), which further reinforces the right to decide on curriculum without seeking approval from Ministry officials.

Even as policy updates focused on bilingual education, Ecuador's worsening economic conditions set the foundation for the largest strike in Ecuador's recent history in June 2022. President Guillermo Lasso, a banker who served as the CEO of one of Ecuador's major banks, assumed office in May 2021 after winning a run-off election against Correa's hand-picked successor. Lasso's right-wing policies have continued much of the neoliberal multiculturalism of his predecessor. After assuming office, his policies exacerbated poverty in Ecuador, including by carrying out increases in gasoline prices mandated by the International Monetary Fund that the 2019 mobilizations had previously fought against; increasing drilling for petroleum and mining in Indigenous territories; and overseeing even more debt for many Ecuadorian families.[17] CONAIE directors attempted to negotiate with his administration for over a year, to no avail. Living conditions had become unbearable, such as high rates of child malnourishment; farmers who do not receive enough income from their crops to live on; and young people experiencing vast un- and underemployment.[18] CONAIE made ten demands of the state, many having to do with gas, mining, and agriculture. One demand was to increase the education and health budgets, with public universities missing basic amenities, impossibly large class sizes, and a shortage of medicines in public hospitals, among many other problems.[19]

Within this context, CONAIE president Leonidas Iza announced a national strike for June 13, 2022, with widespread support of Indigenous organizations. The scale of the strike was massive in terms of how many people were involved, the array of actors who participated, and how much of the country came to a standstill (Figures 8.1–8.4). The strike shut down roads throughout Ecuador and lasted for eighteen days, cutting off food supplies, suspending government services, and halting transportation in and out of cities during many hours of the day. It united the three major national Indigenous organizations in Ecuador: CONAIE, FENOCIN, and FEINE. It also brought together labor unions, high school and university students, teachers, farmers, artists, wings of the Catholic church, among many others.[20] Each day, the protests against the government continued to grow in number and expand to cities throughout the country, and eventually the Lasso administration declared a state of emergency and mobilized the military, at which point they further amplified state-sponsored violence.[21] Over the eighteen days of mobilizations, the protests saw extreme police violence and repression, and the arrest, eventual release, and later legal proceedings against the president of CONAIE Iza.

Figure 8.1 Protesters at the strike marching with the *wiphala* flag in Quito. Photo by author.

Figure 8.2 "Lasso, Murderer" inscribed on a bus stop advertisement near the Universidad Central in Quito, a central site of the protests, with traffic shut down. Photo by author.

Figure 8.3 Protestors at the strike in Quito with shields from the police. Photo by author.

Figure 8.4 The National Assembly during the strike. This file is licensed under the Creative Commons Attribution 3.0 Unported license. Attribution: El Blog de Jota.

At least nine people died, including five protestors, three people whose deaths resulted from road blockages, and one member of the military.[22]

As Chapter 2 showed, public schooling has long been one of the first points of concession of presidential administrations to activists, and this latest strike was no exception. One week into the strike, Lasso responded to CONAIE's ten demands with a commitment to double intercultural bilingual education's budget to more than $4 million.[23] He claimed immediate dispersal of the funds. Other concessions included a fertilizer subsidy, a small increase in government assistance for poor citizens, and debt cancellations.[24] Iza, speaking for CONAIE, said the concessions were insufficient and emphasized their demands for gas subsidies.[25] When the presidential administration finally agreed to negotiate again after more than another week had passed, organizers gained several more significant demands, such as reducing the price of gas by 15 cents a gallon, an agreement to make policies to develop subsidies, and to repeal and rewrite decrees that had promoted increased extraction and mining in the country.[26] This is when the strike subsided.

It was within this immediate context that Lasso's Ministry of Education signed papers to return "*autonomía total*" (total autonomy) of bilingual education.[27] The process had been initiated during Moreno's presidency, and the officials who announced the change emphasized that it had been underway for "more than a year," even as the post-strike timing of the announcement seemed more than coincidental. On August 3, 2022, there was a ceremony to sign a Ministerial Agreement 2022-001 between the Ministry of Education and Intercultural Bilingual Education, which would reiterate the designations of autonomy from the Organic Law of Intercultural Education (LOEI).

The announcements, such as the transfer of job allocations and the furniture of the school system to the Secretariat, largely seemed to put into practice what had been agreed upon in the LOEI back in Moreno's presidency.[28] For example, a member of the Tsachila nationality and the director of higher education noted that "*los representantes de las nacionalidades y pueblos a este consejo plurinacional serán nombrados a través de procesos definidos por el Consejo Nacional Electoral en coordinación con las comunidades, pueblos y nacionalidades respetando derechos colectivos establecidos en la constitución de la república*" (representatives of the nationalities and pueblos for this Plurinational Council will be named through the processes defined by the National Electoral Council in coordination with the communities, *pueblos*, and nationalities respecting collective rights established in the Constitution of the Republic). This language appears verbatim in the LOEI, which continues to name the Educational System as the highest authority for the Council (Article 85), also raising questions about the idea of "total autonomy."

While the advances mark major institutional gains, criticisms surfaced. On Facebook, many teachers lambasted the secretary of the school system's speech at the ceremony for awarding too much credit to the president and not properly acknowledging the strike and the protests. Indeed, he thanked Lasso immediately after thanking "*el hacedor de las cosas*" (the maker of things) and emphasized that the event "*no es nada político*" (isn't at all political) and that it's "*como siempre lo hacemos desde el Ministerio de Educación y desde la Secretaría de la Educación Intercultural Bilingüe*" (as we always do from the Ministry of Education and from the Secretariat of Intercultural Bilingual Education). Such discourses would seem to signify a political strategy that emphasizes the presidential administration as a primary interlocutor and supervisor, which was further compounded by both his and the minister of education's emphasis on Lasso's discourses about the country as "united." As Chapter 2 showed, however, that exact word "united" was used in the late 1980s by both then president Borja and CONAIE activists to establish the autonomous school system, so such political strategies are not necessarily counterproductive to the efforts. At the schooling level, in recent workshops with teachers, directors of the school system aimed to get teachers to systematically apply the intercultural bilingual education model, and teachers emphasized that changes in offices at the level of districts seemed to be taking effect.

As this book has shown, perhaps the biggest concern about the changes is whether they fundamentally rupture the institutional expectations and logics that have made so many teachers, parents, and students disillusioned with the school system. The Ecuadorian online magazine *Plan V*, writing about the primary school system, foregrounded a concern about educational organization and the directionality of knowledge and regulation that this book shows is equally applicable to this case (Quishpe 2022):

Otro de los signos de la educación, en los últimos años, ha sido su carácter vertical. Las decisiones a nivel de políticas generales como de instrumentos normativos, curriculares, de evaluación, entre otros, han sido diseñados con una clara tendencia tecnocrática, externa y ajena al quehacer de los actores educativos. El rol asumido por el Estado—el Ministerio de Educación—ha sido protagónico y ha cubierto todos los espacios y ha ocasionado, entre varios aspectos la exclusión y el opacamiento de los actores educativos.

Another of the signs of education, in these recent years, has been its vertical character. Decisions at the level of general policies as well as regulatory instruments, curricula, of evaluation, among others, have been designed with a clear technocratic tendency, external and alien to the tasks of educational actors. The role assumed by the state—the Ministry of Education—has been protagonist and has covered all spaces and has occasioned, among several aspects, the exclusion and overshadowing of educational actors.

This "vertical character" of state institutions has long stymied efforts toward widespread support for those who direct the bilingual school system, even as they have largely inherited a comparable version of Ecuador's school system writ large. This "technocratic" tendency, once again, positions those who plan as experts and most everyone else as not and as subject to regulation, much of which they may see as standardizing or imposed. Will the current efforts toward autonomy be able to transform this characteristic? From the norms and requirements of Unified Kichwa to crafting textbooks that are used across the country, the scale of "general policies" has set those who plan the school system up to become experts and, inevitably, erase aspects of schooling for the diverse members of society for whom they plan.

These tensions manifest directly in the words of the minister of education at the event in which she simultaneously emphasized greater accountability and more dialogue in yielding more decision-making to members of Indigenous *pueblos* and nationalities:

> A mayor autonomía mayor responsabilidad, ante mayor autonomía mayor rendición de cuentas, ante mayor autonomía mayor diálogo con las nacionalidades y el territorio, ante mayor autonomía requerimos también mayor corresponsabilidad de todos quienes conforman el sistema de educación intercultural bilingüe y la etno educación.

> The greater the autonomy, the greater the responsibility; the greater the autonomy, the greater the accountability; the greater the autonomy, the greater the dialogue with the nationalities and the territory; the greater the autonomy, we also require greater co-responsibility of all those who make up the ethno-education and intercultural bilingual education system.

These tensions aptly describe many of the dynamics that have become contradictory for those who manage the school system. Can more dialogue and influence from "the nationalities" and "the territory" make the school system more plural? Or will the technocratic discourses and the norms of bureaucracies like state institutions predominate these changes? As this book has shown, these are the very struggles of bilingual education in Ecuador that have been predominant over the past thirty years, regardless of how regulated the school system has been by presidential administrations. This book has shown that efforts to reform the school system would also need close examination of how institutional norms, communication, and practices are reproduced.

Notes

Introduction

1. The school system's promotional materials announced fourteen languages, even if others now count eleven or twelve (https://www.elcomercio.com/tendencias/sociedad/lenguas ancestrales-extincion-andoa-zapara-intercultural.html).
2. Gustafson (2009); McCarty & May (2017); McCarty, Nicholas, & Wigglesworth (2019).
3. De la Cadena (2005) examines schools in the Andes as sites of major epistemological differences, with Andean conceptualizations extending beyond the arrival of the modern state.
4. This number reflects the peak of the number of EIB schools in Ecuador. In a speech on August 3, 2022, the minister of education said that there were then 1,736 EIB schools.
5. Becerra-Lubies, Mayo, & Fones (2019); De Korne, López-Gopar, & Rios Rios (2019); McCarty, Lee, Noguera, Yepa, & Nicholas (2022); Postero & Zamosc (2004, 15).
6. https://www.elcomercio.com/tendencias/ecuador-autodefine-indigena-poblacion-etnia.html.
7. This observation follows the significant line of research on raciolinguistics and raciontologies in US-based scholars who research education in the United States (e.g., Rosa & Díaz 2020; Rosa & Flores 2017).
8. E.g., Anyon (2009); Dhillon (2017); Niesz (2019); Piven & Cloward (1977).
9. I follow scholars of Quechua (Mannheim 1991; Albó 1977) in referring to Quechua as an "oppressed" language due to decades of state policy against it, even as Quechua was also the language of an empire and an "oppressor" language. Still, "oppressed" erases some of the relevance and malleability of language use (see, e.g., Viatori & Ushigua 2007) and provides a frame that masks differences and even resistance.
10. E.g., as argued in Niezen (2003).
11. Sumida Huaman (2020); McCarty et al. (2005); and many others.
12. The study of metasemiotic work has become a linguistic anthropological focus (Carr 2011; Nakassis 2016; Shankar 2012).
13. Gayatri Chakravorty Spivak (e.g., 1993, 3–4, as in other writings) emphasizes that such efforts must be accompanied by constant reminders that they are, in fact, essentialist, even if this is counterproductive. Her writings indicate a double bind to strategic essentialism. Research on political movements and Indigeneity in Central and South America has also shown the challenges of "essentialist" discourses with a different genealogy (see Warren 2001, 94; Jackson & Warren 2005, 559–60; Whitten & Whitten 2011, 85).
14. See Flores & Rosa (2015); Rosa & Flores (2017) for racialized talk and commensuration.
15. See versions of this argument in Moore et al. (2010).
16. Scholars have long emphasized this question. For example, Hornberger (2008) asks whether schools can reverse language shift, since they are just one setting in which young people learn and speak. Rockwell & Gomes (2009, 98) emphasize fundamental problems with schools, suggesting that problems arise from focusing on "alternative schooling" for

Indigenous peoples instead of "alternatives to schooling." See also Hornberger & King (1996); Hornberger & De Korne (2018); McCarty (2008); McCarty & Nicholas (2014); Sims (2005).
17. Hale (2002); McNeish (2008); Radcliffe & Webb (2015).
18. See Fenigsen (1999) for a review of literature around linguistic domination.
19. Interview, January 9, 2012.
20. Luykx et al. (2016); De Korne (2021); Mannheim (1991); Romero (2015).
21. Counting speakers of Quechua/Kichwa is hard, as scholars have shown for many other language families. See Howard (2011) for a detailed analysis of statistics throughout the region.
22. See Wortham (2008); Gal & Irvine (2019) for a guide for similar methodological considerations for linguistic anthropological research.
23. See, e.g., critiques by Bourgois (1996); Davis (2020); Heath (1983); Levinson (1999); Schieffelin & Ochs (1986); Varenne (2007).
24. In 2022, as this book was going into production, the Ministry of Education announced a process of returning "autonomy" to the school system. See the Conclusion for the most recent updates.
25. See, e.g., Chapter 7; and similar cases for Indigenous languages in Lee (2009); López Gopar (2016); Valdiviezo (2009, 73).
26. Throughout the world, teaching Indigenous languages in classroom increasingly means teaching them as *second* or nondominant languages with strategies such as linguistic immersion (cf. May 2013; McCarty 2008).
27. https://educacion.gob.ec/wp-content/uploads/downloads/2015/11/Proyecto_Fortalecimiento-Educacion-Intercultural-Bilingue.pdf.
28. See a similar point in King (2001) and Uzendoski (2008).
29. Niezen (2003); Postero (2007); Taylor (1994); Van Cott (2009).
30. Some scholars who have led the way on this topic include Povinelli (2002); García-Sánchez (2016); Wroblewski (2014).
31. Moore (2011); Silverstein (1998); Paz (2019); Urla (2012).
32. Hornberger (2002); Jaffe (1999); May (2007).
33. Hale (2005); Martínez Novo (2014); Paschel (2016); Simpson (2014).
34. Conklin & Graham (1995); Graham & Penny (2014); Loperena (2020); Povinelli (2002).
35. Philosophers have shown how a politics of recognizing difference depends upon how subjects mutually recognize one another (see, e.g., Honneth & Farrell 1997, 17, who focus on the moral aspects of recognition). Philosophers since Hegel have called attention to how legal recognition is just one of several levels of scale (e.g., individual recognition of the self, subjects who recognize one another) in which recognition has moral implications. Here, I focus on the political dimensions of national, state-sponsored recognition and its cultural and linguistic implications.
36. Wroblewski (2014, 66) makes a similar point for Napo Kichwa populations who are, on the one hand, more peripheral (in their location in the Amazonian province of Napo) but associated with regional state institutions like local bilingual education planning offices.
37. Gustafson (2009); Hornberger (2000); Postero (2007); Rodríguez Cruz (2018).
38. Interview, November 8, 2012.
39. See also Mateos Cortés, Selene, & Dietz (2017, 45).

Notes 221

40. Another example is how Peery (2012) shows how standardized Navajo followed a similar process to Kichwa: while the New Deal called for increased schooling and literacy in Navajo, those who would speak or write in the language made standardized Navajo analogous to standardized English. The forms of standardized Navajo and its uses in public spheres like education, law, and politics meant linguistic assimilation occurred in translation and language planning.
41. It is complicated to conclude which language is "dominant" and the various ways in which morphological and syntactic contact manifests. Auer (2014) points out that grammatical borrowing is gradient and often contradictory. Unified Kichwa demonstrates an especially large and systematic degree of calquing based on Spanish.
42. Simultaneity is yet another example of how code-switching as careful, delineated language use between two discrete codes is more of an ideal than a practice (Armstrong-Fumero 2009; Makihara 2008; García & Wei 2014).
43. In Peruvian Quechua, *waway* is an adjectival form of the noun *wawa* that means very cute or very soft (Gobierno Regional de Cusco 2005, 732).

Chapter 1

1. Interview, December 15, 2011.
2. "*un vuelco en el tiempo/espacio, el fin de un ciclo y el inicio de otro, cuando un 'mundo al revés' puede volver sobre sus pies.*"
3. "*todo tiene un Pachakutin, un cambio, una transformación para volver de nuevo.*"
4. Contemporary linguistic anthropology parallels Bateson's claims in writing about pragmatics and metapragmatics, including first- and second-order indexicals (see, e.g., Lucy 1993; Silverstein 1993; 2003a, among many others).
5. In a similar example, Graham (2002) argues that in Brazil and Venezuela, Amazonian spokespeople encounter the predicament of balancing Indigenous language use to signal their identities with the need to convey messages to international audiences, which requires the use of dominant languages. When they speak Portuguese or Spanish, others question their Indigeneity, presenting a dilemma of incompatible expectations but with fewer other functions of Kichwa use in comparison to the Ecuador example.
6. Scholars have long considered how power inevitably yields resistance and, conversely, how resistance still indicates power (e.g., Foucault 1978; Abu-Lughod 1990).
7. Common Unified Kichwa expressions tend to systematically parallel Spanish, albeit in different linguistic and semiotic ways (see, e.g., *mashi* in Chapter 2, or *yupaychani* in Chapter 5).
8. January 15, 2012.
9. https://www.fenocin.org/revolucion-agraria/fenocin-en-la-asamblea.
10. https://archives.lib.umn.edu/repositories/6/resources/5078.
11. E.g., a search for *intercultural* in *American Anthropologist* returns no results before the 1930s, and just one result during the 1930s for a chapter title in a 1938 book review written by Julian Steward. By the 1940s and 1950s, there are many more results, such as Margaret Mead's (1949) obituary of Ruth Benedict throughout the list of Benedict's published work, or an early (Social Science Research Council 1954) formulation of acculturation.
12. "*Cuando hablamos de educación indígena, en realidad, nos estamos refiriendo a la educación intercultural, esto es, a la operación, en las comunidades indígenas pre-alfabetas que carecen de escolarización, de la enseñanza escolar característica de la sociedad nacional.*"

13. *"lenguas vernáculas."*
14. Walsh writes that the meeting occurred in 1982, but 1980 seems to be the correct year.
15. Author interview, August 12, 2015.

Chapter 2

1. E.g., see research on Indigenous movements, such as Gustafson (2009); Postero (2007); Stephen (2002).
2. See Tarlau (2019) for a similar point about Brazil.
3. Chisaguano (2003, 44) lists some of these options.
4. From author interview with Roldos's vice president Osvaldo Hurtado on August 12, 2015.
5. http://www.elcomercio.com/actualidad/discurso-jaime-roldos-constitucion-10deagosto.html.
6. Hurtado would become president in the wake of Roldós's death in 1981, in which many believe the CIA played a part.
7. From Interview, "Yo hablé con ella para que prepararan en la Universidad Católica la traducción, creo que incluso se reunieron con Roldós para enseñarle a pronunciar."
8. Interview with Hurtado on August 12, 2015.
9. Others especially attribute this change closely to the neoliberal president and development interests (e.g., Gustafson 2014).
10. *"Las conversaciones habían demostrado, en efecto, que en el marco de referencia en el cual se inscribía la alfabetización, era muy diferente para los unos y para el otro; que la pluriculturalidad de la sociedad ecuatoriana no era traducida de la misma manera."*
11. Interview, July 23, 2013.
12. The decree that established the National Directorate of Indigenous Intercultural Bilingual Education. Montaluisa later removed the word *Indigenous*.
13. Interview, February 3, 2012.
14. Interview, July 23, 2013.
15. Interview, July 23, 2013.
16. Interview, January 9, 2012.
17. Interview, July 23, 2013.
18. "Después de 500 años de dominación, autodeterminación en 1992!" (After 500 years of domination, Indigenous self-determination in 1992!).
19. Nationalities with smaller populations, many who live further from an urban center, had "nationality" directorates instead of "provincial" ones.
20. Interview, February 29, 2012.
21. Interview, February 23, 2012.
22. In 2007, Rafael Correa established the Ministry of Culture and Patrimony, changing the name of the other entity to simply the Ministry of Education (http://www.ecuadorinmediato.com/Noticias/news_user_view/ecuadorinmediato_noticias--47527).
23. The plan was put to a national election and passed with more than 66 percent of the vote (*Plan Decenal de Educación del Ecuador* 2007, 6).
24. The process of applying to be director was one of "merit" and application. However, I routinely listened to interlocutors from across school system express concern that the traditional directors would tend to rotate the position or appoint supporters to it.
25. https://pueblosencamino.org/?p=1650.

26. https://www.ultimahora.com/acusaciones-terrorismo-agudizan-la-pugna-correa-y-los-lideres-indigenas-n402950.
27. From Article 2: "El castellano es el idioma oficial del Ecuador; el castellano, el kichwa y el shuar son idiomas oficiales de relación intercultural. . . . El Estado respetará y estimulará su conservación y uso."
28. https://www.eluniverso.com/2008/07/25/0001/8/E6580430C16D4C09B0158703AC2852F7.html.
29. https://red.diariocritico.com/noticia/970826/noticias/santi-insatisfecho-por-la-inclusion-del-quichua-como-idioma-oficial.html.
30. "apoyar y fortalecer el Sistema de Educación Intercultural Bilingüe, bajo la rectoría de las políticas públicas del Estado a través de la autoridad educativa nacional . . ., bajo los principios de interculturalidad y plurinacionalidad" (Article 1).
31. Interview, May 14, 2012.
32. http://raulvallejo.com/discursos/educacion-de-calidad-y-calidez-por-la-dignidad-de-la-gente-de-mi-patria.
33. from EIB internal document *Proyecto de Fortalecimiento de la Educación Intercultural Bilingüe* (2011–2014), 4.
34. From internal document, *Proyecto de Fortalecimiento de la Educación Intercultural Bilingüe* (2011–2014), 19–20.
35. When there were around seventy employees in the office during my time of research, most were Kichwa with around ten who identified as *mestizos*, three Shuar employees, and two Chachi employees.
36. http://www.elcomercio.com/actualidad/director-educacion-intercultural-bilinguee-pichincha.html.

Chapter 3

1. See discussions in Hinton, Huss, & Roche (2018); Hornberger (1996).
2. May 5, 2013.
3. Articles 5 & 143.
4. The public voted to accept the Constitution in 1978, and it went into effect in 1979.
5. Interview, May 23, 2013.
6. Interview, July 30, 2013.
7. August 5, 2013; this quote and some of this section's information also appear in Limerick (2018).
8. Proyecto de Mejoramiento de la Calidad de Educación Básica Intercultural Bilingüe de la Nacionalidad Kichwa Andina.
9. Interview, February 22, 2012.
10. I edited a few parts of the transcript for clarity and indicate them with endnotes.
11. Added because her sentence was missing a word to make the idea complete.
12. Corrected to change a elision that made the phrase hard to understand (ñukanchik taytakuna, yuya[*sic*] tapuna).
13. Corrected to make the phrase more comprehensible (shuk yachakuyta *kikin* shimipi).

Chapter 4

1. Interview, January 16, 2012.
2. "*Nosotros terminábamos de estudiar en el colegio, o sea, vacaciones a trabajar en la tierra.*"
3. "*Y se alegran más los papás.*"
4. https://tradingeconomics.com/ecuador/minimum-wages.
5. This information comes from an interview on July 30, 2013.
6. "*No se miraba nada horarios.*"
7. June 5, 2012.
8. I leave this transcript without a date to further conceal the teacher's identity.
9. http://elcomercio.pe/mundo/latinoamerica/ecuador-indigenas-quieren-rafael-correa-193672.
10. July 28, 2011.
11. October 3, 2012.

Chapter 5

1. Fieldnotes, January 16, 2012.
2. E.g., the dialect map at http://www.muturzikin.com/cartesamerique/ameriquedusud2.htm isolates ten different Ecuadorian Kichwa varieties.
3. Interview, date erased to maintain anonymity.
4. Howard (2011, 190) writes that most Kichwa speakers in Ecuador are bilingual in Spanish, whereas Bolivia and Peru both have sizable Quechua-speaking populations that do not speak Spanish.
5. I have edited excerpts here to better maintain flow and context relevant for the theme of this section.
6. Occurred on February 3, 2012.
7. See the final copy of the translation here: https://issuu.com/direccion.comunicacion/docs/ley_org__nica_de_educaci__n_intercu/136.
8. The direct object's grammar is consistent in all examples and is marked by both an accusative case marker [-*ta*] and the affirmative validator [-*mi*].
9. This function is especially common in causative verbs (Adelaar 2004, 216) and is the case here with the verb *yachana* (to know) that appears with the causative -*chi* to form *yachachina* (to cause to know, to teach).
10. E.g., see https://classics.osu.edu/Undergraduate-Studies/Latin-Program/Grammar/Cases/accusative-case.
11. The final version is written this way: "Yachanawasikunapa llankaykunapi tantariynakushpa aynina, shinapash amawta yachaykunapika mana ushay tukunchu" (Ministerio de Educación 2011, 18).

Chapter 6

1. May 2, 2013.
2. June 5, 2013.

3. *Tiya* (Kichwa "madame") and *tía* (Spanish "aunt") are bivalent in sound. I have translated the word as "aunt" from Spanish and written the word in the Spanish alphabet because Ruth mentions a specific aunt in her example here and says "my aunt" in line 7. Mannheim (1991, 98) describes *tiya* as a lexical borrowing from Spanish to Kichwa with a similar semantic range. My experience is that it is more honorific in Kichwa than Spanish.
4. Ochs & Schieffelin (1989) make a similar argument about how children are socialized into adult ways of speaking.
5. Linguistic anthropologists consider iconization across speech events in how linguistic forms resemble ideas (Lempert 2012a; Urban 1986; Wortham & Reyes 2015). I more fully examine this process for a linguistic anthropological audience in Chapter 7.
6. Estermann (2012, 12) traces that Aymara intellectuals translated the concept from Aymara to Spanish and then others translated it from Spanish to Quechua.
7. Participant observation, September 29, 2011.
8. Anderson (2006 [1983], 5) offers the same phrase in his description of how nationality is a universal possession: "in the modern world everyone can, should, will 'have' a nationality, as he or she 'has' a gender."
9. Interview, October 5, 2011.
10. I list no date for this interview to maintain anonymity.

Chapter 7

1. Though Elena corrected the student, Kichwa speakers from the Northern and Central Highlands routinely use this phrase even when they are likely not to see someone the next day.
2. See Wortham & Reyes (2015) for arguments for the greater inclusion of poetics in discourse analysis.
3. Abu El-Haj (2015); García-Sánchez (2013); Luykx (1999); Valdiviezo (2009).
4. See other writing on how behavior can resemble language ideologies in a parallel fashion across extensive speech events, such as Blommaert (2006); Jakobson (1987 [1960]); Parmentier (1997, 20); Wortham and Reyes (2015).
5. See, e.g., Paz (2018, 4).
6. From Ministry document *Proyecto de Fortalecimiento de la Educación Intercultural Bilingüe*, 5.
7. *Propuesta para la conformación de los equipos técnico pedagógo de los pueblos y nacionalidades del Ecuador, para el sistema de educación intercultural bilingüe*, 2.
8. From audio recording, June 4, 2012.

Conclusions

1. E.g., see Chakrabarty (2009), among many others.
2. See also the case of the Mohawks of Kahnawà:ke who have refused many state inscriptions, responsibilities, and privileges, such as using Canadian passports or paying taxes (Simpson 2014, 7).
3. "Al reconocimiento de esta 'doblez' y a la capacidad de vivirla creativamente."
4. Hornberger & De Korne (2018); McCarty (2008); McCarty & Nicholas (2014); Sims (2005).

5. https://www.nytimes.com/2020/04/28/world/americas/peru-indigenous-rap-renata-flores.html.
6. https://www.aljazeera.com/indepth/opinion/2012/08/201285142554706344.html.
7. https://remezcla.com/features/culture/kichwa-hatari-radio-show.
8. https://notimundo.com.ec/educacion-intercultural-bilingue-en-comunidades-entre-los-pedidos-de-la-confeniae-al-gobierno-de-lenin-morno/.
9. From Twitter account of Fander Falconí, minister of education, May 23, 2018.
10. https://lahora.com.ec/noticia/1102090980/moreno-dispone-reemplazar-escuelas-unidocentes-y-suspender-proyecto-de-hospitales.
11. https://www.elcomercio.com/tendencias/sociedad/ruth-moya-carreras-universidad-indigena.html.
12. https://lalineadefuego.info/el-decreto-445-el-racismo-y-la-politica-del-gobierno-por-inti-cartuche-vacacela.
13. https://mutantia.ch/es/paro-nacional-la-historia-que-se-escribe-desde-el-hospital.
14. https://www.thedp.com/article/2021/12/upenn-maria-paula-romo-ecuador-protest-visiting-scholar.
15. https://www.educacionbilingue.gob.ec/seseib-entrega-propuesta-de-reforma-a-la-ley-organica-de-educacion-intercultural-sobre-el-sistema-de-educacion-intercultural-bilingue.
16. https://www.elcomercio.com/actualidad/politica/ejecutivo-reforma-ley-educacion-intercultural.html.
17. https://nacla.org/protest-ecuador-indigenous-criminalization.
18. https://www.washingtonpost.com/es/post-opinion/2022/07/14/paro-nacional-protestas-en-ecuador-2022-guillermo-lasso.
19. https://gk.city/2022/06/14/que-pide-conaie-paro-junio-2022.
20. https://www.historiaypresente.com/ecuador-el-drama-en-las-calles.
21. https://www.elcomercio.com/actualidad/guillermo-lasso-estado-excepcion-conaie.html.
22. https://gk.city/2022/06/30/termina-el-paro-nacional-en-ecuador.
23. https://www.eluniverso.com/noticias/ecuador/aumento-de-presupuesto-para-secretaria-de-educacion-bilingue-superaria-los-4-millones-es-una-de-las-respuestas-del-gobierno-a-las-demandas-de-la-conaie-nota.
24. https://www.expreso.ec/actualidad/movilizaciones-apuntan-capital-culpan-desabastecimiento-gobierno-129817.html.
25. https://www.expreso.ec/actualidad/movilizaciones-apuntan-capital-culpan-desabastecimiento-gobierno-129817.html.
26. https://gk.city/2022/06/30/termina-el-paro-nacional-en-ecuador.
27. https://www.facebook.com/photo/?fbid=445855967552416&set=pcb.445856414219038.
28. https://www.facebook.com/SEIBEec/videos/589699552666187.

References

Abram, Matthias. 1992. *El Proyecto EBI 1985–1990: Lengua, cultura e identidad*. Quito, Ecuador: Abya-Yala.

Abu El-Haj, Thea Renda. 2007. "'I Was Born Here, but My Home, It's Not Here': Educating for Democratic Citizenship in an Era of Transnational Migration and Global Conflict." *Harvard Educational Review* 77 (3): 285–316. https://doi.org/10.17763/haer.77.3.412l7m737q114h5m.

Abu El-Haj, Thea Renda. 2015. *Unsettled Belonging: Educating Palestinian American Youth after 9/11*. 1st edition. Chicago; London: University of Chicago Press.

Abu-Lughod, Lila. 1990. "The Romance of Resistance: Tracing Transformations of Power through Bedouin Women." *American Ethnologist* 17 (1): 41–55.

Academia de la Lengua Kichwa (ALKI). n.d. "Propuesta Para La Constitución de La Academia de La Lengua Kichwa." Ambato, Ecuador.

Adelaar, Willem F. H. 2004. *The Languages of the Andes*. Cambridge: Cambridge University Press.

Agha, Asif. 2005. "Voice, Footing, Enregisterment." *Journal of Linguistic Anthropology* 15 (1): 38–59.

Agha, Asif. 2007. *Language and Social Relations*. New York: Cambridge University Press.

Agha, Asif. 2012. "Mediatized Projects at State Peripheries." *Language & Communication* 32 (2): 98–101. https://doi.org/10.1016/j.langcom.2011.08.002.

Aguirre Beltrán, Gonzalo. 1955. *Programas de salud en la situación intercultural*. México: Instituto Indigenista Interamericano.

Aguirre Beltrán, Gonzalo. 1973. *Teoría y práctica de la educación indígena*. México: Secretaría de Educación Pública.

Ahlers, Jocelyn C. 2006. "Framing Discourse." *Journal of Linguistic Anthropology* 16 (1): 58–75. https://doi.org/10.1525/jlin.2006.16.1.058.

Ahlers, Jocelyn. 2017. "Native California Languages as Semiotic Resources in the Performance of Identity." *Journal of Linguistic Anthropology* 27 (1): 40–53. https://doi.org/10.1111/jola.12142.

Albó, Xavier. 1977. *El futuro de los idiomas oprimidos*. La Paz, Bolivia: Centro de Investigación y Promoción del Campesinado.

Alim, H. Samy. 2016. "Introducing Raciolinguistics." In *Raciolinguistics: How Language Shapes Our Ideas about Race*, edited by H. Samy Alim, John R. Rickford, and Arnetha F. Ball, 33–50. New York: Oxford University Press.

Alim, H. Samy, John R. Rickford, and Arnetha F. Ball, eds. 2016. *Introducing Raciolinguistics*. New York: Oxford University Press.

Almeida, Ileana. 1979. "Códigos Culturales y Movilidad Semántica En El Kechua." *América Indígena* 39 (4): 721–31.

Almeida, Ileana, Nidia Arroba Rodas, and Lautaro Ojeda Segovia. 2005. *Autonomía indígena*. Quito, Ecuador: Abya-Yala.

Almeida Reyes, Eduardo. 2011. *Ecuador: Estado Uninacional o Plurinacional*. Quito, Ecuador: PPL Impresores.

Altmann, Philipp. 2014. "Good Life as a Social Movement Proposal for Natural Resource Use: The Indigenous Movement in Ecuador." *Consilience*, no. 12 (July). https://doi.org/10.7916/consilience.vi12.7550.

Anderson, Benedict. 2006. *Imagined Communities: Reflections on the Origin and Spread of Nationalism*. New York: Verso.

Andrade Ciudad, Luis, and Rosaleen Howard. 2021. "Las lenguas quechuas en tres países andino-amazónicos: De las cifras a la acción ciudadana. Quechua Languages in Three Andean-Amazonian Countries: From Census Data to Citizen Action." *Káñina, Revista de artes y letras* 45 (1): 7–38.

Andronis, Mary Antonia. 2004. "Iconization, Fractal Recursivity, and Erasure: Linguistic Ideologies and Standardization in Quichua-Speaking Ecuador." In *Proceedings of the Eleventh Annual Symposium about Language and Society*, 47:263–69. Austin: Texas Linguistic Forum.

Anyon, Jean. 2009. "Progressive Social Movements and Educational Equity." *Educational Policy* 23 (1): 194–215.

Appadurai, Arjun. 2007. "The Capacity to Aspire: Culture and the Terms of Recognition." In *Cultural Politics in a Global Age: Uncertainty, Solidarity, and Innovation*, edited by David Held and Henrietta L. Moore, 29–36. Oxford: Oneworld Publications.

Armstrong-Fumero, Fernando. 2009. "Old Jokes and New Multiculturalisms: Continuity and Change in Vernacular Discourse on the Yucatec Maya Language." *American Anthropologist* 111 (3): 360–72. https://doi.org/10.1111/j.1548-1433.2009.01138.x.

Asad, Talal. 1986. "The Concept of Cultural Translation in British Social Anthropology." In *Writing Culture: The Poetics and Politics of Ethnography*, edited by James Clifford and George E. Marcus, 141–64. Berkeley: University of California Press.

Atupaña, José M. 2006. "Kukayu pedagógico: Alimento preciado para saciar el hambre de aprender." Discussion Board. *Chaskinanayrampi* (blog). December 18, 2006. https://espanol.groups.yahoo.com/neo/groups/chaskinayrampi/conversations/topics/3358%3e?guccounter=1.

Auer, Peter. 2014. "Language Mixing and Language Fusion: When Bilingual Talk Becomes Monolingual." In *Congruence in Contact-Induced Language Change: Language Families, Typological Resemblance, and Perceived Similarity*, edited by Juliane Besters-Dilger, Cynthia Dermarkar, Stefan Pfänder, and Achim Rabus, 294–336. Berlin; Boston: Walter de Gruyter.

Austin, J. L. 1962. *How to Do Things with Words*. Oxford: Clarendon Press.

Aydarova, Elena. 2019. "Flipping the Paradigm: Studying Up and Research for Social Justice." In *Research Methods for Social Justice and Equity in Education*, edited by Kamden K. Strunk and Leslie Ann Locke, 33–43. Cham: Springer International Publishing. https://doi.org/10.1007/978-3-030-05900-2_3.

Bach, Kent, and Robert M. Harnish. 1979. *Linguistic Communication and Speech Acts*. Cambridge, MA: MIT Press.

Bakhtin, Mikhail. 1981. *The Dialogic Imagination*. Austin: University of Texas Press.

Barriga López, Franklin. 1992. *Las culturas indígenas ecuatorianas y el Instituto Lingüístico de Verano*. Buenos Aires: Ediciones Amauta.

Barros, Maria Cändida. 1995. "The Missionary Presence in Literacy Campaigns in the Indigenous Languages of Latin America (1939–1952)." *International Journal of Educational Development* 15 (3): 277–87. https://doi.org/10.1016/0738-0593(95)00015-U.

Bartlett, Lesley, and Ofelia Garcia. 2011. *Additive Schooling in Subtractive Times: Bilingual Education and Dominican Immigrant Youth in the Heights*. Nashville, TN: Vanderbilt University Press.

Bassnett, Susan. 2009. "Domesticating the Other: English and Translation." In *The Routledge Companion to English Language Studies*, edited by Janet Maybin and Joan Swann, 271–81. London: Routledge.

Bassnett, Susan. 2013. *Translation Studies*. London; New York: Routledge.

Bateson, Gregory. 1987. *Steps to an Ecology of Mind: Collected Essays in Anthropology, Psychiatry, Evolution and Epistemology*. San Francisco, CA: Jason Aronson Inc.

Baudrillard, Jean. 1994. *Simulacra and Simulation*. Translated by Sheila Faria Glaser. Ann Arbor: University of Michigan Press.

Bauman, Richard. 2004. *A World of Others' Words: Cross-Cultural Perspectives on Intertextuality*. Malden, MA: Wiley-Blackwell.

Bauman, Richard, and Charles L. Briggs. 2003. *Voices of Modernity: Language Ideologies and the Politics of Inequality*. New York: Cambridge University Press.

Becerra-Lubies, Rukmini, Simona Mayo, and Aliza Fones. 2019. "Revitalization of Indigenous Languages and Cultures: Critical Review of Preschool Bilingual Educational Policies in Chile (2007–2016)." *International Journal of Bilingual Education and Bilingualism* 24 (8): 1147–62. https://doi.org/10.1080/13670050.2018.1563584.

Becker, Alton L. 2000. *Beyond Translation: Essays toward a Modern Philology*. Ann Arbor: University of Michigan Press.

Becker, Marc. 2008. *Indians and Leftists in the Making of Ecuador's Modern Indigenous Movements*. Durham, NC: Duke University Press.

Becker, Marc. 2010. *Pachakutik: Indigenous Movements and Electoral Politics in Ecuador*. Lanham, MD: Rowman & Littlefield.

Becker, Marc, and Thea N. Riofrancos. 2018. "A Souring Friendship, a Left Divided." *NACLA Report on the Americas* 50 (2): 124–27. https://doi.org/10.1080/10714839.2018.1479452.

Benei, Véronique. 2010. "To Fairly Tell: Social Mobility, Life Histories, and the Anthropologist." *Compare: A Journal of Comparative and International Education* 40 (2): 199–212. https://doi.org/10.1080/03057920903546062.

Benjamin, Walter. 2010. *The Work of Art in the Age of Mechanical Reproduction*. n.p.: Prism.

Benson, Carol. 2005. *The Importance of Mother Tongue-Based Schooling for Educational Quality Stockholm*. Sweden: UNESCO.

Blommaert, Jan. 2006. "Applied Ethnopoetics." *Narrative Inquiry* 16 (1): 181–90. https://doi.org/10.1075/ni.16.1.23blo.

Blommaert, Jan. 2008. "Artefactual Ideologies and the Textual Production of African Languages." *Language & Communication* 28 (4): 291–307. https://doi.org/10.1016/j.langcom.2008.02.003.

Blommaert, Jan. 2010. *The Sociolinguistics of Globalization*. Cambridge: Cambridge University Press.

Blommaert, Jan, Sirpa Leppänen, Päivi Pahta, and Tiina Räisänen. 2012. *Dangerous Multilingualism: Northern Perspectives on Order, Purity and Normality*. Basingstoke: Palgrave Macmillan.

Boas, Franz. 1911. *Handbook of the American Indian Languages: Part 1*. Washington, DC: Smithsonian Institution.

Bonfiglio, Thomas Paul. 2013. "Inventing the Native Speaker." *Critical Multilingualism Studies* 1 (2): 29–58.

Bourdieu, Pierre. 1991. *Language & Symbolic Power*. Cambridge, MA: Harvard University Press.

Bourgois, Philippe. 1996. "Confronting Anthropology, Education, and Inner-City Apartheid." *American Anthropologist* 98 (2): 249–58.

Brayboy, Bryan McKinley Jones. 2005. "Transformational Resistance and Social Justice: American Indians in Ivy League Universities." *Anthropology & Education Quarterly* 36 (3): 193–211.

Brayboy, Bryan McKinley Jones, and Megan Bang. 2019. "Societal Issues Facing Indigenous Education: Introduction." In *Handbook of Indigenous Education*, edited by Elizabeth Ann McKinley and Linda Tuhiwai Smith, 1–7. Singapore: Springer. https://doi.org/10.1007/978-981-10-1839-8_76-2.

Briggs, Charles L., and Richard Bauman. 1992. "Genre, Intertextuality, and Social Power." *Journal of Linguistic Anthropology* 2 (2): 131–72.

Brown, Wendy. 2008. *Regulating Aversion: Tolerance in the Age of Identity and Empire*. Princeton, NJ: Princeton University Press.

Brownell, Cassie J., and Amy Noelle Parks. 2022. "When the Clips Are Down: How Young Children Negotiate a Classroom Management System." *Anthropology & Education Quarterly* 53 (1): 5–26. https://doi.org/10.1111/aeq.12400.

Brysk, A. 2000. *From Tribal Village to Global Village: Indian Rights and International Relations in Latin America*. Stanford, CA: Stanford University Press.

Cachiguango, Luis Enrique, and Julián Pontón. 2010. *Yaku-Mama: La crianza del agua; La música ritual del Hatun Puncha—Inti Raymi en Kotama, Otavalo*. Quito, Ecuador: Ministerio de Cultura del Ecuador.

Canessa, Andrew. 2014. "Conflict, Claim and Contradiction in the New 'Indigenous' State of Bolivia." *Critique of Anthropology* 34 (2): 153–73. https://doi.org/10.1177/0308275X1 3519275.

Cao, Deborah. 2007. *Translating Law*. Tonawanda, NY: Multilingual Matters.

Carnoy, Martin, and Henry M. Levin. 1985. *Schooling and Work in the Democratic State*. Stanford, CA: Stanford University Press.

Carr, Summerson. 2009. "Anticipating and Inhabiting Institutional Identities." *American Ethnologist* 36 (2): 317–36. https://doi.org/10.1111/j.1548-1425.2009.01137.x.

Carr, E. Summerson. 2010. "Enactments of Expertise." *Annual Review of Anthropology* 39 (1): 17–32. https://doi.org/10.1146/annurev.anthro.012809.104948.

Carr, E. Summerson. 2011. *Scripting Addiction: The Politics of Therapeutic Talk and American Sobriety*. Princeton, NJ: Princeton University Press.

Carr, E. Summerson, and Brooke Fisher. 2016. "Interscaling Awe, De-Escalating Disaster." In *Scale: Discourse and Dimensions of Social Life*, edited by E. Summerson Carr and Michæl Lempert, 133–58. Oakland: University of California Press.

Carruthers, Andrew M. 2017. "Grading Qualities and (Un)Settling Equivalences: Undocumented Migration, Commensuration, and Intrusive Phonosonics in the Indonesia-Malaysia Borderlands." *Journal of Linguistic Anthropology* 27 (2): 124–50. https://doi.org/ 10.1111/jola.12153.

Castagno, Angelina E., and Teresa McCarty. 2017. *The Anthropology of Education Policy: Ethnographic Inquiries into Policy As Sociocultural Process*. London: Taylor & Francis Group. http://ebookcentral.proquest.com/lib/teacherscollege-ebooks/detail.action?docID= 4905755.

Cattelino, Jessica R. 2010. "The Double Bind of American Indian Need-Based Sovereignty." *Cultural Anthropology* 25 (2): 235–62. https://doi.org/10.1111/j.1548-1360.2010.01058.x.

Cerrón-Palomino, Rodolfo. 1987. *Lingüística quechua*. Cuzco: Bartolomé de las Casas.

Certeau, Michel de. 1984. *The Practice of Everyday Life*. Berkeley: University of California Press.

Chakrabarty, Dipesh. 2009. *Provincializing Europe: Postcolonial Thought and Historical Difference*. Princeton, NJ: Princeton University Press.

Chango Juarez, Bernardo. 2007. "Algunos fundamentos sobre la lengua Quichua en América." In *Shimiyukkamu diccionario*, 7–12. Quito, Ecuador: Casa de la Cultura Ecuatoriana.

Chimbutane, Feliciano. 2011. *Rethinking Bilingual Education in Postcolonial Contexts*. Bristol: Multilingual Matters.

Chiodi, Francisco. 1990. "Ecuador." In *La Educación Indígena En América Latina*, edited by Francisco Chiodi, 1:329–543. Quito: P.EBI & Abya-Yala.

Chisaguano Malliquinga, Silverio. 2003. "La participación de los indígenas del Ecuador en la institucionalización del sistema de educación intercultural bilingue." Quito, Ecuador: FLACSO.

Citarella, Luca. 1990. "Mexico." In *La educación indígena en América Latina*, edited by Francisco Chiodi, 1:9–156. Quito, Ecuador: P.EBI & Abya-Yala.

Cody, Francis. 2013. *The Light of Knowledge: Literacy Activism and the Politics of Writing in South India*. Ithaca, NY: Cornell University Press.

Colloredo-Mansfeld, Rudi. 2009. *Fighting Like a Community: Andean Civil Society in an Era of Indian Uprisings*. Chicago: University of Chicago Press.

Comaroff, John L., and Jean Comaroff. 2009. *Ethnicity, Inc*. Chicago: University of Chicago Press.

Conejo, Alberto. 2008. "Educación intercultural bilingue en el Ecuador." *Comunicación y Sociedad* 3 (2) (Noviembre): 64–82.

Conklin, Beth A., and Laura R. Graham. 1995. "The Shifting Middle Ground: Amazonian Indians and Eco-Politics." *American Anthropologist* 97 (4): 695–710. https://doi.org/10.1525/aa.1995.97.4.02a00120.

Coronel-Molina, Serafín M. 2015. *Language Ideology, Policy and Planning in Peru*. Bristol: Multilingual Matters.

Cortina, Regina. 2014. "Partnerships to Promote the Education of Indigenous Citizens." In *The Education of Indigenous Citizens in Latin America*, edited by Regina Cortina, 50–73. Bristol; Buffalo, NY: Multilingual Matters.

Cortina, Regina, and Katy De la Garza. 2015. *Educación, pueblos indígenas e interculturalidad en América Latina*. Quito, Ecuador: Abya-Yala.

Costa, James, Haley De Korne, and Pia Lane. 2017. "Standardising Minority Languages." In *Standardizing Minority Languages: Competing Ideologies of Authority and Authenticity in the Global Periphery*, edited by Pia Lane, James Costa, and Haley De Korne, 1–23. New York: Routledge.

Coulthard, Glen Sean. 2014. *Red Skin, White Masks: Rejecting the Colonial Politics of Recognition*. Minneapolis: University of Minnesota Press.

Crawley, Cheryl K. 2020. *Native American Bilingual Education: An Ethnography of Powerful Forces*. Bingley, UK: Emerald Publishing.

Crazy Bull, Cheryl, and Emily R. White Hat. 2019. "Cangleska Wakan: The Ecology of the Sacred Circle and the Role of Tribal Colleges and Universities." *International Review of Education* 65 (1): 117–41. https://doi.org/10.1007/s11159-018-9760-8.

Dar, Wahid Ahmad, and Irshad Ahmad Najar. 2018. "Educational Anthropology, Tribal Education and Responsible Citizenship in India." *South Asia Research* 38 (3): 327–46.

Das, Sonia Neela. 2008. "Between Convergence and Divergence." *Journal of Linguistic Anthropology* 18 (1): 1–23.

Das, Sonia N. 2016. *Linguistic Rivalries: Tamil Migrants and Anglo-Franco Conflicts*. New York: Oxford University Press.

Davis, Christina P. 2020. *The Struggle for a Multilingual Future: Youth and Education in Sri Lanka*. New York: Oxford University Press.

De Korne, Haley. 2021. *Language Activism: Imaginaries and Strategies of Minority Language Equality. Language Activism*. Berlin; Boston: De Gruyter Mouton.

De Korne, Haley, Mario E. López Gopar, and Kiara Rios Rios. 2019. "Changing Ideological and Implementational Spaces for Minoritised Languages in Higher Education: Zapotequización of Language Education in Mexico." *Journal of Multilingual and Multicultural Development* 40 (6): 504–17. https://doi.org/10.1080/01434632.2018.1531876.

De Korne, Haley, and Miranda Weinberg. 2021. "'I Learned That My Name Is Spelled Wrong': Lessons from Mexico and Nepal on Teaching Literacy for Indigenous Language Reclamation." *Comparative Education Review* 65 (2): 288–309. https://doi.org/10.1086/713317.

De la Cadena, Marisol. 2005. "Are Mestizos Hybrids? The Conceptual Politics of Andean Identities." *Journal of Latin American Studies* 37 (2): 259–84. https://doi.org/10.1017/S0022216X05009004.

References

De la Torre, Luz María. 1999. *Un universo femenino en el mundo andino*. Quito, Ecuador: Instituto para el Desarrollo Social y de las Investigaciones Científicas.

Dervin, Fred, Anahy Gajardo, and Anne Lavanchy, eds. 2011. *Politics of Interculturality*. Electronic resource. Newcastle upon Tyne: Cambridge Scholars.

de Waard, Jan, and Eugene A. Nida. 1986. *From One Language to Another: Functional Equivalence in Bible Translation*. Nashville, TN: Thomas Nelson.

Dhillon, Jaskiran K. 2017. *Prairie Rising: Indigenous Youth, Decolonization, and the Politics of Intervention*. Toronto; Buffalo; London: University of Toronto Press, Scholarly Publishing Division.

Dietz, Gunther. 2004. "From Indigenismo to Zapatismo: The Struggle for a Multi-Ethnic Mexican Society." In *The Struggle for Indigenous Rights in Latin America*, edited by Nancy Postero and Leon Zamosc, 32–80. Portland, OR: Sussex Academic Press.

Dietz, Gunther. 2012. *Multiculturalismo, interculturalidad y diversidad en educación: Una aproximación antropológica*. Ciudad de México: Fondo de Cultura Económica.

DuBois, Cora. 1955. "Some Notions of Learning Intercultural Understanding." In *Education and Anthropology*, edited by George Spindler, 89–105. Stanford, CA: Stanford University Press.

DuBois, Rachel Davis, and Corann Okorodudu. 1984. *All This and Something More: Pioneering in Intercultural Education, an Autobiography*. Bryn Mawr, PA: Dorrance.

Duchene, Alexandre, and Monica Heller. 2007. *Discourses of Endangerment: Interest and Ideology in the Defense of Languages*. New York: Continuum.

Duranti, Alessandro. 1992. "Language and Bodies in Social Space: Samoan Ceremonial Greetings." *American Anthropologist* 94 (3): 657–91. https://doi.org/10.1525/aa.1992.94.3.02a00070.

Duranti, Alessandro. 1997. "Universal and Culture-Specific Properties of Greetings." *Journal of Linguistic Anthropology* 7 (1): 63–97. https://doi.org/10.1525/jlin.1997.7.1.63.

Echeverria, Bolivar. 2019. *Modernity and "Whiteness."* Translated by Rodrigo Ferreira. Cambridge, UK; Medford, MA: Polity.

Eisenlohr, Patrick. n.d. "Materialities of Entextualization: The Domestication of Sound Reproduction in Mauritian Muslim Devotional Practices." *Journal of Linguistic Anthropology* 20 (2): 314–33. https://doi.org/10.1111/j.1548-1395.2010.01072.x.

Ennis, Georgia. 2019. "Multimodal Chronotopes: Embodying Ancestral Time on Quichua Morning Radio." *Signs and Society* 7 (1): 6–37. https://doi.org/10.1086/700641.

Ennis, Georgia. 2020. "Linguistic Natures: Method, Media, and Language Reclamation in the Ecuadorian Amazon." *Journal of Linguistic Anthropology* 30 (3): 304–25. https://doi.org/10.1111/jola.12281.

Errington, James Joseph. 2008. *Linguistics in a Colonial World: A Story of Language, Meaning, and Power*. Malden, MA; Oxford: Blackwell Pub.

Estermann, Josef. 2012. "Crisis Civilizatoria y Vivir Bien." *Polis. Revista Latinoamericana* 33: 1–22.

Fabian, Johannes. 1991. *Language and Colonial Power: The Appropriation of Swahili in the Former Belgian Congo 1880–1938*. Berkeley: University of California Press.

Falconi, Elizabeth, and Kathryn E. Graber. 2019. *Storytelling as Narrative Practice: Ethnographic Approaches to the Tales We Tell*. Leiden: Brill.

Fauchois, Anne. 1988. *El quichua serrano frente a la comunicación moderna*. Quito, Ecuador: Proyecto EBI, Abya-Yala.

Faudree, Paja. 2015a. "What Is an Indigenous Author? Minority Authorship and the Politics of Voice in Mexico." *Anthropological Quarterly* 88 (1): 5–35.

Faudree, Paja. 2015b. "Why X Doesn't Always Mark the Spot: Contested Authenticity in Mexican Indigenous Language Politics." *Semiotica* 2015 (203): 179–201. https://doi.org/10.1515/sem-2014-0078.

Fenigsen, Janina. 1999. "'A Broke-Up Mirror': Representing Bajan in Print." *Cultural Anthropology* 14 (1): 61–87. https://doi.org/10.1525/can.1999.14.1.61.

Ferguson, Charles A. 1981. "'Foreigner Talk' as the Name of a Simplified Register." *International Journal of the Sociology of Language* 1981 (28): 9–18. https://doi.org/10.1515/ijsl.1981.28.9.

Flores, Nelson, and Jonathan Rosa. 2015. "Undoing Appropriateness: Raciolinguistic Ideologies and Language Diversity in Education." *Harvard Educational Review* 85 (2): 149–71. https://doi.org/10.17763/0017-8055.85.2.149.

Flores, Nelson, and Jamie L. Schissel. 2014. "Dynamic Bilingualism as the Norm: Envisioning a Heteroglossic Approach to Standards-Based Reform." *TESOL Quarterly* 48 (3): 454–79. https://doi.org/10.1002/tesq.182.

Floyd, Simeon. 2004. "Purismo lingüístico y realidad local: ¿Quichua puro o puro quichuañol?" In *Proceedings of the Conference on Indigenous Languages of Latin America*, 1–15. Austin, TX. http://www-ailla.lib.utexas.edu/site/cilla1/Floyd_Quichua_Spanish.pdf.

Foucault, Michel. 1978. *The History of Sexuality*, Vol. 1: *An Introduction*. Reissue edition. New York: Vintage Books.

Foucault, Michel. 1979. *Discipline and Punish: The Birth of the Prison*. New York: Vintage/Random House.

Foucault, Michel. 1984. *The Foucault Reader*. New York: Pantheon Books.

Foucault, Michel, Graham Burchell, Colin Gordon, and Peter Miller. 1991. *The Foucault Effect: Studies in Governmentality*. Chicago: University of Chicago Press.

Fraser, Nancy. 2000. "Rethinking Recognition." *New Left Review* 3: 107–20.

Fraser, Nancy. 2017. "The End of Progressive Neoliberalism." *Dissent Magazine (blog)*. January 2, 2017. https://www.dissentmagazine.org/online_articles/progressive-neoliberalism-reactionary-populism-nancy-fraser.

Gal, Susan. 2006. "Contradictions of Standard Language in Europe: Implications for the Study of Practices and Publics." *Social Anthropology* 14 (2): 163–81. https://doi.org/10.1017/S0964028206002515.

Gal, Susan. 2015. "Politics of Translation." *Annual Review of Anthropology* 44 (1): 225–40. https://doi.org/10.1146/annurev-anthro-102214-013806.

Gal, Susan. 2017. "Visions and Revisions of Minority Languages: Standardization and Its Dilemmas." In *Standardizing Minority Languages: Competing Ideologies of Authority and Authenticity in the Global Periphery*, edited by Pia Lane, James Costa, and Haley De Korne, 222–42. New York: Routledge.

Gal, Susan, and Judith T. Irvine. 2019. *Signs of Difference: Language and Ideology in Social Life*. New York: Cambridge University Press.

Gal, Susan, and Kathryn Woolard. 2001. "Constructing Languages and Publics: Authority and Representation." In *Languages and Publics: The Making of Authority*, edited by Susan Gal and Kathryn Woolard, 1–12. Manchester: Routledge.

Gamio, Manuel. 2006. *Forjando Patria*. México: Porrúa.

García, María Elena. 2004. "Rethinking Bilingual Education in Peru: Intercultural Politics, State Policy and Indigenous Rights." *International Journal of Bilingual Education and Bilingualism* 7 (5): 348–67. https://doi.org/10.1080/13670050408667819.

García, María Elena. 2005. *Making Indigenous Citizens: Identities, Education, and Multicultural Development in Peru*. Stanford, CA: Stanford University Press.

García, Ofelia. 2009. "En/Countering Indigenous Bilingualism." *Journal of Language, Identity & Education* 8 (5): 376–80. https://doi.org/10.1080/15348450903305155.

García, Ofelia, and Li Wei. 2014. *Translanguaging: Language, Bilingualism and Education*. Basingstoke, Hampshire; New York: Palgrave Pivot.

García-Sánchez, Inmaculada M. 2013. "The Everyday Politics of 'Cultural Citizenship' among North African Immigrant School Children in Spain." *Language & Communication* 33 (4, Part B): 481–99.

García-Sánchez, Inmaculada M. 2014. *Language and Muslim Immigrant Childhoods: The Politics of Belonging*. Wiley Blackwell Studies in Discourse and Culture. Chichester, UK; Malden, MA: Wiley Blackwell.

García-Sánchez, Inmaculada M. 2016. "Multiculturalism and Its Discontents: Essentializing Ethnic Moroccan and Roma Identities in Classroom Discourse in Spain." In *Raciolinguistics: How Language Shapes Our Ideas about Race*, edited by H. Samy Alim, John R. Rickford, and Arnetha F. Ball, 291–308. New York: Oxford University Press.

García-Sánchez, Inmaculada M., and Marjorie Faulstich Orellana. 2019. "Introduction." In *Language and Cultural Practices in Communities and Schools: Bridging Learning for Students from Non-Dominant Groups*, edited by Inmaculada M. García-Sánchez and Marjorie Faulstich Orellana, 1–23. Milton, UK: Taylor & Francis Group.

Gobierno Regional de Cusco. 2005. *Diccionario/Simi Taqe*. Cusco, Peru: Gobierno Regional de Cusco.

Goffman, Erving. 1974. *Frame Analysis: An Essay on the Organization of Experience*. Vol. ix. Cambridge, MA: Harvard University Press.

Gómez Rendón, Jorge. 2017. "Grammatical Borrowing in Imbabura Quechua." In *Grammatical Borrowing in Cross-Linguistic Perspective*, edited by Yaron Matras and Jeanette Sakel, 481–521. New York: De Gruyter Mouton.

González Terreros, María Isabel. 2011. *Movimiento indígena y educación intercultural en Ecuador*. México DF: CLACSO, UNAM.

Goodman, Jane, Matt Tomlinson, and Justin Richland. 2014. "Citational Practices: Knowledge, Personhood, and Subjectivity." *Annual Review of Anthropology* 43 (October): 449–63. https://doi.org/10.1146/annurev-anthro-102313-025828.

Graham, Laura R. 2002. "How Should an Indian Speak? Amazonian Indians and the Symbolic Politics of Language in the Global Public Sphere." In *Indigenous Movements, Self-Representation, and the State in Latin America*, edited by Kay B. Warren and Jean E. Jackson, 181–228. Austin: University of Texas Press.

Graham, Laura R., and H. Glenn Penny, eds. 2014. *Performing Indigeneity: Global Histories and Contemporary Experiences*. Lincoln: University of Nebraska Press.

Grzech, Karolina, Anne Schwarz, and Georgia Ennis. 2019. "Divided We Stand, Unified We Fall? The Impact of Standardisation on Oral Language Varieties: A Case Study of Amazonian Kichwa." *Revista de llengua i dret*, June, 123–45. https://doi.org/10.2436/rld.i71.2019.3253.

Guerrettaz, Anne Marie. 2015. "Ownership of Language in Yucatec Maya Revitalization Pedagogy." *Anthropology & Education Quarterly* 46 (2): 167–85. https://doi.org/10.1111/aeq.12097.

Guerrettaz, Anne Marie. 2019. "Yucatec Maya Language Planning and the Struggle of the Linguistic Standardization Process." *International Journal of the Sociology of Language* 2019 (260): 61–83. https://doi.org/10.1515/ijsl-2019-2048.

Gundaker, Grey. 1998. *Signs of Diaspora / Diaspora of Signs: Literacies, Creolization, and Vernacular Practice in African America*. Oxford: Oxford University Press.

Gustafson, Bret. 2009. *New Languages of the State: Indigenous Resurgence and the Politics of Knowledge in Bolivia*. Durham, NC: Duke University Press.

Gustafson, Bret. 2014. "Intercultural Bilingual Education in the Andes." In *The Education of Indigenous Citizens in Latin America*, edited by Regina Cortina, 74–97. Bristol; Buffalo, NY: Multilingual Matters.

Haboud, Marleen. 2004. "Quichua Language Vitality: An Ecuadorian Perspective." *International Journal of the Sociology of Language* 167: 69–81. https://doi.org/10.1515/ijsl.2004.022.

Haboud, Marleen. 2010. "South America and the Andean Region." In *Atlas de las lenguas del mundo en peligro*, edited by Christopher Moseley, 95–102. Valencia: UNESCO.

Hacking, Ian. 2015. "Biopower and the Avalanche of Printed Numbers." In *Biopower: Foucault and Beyond*, edited by Vernon W. Cisney and Nicolae Morar, 65–81. Chicago: University of Chicago Press.

Hale, Charles. 2004. "Rethinking Indigenous Politics in the Era of the 'Indio Permitido.'" *NACLA Report on the Americas*. https://nacla.org/article/rethinking-indigenous-politics-era-indio-permitido.

Hale, Charles R. 2002. "Does Multiculturalism Menace? Governance, Cultural Rights and the Politics of Identity in Guatemala." *Journal of Latin American Studies* 34 (3): 485–524. https://doi.org/10.1017/S0022216X02006521.

Hale, Charles R. 2005. "Neoliberal Multiculturalism." *PoLAR: Political and Legal Anthropology Review* 28 (1): 10–19. https://doi.org/10.1525/pol.2005.28.1.10.

Hale, Charles R. 2006. "Activist Research v. Cultural Critique: Indigenous Land Rights and the Contradictions of Politically Engaged Anthropology." *Cultural Anthropology* 21 (1): 96–120. https://doi.org/10.1525/can.2006.21.1.96.

Hale, Charles R. 2011. "*Resistencia para que?* Territory, Autonomy and Neoliberal Entanglements in the 'Empty Spaces' of Central America." *Economy and Society* 40 (2): 184–210. https://doi.org/10.1080/03085147.2011.548947.

Hale, Charles R. 2020. "Using and Refusing the Law: Indigenous Struggles and Legal Strategies after Neoliberal Multiculturalism." *American Anthropologist* 122 (3): 618–31.

Hale, Charles R., and Leith Mullings. 2020. "A Time to Recalibrate." In *Black and Indigenous Resistance in the Americas: From Multiculturalism to Racist Backlash*, edited by Juliet Hooker, 21–65. Lanham: Lexington Books. http://ebookcentral.proquest.com/lib/columbia/detail.action?docID=6141110.

Hamel, Rainer Enrique. 2008. "Bilingual Education for Indigenous Communities in Mexico." In *Encyclopedia of Language and Education*, edited by Jim Cummins and Nancy H. Hornberger, 2nd edition, 5:311–22. New York: Springer.

Handman, Courtney. 2017. "Discussion: The Monologic Imagination of Social Groups." In *The Monologic Imagination*, edited by Matt Tomlinson and Julian Millie, 251–57. Oxford; New York: Oxford University Press.

Hanks, William F. 2010. *Converting Words: Maya in the Age of the Cross*. Berkeley: University of California Press.

Heath, Shirley Brice. 1983. *Ways with Words: Language, Life and Work in Communities and Classrooms*. New York: Cambridge University Press.

Heller, Monica, and Bonnie McElhinny. 2017. *Language, Capitalism, Colonialism: Toward a Critical History*. Toronto, Ontario: University of Toronto Press, Higher Education Division.

Hetherington, Kregg. 2011. *Guerrilla Auditors: The Politics of Transparency in Neoliberal Paraguay*. https://doi.org/10.1215/9780822394266.

Hill, Jane H. 1998. "Language, Race, and White Public Space." *American Anthropologist* 100 (3): 680–89.

Hill, Jane H. 2002. "'Expert Rhetorics' in Advocacy for Endangered Languages: Who Is Listening, and What Do They Hear?" *Journal of Linguistic Anthropology* 12 (2): 119–33. https://doi.org/10.1525/jlin.2002.12.2.119.

Hillewaert, Sarah. 2016. "Tactics and Tactility: A Sensory Semiotics of Handshakes in Coastal Kenya." *American Anthropologist* 118 (1): 49–66. https://doi.org/10.1111/aman.12517.

Hinton, Leanne, Leena Huss, and Gerald Roche. 2018. "Language Revitalization as a Growing Field of Study and Practice." In *The Routledge Handbook of Language Revitalization*, edited by Leanne Hinton, Leena Huss, and Gerald Roche, xxi–xxx. New York: Routledge.

Honneth, Axel, and John Farrell. 1997. "Recognition and Moral Obligation." *Social Research* 64 (1): 16–35.

Hooker, Juliet, Jakelin Curaqueo Mariano, Giorleny Altamirano Rayo, Aileen Ford, Steven Lownes, Jaime Antimil Caniupan, Eliana Fernanda Antonio Rosero, Pamela

Calla, Roosbelinda Cárdenas, and Rigoberto Ajcalón Choy. 2020. *Black and Indigenous Resistance in the Americas: From Multiculturalism to Racist Backlash*. Lanham, MD: Lexington Books.

Hornberger, Nancy H. 1988. *Bilingual Education and Language Maintenance*. Providence, RI: Foris.

Hornberger, Nancy H. 1989. "Can Peru's Rural Schools Be Agents for Quechua Language Maintenance?" *Journal of Multilingual and Multicultural Development* 10 (2): 145–59.

Hornberger, Nancy H., ed. 1996. "Indigenous Literacies in the Americas." In *Indigenous Literacies in the Americas: Language Planning from the Bottom Up*, edited by Nancy H. Hornberger, 2012 ed., 3–18. Berlin; New York: De Gruyter Mouton.

Hornberger, Nancy H. 1998. "Language Policy, Language Education, Language Rights: Indigenous, Immigrant, and International Perspectives." *Language in Society* 27 (4): 439–58.

Hornberger, Nancy H. 2000. "Bilingual Education Policy and Practice in the Andes: Ideological Paradox and Intercultural Possibility." *Anthropology & Education Quarterly* 31 (2): 173–201. https://doi.org/10.1525/aeq.2000.31.2.173.

Hornberger, Nancy H. 2002. "Multilingual Language Policies and the Continua of Biliteracy: An Ecological Approach." *Language Policy* 1 (1): 27.

Hornberger, Nancy H. 2008. "Introduction: Can Schools Save Indigenous Languages? Policy and Practice on Four Continents." In *Can Schools Save Indigenous Languages?*, edited by Nancy H. Hornberger, 1–12. London: Palgrave Macmillan UK. https://doi.org/10.1057/9780230582491_1.

Hornberger, Nancy H. 2014. "'Until I Became a Professional, I Was Not, Consciously, Indigenous': One Intercultural Bilingual Educator's Trajectory in Indigenous Language Revitalization." *Journal of Language, Identity & Education* 13 (4): 283–99. https://doi.org/10.1080/15348458.2014.939028.

Hornberger, Nancy H., and Haley De Korne. 2018. "Is Revitalization through Education Possible?" In *The Routledge Handbook of Language Revitalization*, by Leanne Hinton, Leena Huss, and Gerald Roche, 94–105. New York: Routledge.

Hornberger, Nancy H., and Kenda A. King. 1996. "Bringing the Language Forward: School-Based Initiatives for Quechua Language Revitalization in Ecuador and Bolivia." In *Indigenous Literacies in the Americas: Language Planning from the Bottom Up*, by Nancy H. Hornberger, 299–320. Berlin: Walter de Gruyter.

Hornberger, Nancy H., and Kendall A. King. 1998. "Authenticity and Unification in Quechua Language Planning." *Language, Culture and Curriculum* 11 (3): 390–410. https://doi.org/10.1080/07908319808666564.

Hornberger, Nancy H., and Kendall A. King. 2001. "Reversing Quechua Language Shift in South America." In *Can Threatened Languages Be Saved?*, by Joshua A. Fishman, 166–93. Buffalo, NY: Multilingual Matters.

Howard, Rosaleen. 2008. "Language Ideologies, Identities and the Discourse of Interculturalism in the Andes." In *Lengua, nación e identidad. La regulación del plurilingüismo en España y América Latina*, edited by Kirsten Süselbeck, Ulrike Mühlschlegel, and Peter Masson, 367–86. Madrid/Frankfurt: Iberoamericana/Vervuert.

Howard, Rosaleen. 2011. "The Quechua Language in the Andes Today: Between Statistics, the State, and Daily Life." In *History and Language in the Andes*, edited by P. Heggarty and A. J. Pearce, 189–213. New York: Palgrave Macmillan.

Howard, Rosaleen. 2014. *Kawsay Vida: A Multimedia Quechua Course for Beginners and Beyond*. Austin: University of Texas Press.

Howard, Rosaleen, Luis Andrade Ciudad, and Raquel de Pedro Ricoy. 2018. "Translating Rights: The Peruvian Indigenous Languages Act in Quechua and Aymara." *Amerindia* 40: 219–45.

Howard, Rosaleen, Raquel De Pedro Ricoy, and Luis Andrade Ciudad. 2018. "Translation Policy and Indigenous Languages in Hispanic Latin America." *International Journal of the Sociology of Language* 2018 (251): 19–36. https://doi.org/10.1515/ijsl-2018-0002.

Ilich, Ivan. 1977. "Disabling Professions." *Panarchy*. https://www.panarchy.org/illich/professions.html.

"Informe final de la Reunión Regional de Especialistas sobre Educación Bicultural y Bilingue." 1982. *América Indígena* 42 (2): 333–48.

Inoue, Miyako. 2006. *Vicarious Language: Gender and Linguistic Modernity in Japan*. Berkeley: University of California Press.

Irvine, Judith T., and Susan Gal. 2000. "Language Ideology and Linguistic Differentiation." In *Regimes of Language: Ideologies, Polities, and Identities*, edited by Paul Kroskrity, 35–84. Santa Fe, NM: School of American Research Press.

Jackson, Jean E. 2019. *Managing Multiculturalism: Indigeneity and the Struggle for Rights in Colombia*. Stanford, CA: Stanford University Press.

Jackson, Jean E., and Kay B. Warren. 2005. "Indigenous Movements in Latin America, 1992–2004: Controversies, Ironies, New Directions." *Annual Review of Anthropology* 34: 549–73.

Jaffe, Alexandra. 1999. *Ideologies in Action: Language Politics on Corsica*. Berlin: Mouton de Gruyter.

Jakobson, Roman. 1987. "Linguistics and Poetics." In *Language in Literature*, edited by Roman Jakobson. Cambridge, MA: Harvard University Press.

Johnston, Hank, and John A. Noakes. 2005. *Frames of Protest: Social Movements and the Framing Perspective*. Lanham, MD: Rowman & Littlefield.

Joseph, John E. 1995. "Indeterminacy, Translation and the Law." In *Translation and the Law*, edited by Marshall Morris, 13–36. Philadelphia: John Benjamins Publishing.

Joseph Mbembe, Achille. 2016. "Decolonizing the University: New Directions." *Arts and Humanities in Higher Education* 15 (1): 29–45. https://doi.org/10.1177/1474022215618513.

Kaarhus, Randi. 1989. *Historias en el tiempo, historias en el espacio*. Quito, Ecuador: Abya-Yala.

Kawsaypura Yachaypa Hatun Kamachiy. 2011. Quito, Ecuador: Ministerio de Educación.

Khan, Kamran. 2019. *Becoming a Citizen: Linguistic Trials and Negotiations in the UK*. London; New York: Bloomsbury Publishing.

King, Kendall. 2001. *Language Revitalization Processes and Prospects*. Tonawanda, NY: Multilingual Matters.

King, Kendall, and Marleen Haboud. 2007. "Language Planning and Policy in Ecuador." In *Language Planning & Policy, Latin America*, Vol. 1: *Ecuador, Mexico, and Paraguay*, edited by Richard B. Bauldauf and Robert B. Kaplan, 39–104. Tonawanda, NY: Multilingual Matters.

King, Kendall A., and Nancy H. Hornberger. 2006. "Quechua as a Lingua Franca." *Annual Review of Applied Linguistics* 26: 177–94.

Kockelman, Paul. 2016. *The Chicken and the Quetzal: Incommensurate Ontologies and Portable Values in Guatemala's Cloud Forest*. Durham, NC: Duke University Press Books.

Korne, Haley De. 2021. *Language Activism: Imaginaries and Strategies of Minority Language Equality*. De Gruyter Mouton. https://doi.org/10.1515/9781501511561.

Kosonen, Kimmo, and Carol Benson. 2013. "Introduction." In *Language Issues in Comparative Education: Inclusive Teaching and Learning in Non-Dominant Languages and Cultures*, edited by Carol Benson and Kimmo Kosonen, 1–18. Rotterdam: Brill.

Kowii, Ariruma. 2017. *(In)Visibilización del Kichwa: Políticas lingüísticas en Ecuador*. Quito, Ecuador: Universidad Andina Simón Bolívar, Abya-Yala.

Kowii Maldonado, Ariruma. 2011. "Diversidad e interculturalidad." In *Interculturalidad y diversidad*, edited by Ariruma Kowii Maldonado, 11–32. Quito, Ecuador: Biblioteca General de Cultura.

Krainer, Anita. 1996. *Educación intercultural bilingue en el Ecuador [Bilingual Intercultural Education in Ecuador]*. Quito, Ecuador: Abya-Yala.

Krainer, Anita. 2010. "La educación intercultural en Ecuador: Logros, desafíos, y situación actual." In *Construyendo interculturalidad: Pueblos indígenas, educación y políticas de identidad en América Latina*, edited by Juliana Strobele-Gregor, Olaf Kaltmeier, and Cornelia Glebeler, 38–44. Frankfurt: Deutsche Gesellschaft für Technische Zusammenarbeit.

Kroskrity, Paul. 2000. "Language Ideologies in the Expression and Representation of Arizona Tewa Ethnic Identity." In *Regimes of Language*, edited by Paul V. Kroskrity, 329–60. Santa Fe, NM: School of American Research Press.

Kroskrity, Paul V. 2009. "Narrative Reproductions: Ideologies of Storytelling, Authoritative Words, and Generic Regimentation in the Village of Tewa1." *Journal of Linguistic Anthropology* 19 (1): 40–56. https://doi.org/10.1111/j.1548-1395.2009.01018.x.

Kroskrity, Paul. 2010. "Language Ideologies—Evolving Perspectives." In *Society and Language Use*, edited by Jürgen Jaspers, Jef Verschueren, and Jan-Ola Östman, 192–211. Philadelphia: John Benjamins Publishing.

Kroskrity, Paul. 2018. "On Recognizing Persistence in the Indigenous Language Ideologies of Multilingualism in Two Native American Communities." *Language & Communication* 62 (September): 133–44. https://doi.org/10.1016/j.langcom.2018.04.012.

Krupa, Christopher, and David Nugent. 2015. *State Theory and Andean Politics: New Approaches to the Study of Rule*. Philadelphia: University of Pennsylvania Press.

Kvietok Dueñas, Frances. 2019. "Youth Bilingualism, Identity and Quechua Language Planning and Policy in the Urban Peruvian Andes." *Publicly Accessible Penn Dissertations*, January. https://repository.upenn.edu/edissertations/3293.

Kvietok Dueñas, Frances. 2021. "'Llegando a secundaria les ha dado amnesia ... ya no quieren hablar': Indigenous Speakerhood Socialization and the Creation of Language Deniers in Quechua Education." *Linguistics and Education* 61 (February): 100888. https://doi.org/10.1016/j.linged.2020.100888.

Lahn, Julie. 2018. "Being Indigenous in the Bureaucracy: Narratives of Work and Exit." *International Indigenous Policy Journal* 9 (1): 1–17. https://doi.org/10.18584/iipj.2018.9.1.3.

Lahn, Julie, and Elizabeth Ganter. n.d. "Aboriginal and Torres Strait Islander People in Public Service Roles: Representation, Recognition and Relationships in Australian Government Bureaucracies." *Journal of Australian Political Economy* 82: 133–48. https://doi.org/10.3316/informit.212850135499005.

Lane, Pia, James Costa, and Haley De Korne, eds. 2017. *Standardising Minority Languages*. New York: Routledge.

Latour, Bruno. 2007. *Reassembling the Social: An Introduction to Actor-Network-Theory*. Oxford: Oxford University Press.

Latour, Bruno. 2009. *The Making of Law: An Ethnography of the Conseil d'Etat*. Cambridge, UK; Malden, MA: Polity.

Laurie, Nina, Robert Andolina, and Sarah Radcliffe. 2003. "Indigenous Professionalization: Transnational Social Reproduction in the Andes." *Antipode* 35 (3): 463–91. https://doi.org/10.1111/1467-8330.00335.

Laurie, Nina, Robert Andolina, and Sarah Radcliffe. 2005. "Ethnodevelopment: Social Movements, Creating Experts and Professionalising Indigenous Knowledge in Ecuador." *Antipode* 37 (3): 470–96. https://doi.org/10.1111/j.0066-4812.2005.00507.x.

Leach, Darcy K. 2005. "The Iron Law of What Again? Conceptualizing Oligarchy across Organizational Forms." *Sociological Theory* 23 (3): 312–37.

Lee, Tiffany S. 2009. "Language, Identity, and Power: Navajo and Pueblo Young Adults' Perspectives and Experiences with Competing Language Ideologies." *Journal of Language, Identity & Education* 8 (5): 307–20. https://doi.org/10.1080/15348450903305106.

Lefevere, André, and Susan Bassnett. 1998. "Introduction." In *Constructing Cultures: Essays on Literary Translation*, by Susan Bassnett and André Lefevere, 1–24. Tonawanda, NY: Multilingual Matters.

Lemke, Thomas. 2001. "'The Birth of Bio-Politics': Michel Foucault's Lecture at the Collège de France on Neo-Liberal Governmentality." *Economy and Society* 30 (2): 190–207. https://doi.org/10.1080/03085140120042271.

Lempert, Michael. 2012a. *Discipline and Debate: The Language of Violence in a Tibetan Buddhist Monastery*. Berkeley and Los Angeles: University of California Press.

Lempert, Michael. 2012b. "Interaction Rescaled: How Monastic Debate Became a Diasporic Pedagogy." *Anthropology & Education Quarterly* 43 (2): 138–56. https://doi.org/10.1111/j.1548-1492.2012.01166.x.

Leonard, Wesley Y. 2017. "Producing Language Reclamation by Decolonising 'Language.'" *Language Documentation and Description* 14: 15–36.

Levinson, Bradley A. 1999. "Resituating the Place of Educational Discourse in Anthropology." *American Anthropologist* 101 (3): 594–604. https://doi.org/10.1525/aa.1999.101.3.594.

Levinson, Bradley A. 2005. "Programs for Democratic Citizenship in Mexico's Ministry of Education: Local Appropriations of Global Cultural Flows." *Indiana Journal of Global Legal Studies* 12 (1): 251–84. https://doi.org/10.2979/gls.2005.12.1.251.

Levinson, Bradley A. U. 2011. "Toward an Anthropology of (Democratic) Citizenship Education." In *A Companion to the Anthropology of Education*, edited by Bradley A. U. Levinson and Mica Pollock, 279–98. Malden, MA. https://doi.org/10.1002/9781444396713.ch17.

Levinson, Bradley A., and Dorothy Holland. 1996. "The Cultural Production of the Educated Person: An Introduction." In *The Cultural Production of the Educated Person: Critical Ethnographies of Schooling and Local Practice*, edited by Bradley A. Levinson, Douglas E. Foley, and Dorothy C. Holland, 1–25. Albany: State University of New York Press.

Limerick, Nicholas. 2018. "Kichwa or Quichua? Competing Alphabets, Political Histories, and Complicated Reading in Indigenous Languages." *Comparative Education Review* 62 (1): 103–24. https://doi.org/10.1086/695487.

Limerick, Nicholas. 2020. "What's the Linguistic Variety of Audit Culture? Administering an Indigenous Language Proficiency Exam in Ecuador's Intercultural Bilingual Education." *Anthropology & Education Quarterly* 51 (3): 282–303. https://doi.org/10.1111/aeq.12343.

Lomawaima, K. Tsianina, and Teresa L. McCarty. 2002. "When Tribal Sovereignty Challenges Democracy: American Indian Education and the Democratic Ideal." *American Educational Research Journal* 39 (2): 279–305. https://doi.org/10.3102/00028312039002279.

Lomawaima, K. Tsianina, and Teresa L. McCarty. 2014. "Introduction to the Special Issue Examining and Applying Safety Zone Theory: Current Policies, Practices, and Experiences." *Journal of American Indian Education* 53 (3): 1–10.

Loperena, Christopher. 2016. "Radicalize Multiculturalism? Garifuna Activism and the Double-Bind of Participation in Postcoup Honduras." *The Journal of Latin American and Caribbean Anthropology* 21 (3): 517–38.

Loperena, Christopher A. 2020. "Adjudicating Indigeneity: Anthropological Testimony in the Inter-American Court of Human Rights." *American Anthropologist* 122 (3): 595–605. https://doi.org/10.1111/aman.13415.

López, Galán, Felipe Javier, and Sergio Iván Navarro Martínez. 2016. "Indigenismo y Educación Intercultural: Una Discusión Necesaria." *Descatos* 52: 144–59.

López, Luis E. 1991. "La educación bilingue en Puno: Hacia un ajuste de cuentas." In *Educación bilingue intercultural: Reflexiones y desafios*, 173–217. Lima, Peru: Fomciencias.

López, Luis E. 2005. *De resquicios a boquerones: La educación intercultural bilingue en Bolivia*. Bolivia: PROEIB.

López, Luis E. 2021. "What Is Educación Intercultural Bilingüe in Latin America Nowadays: Results and Challenges." *Journal of Multilingual and Multicultural Development* 42 (10): 955–68. https://doi.org/10.1080/01434632.2020.1827646.

References

Lopez-Gopar, Mario E. 2016. *Decolonizing Primary English Language Teaching*. Bristol; Buffalo, NY: Multilingual Matters.

Löwenheim, Oded, and Orit Gazit. 2009. "Power and Examination: A Critique of Citizenship Tests." *Security Dialogue* 40 (2): 145–67. https://doi.org/10.1177/0967010609103074.

Lucero, Jose Antonio. 2008. *Struggles of Voice: The Politics of Indigenous Representation in the Andes*. Pittsburgh: University of Pittsburgh Press.

Lucy, John A. 1993. *Reflexive Language: Reported Speech and Metapragmatics*. Cambridge: Cambridge University Press.

Luykx, Aurolyn. 1999. *The Citizen Factory: Schooling and Cultural Production in Bolivia*. Albany: State University of New York Press.

Luykx, Aurolyn, Rivera Fernando García, and Guerrero Félix Julca. 2016. "Communicative Strategies across Quechua Languages." *International Journal of the Sociology of Language* 2016 (240): 159–91. https://doi.org/10.1515/ijsl-2016-0018.

Makihara, Miki. 2008. "Linguistic Syncretism and Language Ideologies: Transforming Sociolinguistic Hierarchy on Rapa Nui (Easter Island)." *American Anthropologist* 106 (3): 529–40. https://doi.org/10.1525/aa.2004.106.3.529.

Malinowski, Bronislaw. 1923. "The Problem of Meaning in Primitive Languages." In *The Meaning of Meaning*, edited by C. K. Ogden and Ivor A. Richards, 296–336. New York: Harcourt, Brace and World.

Mannheim, Bruce. 1991. *The Language of the Inka since the European Invasion*. Austin: University of Texas Press.

Mannheim, Bruce. 2018. "Three Axes of Variability in Quechua." In *The Andean World*, edited by Linda J. Seligmann and Kathleen S. Fine-Dare, 507–23. New York: Routledge.

Martínez Novo, Carmen. 2014a. "Intercultural Bilingual Education in the Andes." In *The Education of Indigenous Citizens in Latin America*, edited by Regina Cortina, 98–123. Bristol; Buffalo, NY: Multilingual Matters.

Martínez Novo, Carmen. 2014b. "Is the Cultural Project of the Indigenous Movement in Crisis? Some Ethnographic Remarks on the Ambiguities of Intercultural Bilingual Education in Ecuador." In *New World Colors: Ethnicity, Belonging, and Difference in the Americas*, edited by Josef Raab. Tempe, AZ: Bilingual Review Press.

Martínez Novo, Carmen, and Carlos de la Torre. 2010. "Racial Discrimination and Citizenship in Ecuador's Educational System." *Latin American and Caribbean Ethnic Studies* 5 (1): 1–26. https://doi.org/10.1080/17442220903506875.

Mateos Cortés, Laura Selene. 2010. "La migración transnacional del discurso intercultural." Granada, Spain: Universidad de Granada.

Mateos Cortés, Laura Selene, and Gunther Dietz. 2017. "Local Resignifications of Transnational Discourses in Intercultural Higher Education: The Case of the Universidad Veracruzana Intercultural in Mexico." *Arts and Humanities in Higher Education* 16 (1): 28–50. https://doi.org/10.1177/1474022216633679.

May, Stephen. 2007. *Language and Minority Rights: Ethnicity, Nationalism and the Politics of Language*. New York: Routledge.

May, Stephen. 2013. "Indigenous Immersion Education: International Developments." *Journal of Immersion and Content-Based Language Education* 1 (1): 34–69. https://doi.org/10.1075/jicb.1.1.03may.

McCarty, Teresa. 2008. "Schools as Strategic Tools for Indigenous Language Revitalization: Lessons from Native America." In *Can Schools Save Indigenous Languages?*, edited by Nancy Hornberger, 161–79. New York: Palgrave Macmillan.

McCarty, Teresa L., Tamara Borgoiakova, Perry Gilmore, K. Tsianina Lomawaima, and Mary Eunice Romero. 2005. "Indigenous Epistemologies and Education—Self-Determination, Anthropology, and Human Rights." *Anthropology & Education Quarterly* 36 (1): 1–7. https://doi.org/10.1525/aeq.2005.36.1.001.

McCarty, Teresa L., Tiffany S. Lee, Joaquín Noguera, Winoka Yepa, and Sheilah E. Nicholas. 2022. "'You Should Know the Name of the Wind Where You Live'—Relationality and Relational Accountability in Indigenous-Language Education." *Comparative Education Review* 66 (3): 417–41. https://doi.org/10.1086/720509.

McCarty, Teresa L., and Stephen May, eds. 2017. *Language Policy and Political Issues in Education*. 3rd edition. New York: Springer.

McCarty, Teresa L., and Sheilah E. Nicholas. 2014. "Reclaiming Indigenous Languages: A Reconsideration of the Roles and Responsibilities of Schools." *Review of Research in Education* 38 (1): 106–36. https://doi.org/10.3102/0091732X13507894.

McCarty, Teresa L., Sheilah E. Nicholas, and Gillian Wigglesworth. 2019. *A World of Indigenous Languages: Politics, Pedagogies and Prospects for Language Reclamation*. Bristol: Multilingual Matters.

McCarty, Teresa L., Joaquín Noguera, Tiffany S. Lee, and Sheilah E. Nicholas. 2021. "'A Viable Path for Education'—Indigenous-Language Immersion and Sustainable Self-Determination." *Journal of Language, Identity & Education* 20 (5): 340–54. https://doi.org/10.1080/15348458.2021.1957681.

McGee Banks, Cherry A. 2010. "Becoming American: Intercultural Education and European Immigrants." In *Intercultural and Multicultural Education: Enhancing Global Interconnectedness*, edited by Carl A. Grant and Agostino Portera, 124–37. New York: Routledge.

McNeish, John-Andrew. 2008. "Beyond the Permitted Indian? Bolivia and Guatemala in an Era of Neoliberal Developmentalism." *Latin American and Caribbean Ethnic Studies* 3 (1): 33–59. https://doi.org/10.1080/17442220701865838.

Mead, Margaret. 1949. "Ruth Fulton Benedict 1887–1948." *American Anthropologist* 51 (3): 457–68. https://doi.org/10.1525/aa.1949.51.3.02a00080.

Meek, Barbara A. 2016. "Shrinking Indigenous Language in the Yukon." In *Scale: Discourse and Dimensions of Social Life*, edited by E. Summerson Carr and Michæl Lempert, 70–90. Oakland: University of California Press.

Meek, Barbra A., and Jacqueline H. E. Messing. 2008. "Framing Indigenous Languages as Secondary to Matrix Languages." *Anthropology & Education Quarterly* 38 (2): 99–118. https://doi.org/10.1525/aeq.2007.38.2.99.

Merlan, Francesca. 2014. "Recent Rituals of Indigenous Recognition in Australia: Welcome to Country." *American Anthropologist* 116 (2): 296–309. https://doi.org/10.1111/aman.12089.

Mertz, Elizabeth. 2007. *The Language of Law School: Learning to "Think Like a Lawyer."* New York: Oxford University Press.

Messing, Jacqueline H. E. 2009. "Ambivalence and Ideology among Mexicano Youth in Tlaxcala, Mexico." *Journal of Language, Identity & Education* 8 (5): 350–64. https://doi.org/10.1080/15348450903307680.

Meyer, Lois M. 2018. "'Carrying on the Word That I Know': Teacher-Community Language Revitalization Collaborations in Indigenous Oaxaca, Mexico." In *The Routledge Handbook of Language Revitalization*, edited by Leanne Hinton, Leena Huss, and Gerald Roche, 384–94. New York: Routledge.

Miller, Peter, and Nikolas Rose. 1990. "Governing Economic Life." In *Foucault's New Domains*, by Mike Gane and Terry Johnson, 75–105. New York: Routledge.

Ministerio de Educación. 2009. *Kichwa Yachakukkunapa Shimiyuk Kamu*. Quito, Ecuador: Ministerio de Educación.

"Modelo del Sistema de Educación Intercultural Bilingue (MOSEIB)." 2013. Quito, Ecuador: Ministerio de Educación.

Montaluisa, Luis. n.d. "Historia de la educación intercultural bilingue del Ecuador." Unpublished Manuscript, 1–28.

Montaluisa, Luis. 1980a. "El vocabulario general de la lengua Quichua para el Ecuador." *Revista de la Universidad Católica* 25: 99–118.

Montaluisa, Luis. 1980b. "Historia de la escritura del Quichua." *Revista de la Universidad Católica* 28: 121–46.

Montaluisa, Luis. 2011. "A los dos años de invasión colonialista al sistema de educación intercultural bilingue." Blogspot. *Educación Intercultural Bilingue* (blog). February 11, 2011. http://eibecuador.blogspot.com/search?updated-max=2009-10-19T16:08:00-05:00&max-results=7&start=7&by-date=false.

Montaluisa-Chasiquiza, Luis. 2019. *La estandarización ortográfica del Quichua ecuatoriano*. Quito, Ecuador: Ediciones Abya-Yala.

Moore, Robert. 2011. "Standardisation, Diversity and Enlightenment in the Contemporary Crisis of EU Language Policy." *King's College London Working Papers in Urban Language and Literacies* 74: 1–31.

Moore, Robert E., Sari Pietikainen, and Jan Blommaert. 2010. "Counting the Losses: Numbers as the Language of Language Endangerment." *Sociolinguistic Studies* 4 (1): 1–26.

Mora, Mariana. 2017. *Kuxlejal Politics: Indigenous Autonomy, Race, and Decolonizing Research in Zapatista Communities*. Austin: University of Texas Press.

Moya, Ruth. 1998. "Reformas educativas e interculturalidad en América Latina." *Revista iberoamericana de educación* 17: 105–87.

Muehlmann, Shaylih. 2008. "'Spread Your Ass Cheeks': And Other Things That Should Not Be Said in Indigenous Languages." *American Ethnologist* 35 (1): 34–48. https://doi.org/10.1111/j.1548-1425.2008.00004.x.

Muysken, Pieter. 1977. *Syntactic Developments in the Verb Phrase of Ecuadorian Quechua*. Amsterdam: Pieter de Ridder Press.

Muysken, Pieter. 2019. *El Kichwa ecuatoriano*. Quito, Ecuador: Ediciones Abya-Yala.

Nakassis, Constantine V. 2012. "Brand, Citationality, Performativity." *American Anthropologist* 114 (4): 624–38. https://doi.org/10.1111/j.1548-1433.2012.01511.x.

Nakassis, Constantine V. 2016. "Linguistic Anthropology in 2015: Not the Study of Language." *American Anthropologist* 118 (2): 330–45. https://doi.org/10.1111/aman.12528.

Niesz, Tricia. 2019. "Social Movement Knowledge and Anthropology of Education." *Anthropology & Education Quarterly* 50 (2): 223–34. https://doi.org/10.1111/aeq.12286.

Niesz, Tricia, Aaron M. Korora, Christy Burke Walkuski, and Rachel E. Foot. 2018. "Social Movements and Educational Research: Toward a United Field of Scholarship." *Teachers College Record* 120 (3): 1–41. https://doi.org/10.1177/016146811812000305.

Ng, Kwai Hang. 2009. *The Common Law in Two Voices: Language, Law, and the Postcolonial Dilemma in Hong Kong*. Stanford, CA: Stanford University Press.

Ng, Kwai Hang. 2014. "Legal Translation and the Problem of Heteroglossia." In *Comparative Law—Engaging Translation*, edited by Simone Glanert, 49–66. New York: Routledge.

Niezen, Ronald. 2003. *The Origins of Indigenism: Human Rights and the Politics of Identity*. Berkeley: University of California Press.

Ochs, Elinor, and Bambi B. Schieffelin. 1989. "Language Has a Heart." *Text* 9 (1): 7–25.

Oróstegui Durán, Sandra Liliana. 2008. "Traducción de la Constitución colombiana de 1991 a siete lenguas vernáculas." *Reflexión política* 10 (19): 164–75.

Ortiz-T., Pablo. 2016. "Políticas estatales, territorios, y derechos de los pueblos indígenas en Ecuador (1983–2012)." In *Los desafíos de la plurinacionalidad*, edited by Pablo Ortiz-T., Iván Narváez Q., and Víctor Bretón Solo de Zaldívar, 13–72. Quito, Ecuador: Abya-Yala.

Oxa, Justo. 2004. "Vigencia de la cultura andina en la escuela." In *Arguedas y el Perú de Hoy*, edited by Carmen Pinilla, 235–43. Lima, Peru: Sur Casa de Estudios del Socialismo.

Pallares, Amalia. 2007. "Contesting Membership: Citizenship, Pluriculturalism(s), and the Contemporary Indigenous Movement." In *Highland Indians and the State in Modern Ecuador*, edited by A. Kim Clark and Marc Becker, 139–54. Pittsburgh: University of Pittsburgh Press.

Parmentier, Richard. 1997. *The Pragmatic Semiotics of Cultures*. Berlin: Mouton de Gruyter.

Paschel, Tianna S. 2016. *Becoming Black Political Subjects: Movements and Ethno-Racial Rights in Colombia and Brazil*. Princeton, NJ: Princeton University Press. Electronic edition. http://hdl.handle.net/2027/heb34127.0001.001.

Paz, Alejandro I. 2018. *Latinos in Israel: Language and Unexpected Citizenship*. Bloomington: Indiana University Press.

Paz, Alejandro I. 2019. "Communicating Citizenship." *Annual Review of Anthropology* 48 (1): 77–93. https://doi.org/10.1146/annurev-anthro-102317-050031.

Peery, Char. 2012. "New Deal Navajo Linguistics: Language Ideology and Political Transformation." *Language & Communication* 32 (2): 114–23. https://doi.org/10.1016/j.langcom.2011.05.003.

Pennycook, Alastair, and Sinfree Makoni. 2019. *Innovations and Challenges in Applied Linguistics from the Global South*. New York: Routledge.

Pérez Silva, Jorge, and Virginia Zavala Cisneros. 2010. "Aspectos cognitivos e ideológicos del 'motoseo' en el Perú." In *América en la lengua española*, 1–10. Valparaiso, Chile: Instituto Cervantes.

Peters, Stephen K. H. 2016. "Loaded Speech: Between Voices in Indigenous Public Speaking Events." *Journal of Linguistic Anthropology* 26 (3): 315–34. https://doi.org/10.1111/jola.12130.

Piven, Frances Fox, and Richard Cloward. 1977. *Poor People's Movements: Why They Succeed, How They Fail*. New York: Vintage.

Plan Decenal de Educación del Ecuador 2006–2015. 2007. Quito, Ecuador: Consejo Nacional de Educación y Ministerio de Educación. https://educacion.gob.ec/wp-content/uploads/downloads/2012/08/Rendicion_2007.pdf.

Postero, Nancy. 2004. "Articulations and Fragmentations: Indigenous Politics in Bolivia." In *The Struggle for Indigenous Rights in Latin America*, edited by Nancy Postero and Leon Zamosc, 189–216. Portland, OR: Sussex Academic Press.

Postero, Nancy. 2006. *Now We Are Citizens: Indigenous Politics in Postmulticultural Bolivia*. 1st edition. Stanford, CA: Stanford University Press.

Postero, Nancy Grey. 2007. *Now We Are Citizens: Indigenous Politics in Postmulticultural Bolivia*. Stanford, CA: Stanford University Press.

Postero, Nancy, and Leon Zamosc. 2004. "Indigenous Movements and the Indian Question in Latin America." In *The Struggle for Indigenous Rights in Latin America*, edited by Leon Zamosc and Nancy Grey Postero, 2006 ed., 1–31. Brighton: Sussex Academic Press.

Povinelli, Elizabeth A. 2001. "Radical Worlds: The Anthropology of Incommensurability and Inconceivability." *Annual Review of Anthropology* 30: 319–34.

Povinelli, Elizabeth A. 2002. *The Cunning of Recognition: Indigenous Alterities and the Making of Australian Multiculturalism*. Durham, NC: Duke University Press.

Pozzi-Escot, Inés. 1991. "Ideas y planteamientos propuestos en el desarrollo y debate de la educación bilingue en el país." In *Educación bilingüe intercultural: Reflexiones y desafíos*, edited by Luis Enrique Lopez, Inés Pozzi-Escot, and Madeleine Zuñiga, 121–48. Lima, Peru: FOMCIENCIAS.

"Proyecto de fortalecimiento de la educación intercultural bilingue, 2011–2014." n.d. Ministerio de Educación. https://educacion.gob.ec/wp-content/uploads/downloads/2015/11/Proyecto_Fortalecimiento-Educacion-Intercultural-Bilingue.pdf.

Quick, Joe, and James T. Spartz. 2018. "On the Pursuit of Good Living in Highland Ecuador: Critical Indigenous Discourses of Sumak Kawsay." *Latin American Research Review* 53 (4): 757–69. https://doi.org/10.25222/larr.132.

Quillen, James. 1955. "Third Session of the Conference." In *Education and Anthropology*, edited by George Spindler, 106. Stanford, CA: Stanford University Press.

Quishpe, Andrés. 2022. "En Las Reformas a La Ley Orgánica de Educación, ¿ganó El País o La UNE?" *Plan V*, May 30, 2022. https://www.planv.com.ec/historias/sociedad/reformas-la-ley-organica-educacion-gano-el-pais-o-la-une.

Quishpe Lema, Cristobal. 2013. "Kichwa Shimita Yachakushunchik." *La gaceta*, March 9. http://www.lagaceta.com.ec/index.php/dominical/187-shayruco/11120-kichwa-shimita-yachakushunchik.

Radcliffe, Sarah A., and Andrew J. Webb. 2015. "Subaltern Bureaucrats and Postcolonial Rule: Indigenous Professional Registers of Engagement with the Chilean State." *Comparative Studies in Society and History* 57 (1): 248–73. https://doi.org/10.1017/S0010417514000668.

Ranta, Eija. 2018. *Vivir Bien as an Alternative to Neoliberal Globalization: Can Indigenous Terminologies Decolonize the State?* London: Routledge.

Rappaport, Joanne. 2005. *Intercultural Utopias: Public Intellectuals, Cultural Experimentation, and Ethnic Pluralism in Colombia*. Durham, NC: Duke University Press.

Rayner, Jeremy. 2021. "Cardboard Coffins and Vaults of Gold: Debt, Obligation and Scandal in Ecuador's Response to Covid-19:" *Open Anthropological Research* 1 (1): 143–58. https://doi.org/10.1515/opan-2020-0111.

Resina de la Fuente, Jorge. 2012. *La plurinacionalidad en disputa: El pulso entre correa y La CONAIE*. Quito, Ecuador: Abya-Yala.

Reyes, Angela. 2017. "Inventing Postcolonial Elites: Race, Language, Mix, Excess." *Journal of Linguistic Anthropology* 27 (2): 210–31. https://doi.org/10.1111/jola.12156.

Reyhner, Jon. 2015. *Teaching Indigenous Students: Honoring Place, Community, and Culture*. University of Oklahoma Press.

Rhodes, Catherine, Irma Pomol Cahum, and Miguel Chan Dzul. 2018. "Exploración lexicográfica de seis diccionarios del Maya Yucateco." *Estudios de lingüística aplicada* 36 (68): 9–57.

Richland, Justin B. 2008. *Arguing with Tradition: The Language of Law in Hopi Tribal Court*. Chicago: University of Chicago Press.

Rindstedt, Camilla, and Karin Aronsson. 2002. "Growing Up Monolingual in a Bilingual Community: The Quichua Revitalization Paradox." *Language in Society* 31 (5): 721–42.

Riofrancos, Thea. 2020. *Resource Radicals: From Petro-Nationalism to Post-Extractivism in Ecuador*. Durham, NC: Duke University Press.

Rivera Cusicanqui, Silvia. 2018. *Un mundo Ch'ixi es posible*. Buenos Aires: Tinta Limón.

Rivera Cusicanqui, Silvia. 2019. "Ch'ixinakax Utxiwa: A Reflection on the Practices and Discourses of Decolonization." *Language, Culture and Society* 1 (1): 106–19.

Rivera Cusicanqui, Silvia. 2020. *Ch'ixinakax Utxiwa: On Decolonising Practices and Discourses*. Translated by Molly Geidel. Cambridge, UK; Medford, MA: Polity.

Rockwell, Elsie. 2007. *Hacer escuela, hacer estado: La educación posrevolucionaria vista desde Tlaxcala*. México DF: CIESAS.

Rockwell, Elsie, and Ana Maria R. Gomes. 2009. "Introduction to the Special Issue: Rethinking Indigenous Education from a Latin American Perspective." *Anthropology & Education Quarterly* 40 (2): 97–109. https://doi.org/10.1111/j.1548-1492.2009.01030.x.

Rodriguez, Juan Luis. 2016. "The National Anthem in Warao: Semiotic Ground and Performative Affordances of Indigenous Language Texts in Venezuela." *Journal of Linguistic Anthropology* 26 (3): 335–51. https://doi.org/10.1111/jola.12129.

Rodríguez Cruz, Marta. 2018. *Educacion intercultural bilingüe, interculturalidad y plurinacionalidad en el Ecuador*. Vol. I. Quito, Ecuador: Abya-Yala.

Romero, Sergio. 2015. *Language and Ethnicity among the K'ichee' Maya*. Salt Lake City: University of Utah Press.

Rosa, Jonathan Daniel. 2016. "Standardization, Racialization, Languagelessness: Raciolinguistic Ideologies across Communicative Contexts." *Journal of Linguistic Anthropology* 26 (2): 162–83. https://doi.org/10.1111/jola.12116.

Rosa, Jonathan. 2019. *Looking like a Language, Sounding like a Race: Raciolinguistic Ideologies and the Learning of Latinidad*. 1st edition. New York: Oxford University Press.

Rosa, Jonathan, and Vanessa Díaz. 2020. "Raciontologies: Rethinking Anthropological Accounts of Institutional Racism and Enactments of White Supremacy in the United States." *American Anthropologist* 122 (1): 120–32. https://doi.org/10.1111/aman.13353.

Rosa, Jonathan, and Nelson Flores. 2017. "Unsettling Race and Language: Toward a Raciolinguistic Perspective." *Language in Society* 46 (5): 621–47. https://doi.org/10.1017/S0047404517000562.

Roseberry, William. 1994. "Hegemony and the Language of Contention." In *Everyday Forms of State Formation: Revolution and the Negotiation of Rule in Modern Mexico*, edited by Gilbert Michael Joseph and Daniel Nugent, 355–66. Durham, NC: Duke University Press.

Santana, Roberto. 1987. "La cuestión étnica y la democracia en Ecuador." *Revista mexicana de sociología* 49 (2): 127–44.

Schegloff, Emanuel A, and Harvey Sacks. 1973. "Opening Up Closings." *Semiotica* 8 (4): 289–327.

Schieffelin, Bambi B., and Elinor Ochs. 1986. "Language Socialization." *Annual Review of Anthropology* 15: 163–91. https://doi.org/10.1146/annurev.an.15.100186.001115.

Schissel, Jamie L. 2019. *Social Consequences of Testing for Language-Minoritized Bilinguals in the United States*. Blue Ridge Summit: Multilingual Matters.

Scott, James C. 1998. *Seeing Like a State: How Certain Schemes to Improve the Human Condition Have Failed*. New Haven, CT; London: Yale University Press.

Searle, John. 1969. *Speech Acts: An Essay in the Philosophy of Language*. Cambridge: Cambridge University Press.

Searle, John R., and Daniel Vanderveken. 1985. "Speech Acts and Illocutionary Logic." In *Logic, Thought and Action*, edited by Daniel Vanderveken, 109–32. Logic, Epistemology, and the Unity of Science. Dordrecht: Springer. https://doi.org/10.1007/1-4020-3167-X_5.

Shange, Savannah. 2019. *Progressive Dystopia: Abolition, Antiblackness, + Schooling in San Francisco*. Durham, NC: Duke University Press.

Shankar, Shalini. 2012. "Creating Model Consumers: Producing Ethnicity, Race, and Class in Asian American Advertising." *American Ethnologist* 39 (3): 578–91. https://doi.org/10.1111/j.1548-1425.2012.01382.x.

Sieder, Rachel, and Jessica Witchell. 2001. "Advancing Indigenous Claims through the Law: Reflections on the Guatemalan Peace Process." In *Culture and Rights*, edited by Jane Cowan, Marie-Bénédicte Dembour, and Richard Wilson, 201–25. Cambridge: Cambridge University Press.

Silverstein, M. 1998. "Contemporary Transformations of Local Linguistic Communities." *Annual Review of Anthropology* 27 (1): 401–26. https://doi.org/10.1146/annurev.anthro.27.1.401.

Silverstein, Michael. 1981. "The Limits of Awareness." In *Southwest Educational Development Laboratory*, 1–31. Austin, TX: SEDL.

Silverstein, Michael. 1993. "Metapragmatic Discourse and Metapragmatic Function." In *Reflexive Language: Reported Speech and Metapragmatics*, edited by John A. Lucy, 33–58. Cambridge: Cambridge University Press.

Silverstein, Michael. 1996. "Monoglot 'Standard' in America: Standardization and Metaphors of Linguistic Hegemony." In *The Matrix of Language: Contemporary Linguistic Anthropology*, edited by Donald Brenneis and Ronald H.S. McCaulay 284–306. Boulder, CO: Westview Press.

Silverstein, Michael. 2003a. "Indexical Order and the Dialectics of Sociolinguistic Life." *Language & Communication* 23 (3–4): 193–229.

Silverstein, Michael. 2003b. "Translation, Transduction, Transformation: Skating 'Glossando' on Thin Semiotic Ice." In *Translating Cultures: Perspectives on Translation and Anthropology*, edited by Paula G. Rubel and Abraham Rosman, 75–108. New York: Berg.

Silverstein, Michael, and Greg Urban. 1996a. *Natural Histories of Discourse*. Chicago: University of Chicago Press.

Silverstein, Michael, and Greg Urban. 1996b. "The Natural History of Discourse." In *Natural Histories of Discourse*, edited by Michael Silverstein and Greg Urban, 1–20. Chicago: University of Chicago Press.

Simpson, Audra. 2007. "On Ethnographic Refusal: Indigeneity, 'Voice' and Colonial Citizenship - Document - Gale Academic OneFile Select." *Junctures: The Journal for Thematic Dialogue* 9. https://go-gale-com.ezproxy.cul.columbia.edu/ps/i.do?p=EAIM&u=columbiau&id=GALE|A176129665&v=2.1&it=r&sid=summon.

Simpson, Audra. 2014. *Mohawk Interruptus: Political Life Across the Borders of Settler States*. Durham, NC: Duke University Press.

Sims, Christine P. 2005. "Tribal Languages and the Challenges of Revitalization." *Anthropology & Education Quarterly* 36 (1): 104–6. https://doi.org/10.1525/aeq.2005.36.1.104.

Social Science Research Council Summer Seminar on Acculturation. 1954. "Acculturation: An Exploratory Formulation." *American Anthropologist* 56 (6): 973–1000. https://doi.org/10.1525/aa.1954.56.6.02a00030.

Sørensen, Birgitte Refslund. 2008. "The Politics of Citizenship and Difference in Sri Lankan Schools." *Anthropology & Education Quarterly* 39 (4): 423–43. https://doi.org/10.1111/j.1548-1492.2008.00031.x.

Speed, Shannon. 2005. "Dangerous Discourses." *PoLAR: Political and Legal Anthropology Review* 28 (1): 29–51. https://doi.org/10.1525/pol.2005.28.1.29.

Spivak, Gayatri Chakravorty. 1990. *The Post-Colonial Critic: Interviews, Strategies, Dialogues*. New York: Routledge.

Spivak, Gayatri Chakravorty. 1993. *Outside in the Teaching Machine*. Psychology Press.

Spivak, Gayatri Chakravorty. 2012. *An Aesthetic Education in the Era of Globalization*. Cambridge, MA: Harvard University Press.

Stephen, Lynn. 2002. *Zapata Lives! Histories and Cultural Politics in Southern Mexico*. Berkeley: University of California Press.

Stephen, Lynn. 2013. *We Are the Face of Oaxaca: Testimony and Social Movements*. Durham, NC: Duke University Press Books.

Stroud, Christopher. 2001. "African Mother-Tongue Programmes and the Politics of Language: Linguistic Citizenship versus Linguistic Human Rights." *Journal of Multilingual and Multicultural Development* 22 (4): 339–55. https://doi.org/10.1080/01434630108666440.

Sumida Huaman, Elizabeth. 2017. "Indigenous Rights Education (IRE): Indigenous Knowledge Systems and Transformative Human Rights in the Peruvian Andes." *International Journal of Human Rights Education* 1 (September): 1–34.

Sumida Huaman, Elizabeth. 2020. "Small Indigenous Schools: Indigenous Resurgence and Education in the Americas." *Anthropology & Education Quarterly* 51 (3): 262–81. https://doi.org/10.1111/aeq.12335.

Sumida Huaman, Elizabeth, and Bryan Brayboy. 2017. *Indigenous Innovations in Higher Education: Local Knowledge and Critical Research*. Rotterdam: Sense Publishers.

Sumida Huaman, Elizabeth, and Laura Valdiviezo. 2020. "Indigenous Community, Youth, and Educational Research in the Andean World." In *Critical Youth Research in Education: Methodologies and Praxis*, edited by Arshad Imtiaz Ali and T. L. McCarty, 80–98. New York: Routledge.

Swinehart, Karl F. 2012. "Metadiscursive Regime and Register Formation on Aymara Radio." *Language & Communication, Languages and Publics in Stateless Nations* 32 (2): 102–13. https://doi.org/10.1016/j.langcom.2011.05.004.

Tarlau, Rebecca. 2019. *Occupying Schools, Occupying Land: How the Landless Workers Movement Transformed Brazilian Education*. New York: Oxford University Press.

Taylor, Charles. 1994. "The Politics of Recognition." In *Multiculturalism: Examining the Politics of Recognition*, edited by Amy Gutmann, 25–74. Princeton, NJ: Princeton University Press.

Throop, C. Jason, and Alessandro Duranti. 2014. "Attention, Ritual Glitches, and Attentional Pull: The President and the Queen." *Phenomenology and the Cognitive Sciences* (November): 1–28. https://doi.org/10.1007/s11097-014-9397-4.

Throop, C. Jason, and Alessandro Duranti. 2015. "Attention, Ritual Glitches, and Attentional Pull: The President and the Queen." *Phenomenology and the Cognitive Sciences* 14 (4) (November): 1–28. https://doi.org/10.1007/s11097-014-9397-4.

Tomlinson, Matt. 2017. "Introduction: Imagining the Monologic." In *The Monologic Imagination*, edited by Matt Tomlinson and Julian Millie, 1–18. Oxford; New York: Oxford University Press.

Urban, Greg. 1986. "Ceremonial Dialogues in South America." *American Anthropologist*, n.s., 88 (2): 371–86.

Urciuoli, Bonnie. 2011. "Neoliberal Education: Preparing the Student for the New Workplace." In *Ethnographies of Neoliberalism*, edited by Carol J. Greenhouse, 162–76. Philadelphia: University of Pennsylvania Press.

Urla, Jacqueline. 2012. *Reclaiming Basque: Language, Nation, and Cultural Activism*. Reno: University of Nevada Press.

Urla, Jacqueline. 2019. "Governmentality and Language." *Annual Review of Anthropology* 48: 261–78. https://doi.org/10.1146/annurev-anthro-102317-050258.

Urla, Jacqueline, Estibaliz Amorrortu, Ana Ortega, and Jone Goirigolzarri. 2017. "Basque Standardization and the New Speaker." In *Standardizing Minority Languages: Competing Ideologies of Authority and Authenticity in the Global Periphery*, edited by Pia Lane, James Costa, and Haley De Korne, 24–46. New York: Routledge.

Uzendoski, Michael. 2008. "La textualidad oral Napo Kichwa y las paradoas de la educación bilingue intercultural." In *Repensando las identidades y políticas indígenas en América Latina*, 147–72. Quito, Ecuador: Abya-Yala.

Uzendoski, Michael A. 2012. "Beyond Orality: Textuality, Territory, and Ontology among Amazonian Peoples." *HAU: Journal of Ethnographic Theory* 2 (1): 55–80. https://doi.org/10.14318/hau2.1.005.

Valdiviezo, Laura. 2009. "Bilingual Intercultural Education in Indigenous Schools: An Ethnography of Teacher Interpretations of Government Policy." *International Journal of Bilingual Education and Bilingualism* 12 (1): 61–79. https://doi.org/10.1080/13670050802149515.

Valdiviezo, Laura. 2014. "Political Discourse and School Practice in Multilingual Peru." In *The Education of Indigenous Citizens in Latin America*, edited by Regina Cortina, 187–210. Bristol; Buffalo, NY: Multilingual Matters.

Van Cott, Donna Lee. 2009. "Indigenous Movements Lose Momentum." *Current History* 108 (715): 83–89.

Varenne, Herve. 2007. "Difficult Collective Deliberations; Anthropological Notes toward a Theory of Education." *Teachers College Record* 109: 1559–88.

Vavrus, Frances. 2021. *Schooling as Uncertainty: An Ethnographic Memoir in Comparative Education*. Bloomsbury Academic.

Venuti, Lawrence. 1994. *The Translator's Invisibility: A History of Translation*. London; New York: Routledge.

Venuti, Lawrence. 2008. *The Translator's Invisibility: A History of Translation*. 2nd ed. London; New York: Routledge.

Viatori, Maximilian. 2009. *One State, Many Nations: Indigenous Rights Struggles in Ecuador*. Santa Fe, NM: School for Advanced Research Press.

Viatori, Maximilian Stefan, and Gloria Ushigua. 2007. "Speaking Sovereignty: Indigenous Languages and Self-Determination." *Wicazo Sa Review* 22 (2): 7–21. https://doi.org/10.1353/wic.2007.0022.

Von Gleich, Utta. 2006. "La lucha de ideologias linguisticas en sistemas educativos." *Pueblos indígenas y educación* 59: 39–64.

References

Walsh, Catherine. 2009. *Interculturalidad, Estado, Sociedad*. Quito, Ecuador: Abya-Yala.

Walsh, Catherine E. 2018. "Interculturality and Decoloniality." In *On Decoloniality: Concepts, Analytics, Praxis*, edited by Walter D. Mignolo and Catherine E. Walsh, 33–56. Durham, NC: Duke University Press Books.

Warren, Jonathan. 2001. *Racial Revolutions: Antiracism and Indian Resurgence in Brazil*. Durham, NC: Duke University Press.

Warren, Kay B. 1998. *Indigenous Movements and Their Critics: Pan-Maya Activism in Guatemala*. Princeton, NJ: Princeton University Press.

Waterman, Stephanie J. 2012. "Home-Going as a Strategy for Success Among Haudenosaunee College and University Students." *Journal of Student Affairs Research and Practice* 49 (2): 193–209. https://doi.org/10.1515/jsarp-2012-6378.

Weber, David. 2005. *Writing Quechua*. Los Angeles: UCLA Latin American Center Publications.

Webster, Anthony K. 2014. "'Dif' G'one' and Semiotic Calquing: A Signography of the Linguistic Landscape of the Navajo Nation." *Journal of Anthropological Research* 70 (3): 385–410.

Whitten, Norman E. Jr. 2003. *Millennial Ecuador: Critical Essays on Cultural Transformations and Social Dynamics*. Iowa City: University Of Iowa Press.

Whitten, Norman E., and Dorothea S. Whitten. 2011. *Histories of the Present: People and Power in Ecuador*. Urbana: University of Illinois Press.

Wibbelsman, Michelle. 2018. "Northern Andean Cosmology and Otavalan Hip Hop." In *The Andean World*, edited by Linda J. Seligmann and Kathleen S. Fine-Dare, 128–42. 1st edition. New York: Routledge.

Woolard, Kathryn A. 1998. "Simultaneity and Bivalency as Strategies in Bilingualism." *Journal of Linguistic Anthropology* 8 (1): 3–29. https://doi.org/10.1525/jlin.1998.8.1.3.

Woolard, Kathryn A. 2005. "Codeswitching." In *A Companion to Linguistic Anthropology*, edited by Alessandro Duranti, 73–94. Malden, MA: Wiley-Blackwell.

Woolard, Kathryn A. 2016. *Singular and Plural: Ideologies of Linguistic Authority in 21st Century Catalonia*. Oxford; New York: Oxford University Press.

Wortham, Stanton. 2005. *Learning Identity: The Joint Emergence of Social Identification and Academic Learning*. New York: Cambridge University Press.

Wortham, Stanton. 2008. "Linguistic Anthropology of Education." *Annual Review of Anthropology* 37: 37–51.

Wortham, Stanton, and Angela Reyes. 2015. *Discourse Analysis beyond the Speech Event*. Routledge.

Wortham, Stanton, and Betsy Rymes. 2003. *The Linguistic Anthropology of Education*. Westport, CT: Praeger.

Wroblewski, Michael. 2012. "Amazonian Kichwa Proper: Ethnolinguistic Domain in Pan-Indian Ecuador." *Journal of Linguistic Anthropology* 22 (1): 64–86. https://doi.org/10.1111/j.1548-1395.2012.01134.x.

Wroblewski, Michael. 2014. "Public Indigeneity, Language Revitalization, and Intercultural Planning in a Native Amazonian Beauty Pageant." *American Anthropologist* 116 (1): 65–80. https://doi.org/10.1111/aman.12067.

Wroblewski, Michael. 2021. *Remaking Kichwa: Language and Indigenous Pluralism in Amazonian Ecuador*. Bloomsbury Studies in Linguistic Anthropology. London; New York: Bloomsbury Academic.

Wyman, Leisy T. 2009. "Youth, Linguistic Ecology, and Language Endangerment: A Yup'ik Example." *Journal of Language, Identity & Education* 8 (5): 335–49. https://doi.org/10.1080/15348450903305122.

Yánez Cossío, Consuelo. 1991. *MACAC teoria y práctica de la educación indígena*. Cali, Colombia: Celater, Macac.

Yánez Cossío, Consuelo. 1997. *La educación indígena en el Ecuador*. Quito, Ecuador: Abya-Yala.

Zavala, Virginia. 2011. "Racialization of the Bilingual Student in Higher Education: A Case from the Peruvian Andes." *Linguistics and Education, Discipline in Classroom* 22 (4): 393–405. https://doi.org/10.1016/j.linged.2011.08.004.

Zavala, Virginia. 2014. "An Ancestral Language to Speak with the 'Other': Closing Down Ideological Spaces of a Language Policy in the Peruvian Andes." *Language Policy* 13 (1): 1–20. https://doi.org/10.1007/s10993-013-9297-4.

Zavala, Virginia. 2019. "Youth and the Repoliticization of Quechua." *Language, Culture and Society* 1 (1): 59–82.

Zúñiga, Madeleine, and Modesto Gálvez. 2002. "Repensando la educación bilingüe intercultural en el Perú: Bases para una propuesta de política." In *Interculturalidad y política: Desafíos y posibilidades*, edited by Norma Fuller, 309–30. Lima: Red para el Desarrollo de las Ciencias Sociales en el Perú.

Index

For the benefit of digital users, indexed terms that span two pages (e.g., 52–53) may, on occasion, appear on only one of those pages.

Figures are indicated by *f* following the page number

Aguirre Beltrán, Gonzalo, 42, 43
alphabets:
   in languages other than Kichwa, 24, 25
   See also Kichwa alphabets
Amaguaña, Tránsito 85, 98
analogy, 7, 36, 197
   examples of 24, 26–27, 31, 36–37, 147–48, 155–56, 158, 180, 221n.40
   See also equivalence
autonomy, for schooling: 7, 48, 73–74, 77, 196, 207–8, 217
   for land: 72, 73–74, 200
   specifics as related to the intercultural bilingual school system: 7, 61, 72, 73–74, 120–21, 196, 215–16, 217

Bakhtin, Mikhail, 23, 26
Basque, 25, 36–37, 83, 197, 202–3
Bateson, Gregory, 7–8, 33–35, 199, 200, 203, 221n.4
bicultural, 44
   bicultural education, 43
bilingualism. *See* multilingualism
bivalency, 23–24, 93–94, 106
Bolivia, 5, 22, 47, 49, 52, 57, 60, 65, 70–71, 80, 81, 83, 85–87, 89, 90–91, 161–62, 201
Borja, Rodrigo, 3–4, 48–49, 58, 59, 60, 64, 65, 68–69, 215–16
buen vivir. *See sumak kawsay*

Cacuango, Dolores, 52, 85, 98
calque, 23–24, 27, 36–37, 83–84, 93–94, 103–4, 106, 132, 145, 156, 158–59, 170, 176, 177, 188, 197, 203, 221n.41
   See also *translation*
Center of Research on Indigenous Education (CIEI), 55, 56, 57–58, 59, 66–67, 88–89, 92, 93

cohesion, 131–32, 133–34, 139, 140, 142–43, 147, 152, 153, 154
Colombia, 110, 116–17, 131–32
colonial:
   500 years, 24
   anti-, 21, 24
   decolonial studies, 197–98
   decolonizing, 65, 153
   forms of language contact, 12–13, 23, 24, 61, 106, 132, 197
   governance, 3–4, 5, 9–10, 24, 41, 49–50, 72, 81, 179
   ideologies, 9–10, 23
   languages, 9–10, 24, 61, 154, 204–5
   linguistics, 12–13, 24
   reproduction, 9, 23, 24, 41, 106, 132, 197
Columbia University, 41
CONAIE, 30, 53–54, 56, 58, 59–60, 65–67, 69–72, 90, 114, 120–21, 122, 130, 132–33, 136, 138, 209, 211, 212–16
constitution:
   constitutional recognition, 21, 37, 60, 85–86, 129, 163
   in Indigenous languages, 7*f*, 37, 203
   1945 Constitution, 81, 85
   1979 Constitution, 85–86
   1991 Colombian constitution, 131–32
   talk about, 11, 73–74, 100, 102–3, 104–5, 130, 133–35, 138–39, 140, 141, 142, 163, 169, 170, 171, 177, 181–82, 215
   2008 Constitution, 3–4, 40, 51, 71–72, 73–74, 129, 196
Correa, Rafael 70, 70*f*, 71, 161–62, 176, 201, 209, 212, 222n.22
   related to intercultural bilingual education, 5, 15–16, 30, 48–49, 72, 74–75, 96–97, 120–21, 125–26, 135–36, 165–66, 199–200, 201, 209

Correa, Rafael (*cont.*)
  and Kichwa, 71, 83–84
  and plurinationality, 40
  related to CONAIE, 70–71, 120–21, 135–36, 165–66, 199–200
Cosmovision. *See* worldview

dialects. *See* registers
decentralization, 53, 75, 201, 202–3
Decree 1585, 72
democracy:
  democratic citizenship, 180
  demonstrating democracy for recognition, 47, 60
  manner of choosing directors in DINEIB, 72
  presidential focus, 47, 58
development industry, 17–18, 43, 52, 53–54, 55, 65, 68, 70–71, 108, 110, 161–62
DINEIB. *See* National Directorate
double bind, 7–8, 9–10, 15, 17–18, 27–28, 29–30, 31–32, 33–35, 37, 40, 44, 78, 79–80, 108–9, 126, 130, 153–54, 156, 157–58, 173, 174–75, 195, 196, 197–98, 199, 200–2, 203, 204, 205–6, 207, 219n.13

essentialism:
  in interculturality, 32, 33–34, 40, 44
  strategic, 9, 16, 219n.13
enregister, 34, 156, 163–64
  See also register
equivalence. *See also* analogy
  across other languages, 25, 132–33, 192
  between Ecuadorian school systems, 61–62
  in Kichwa with standardized Spanish, 23, 26, 28, 34–35, 83–84, 93–94, 95, 134, 144, 156, 158, 160, 165, 170, 174–75, 178, 180, 194, 195
  in recognition, 23, 31, 158, 170, 174–75, 178, 193, 195, 196
expertise, 35–36, 66–67, 106, 124, 136, 137, 141, 147, 201–2, 206, 207–9, 217

FEINE, Council of Evangelical Indigenous Pueblos and Organizations of Ecuador, 54, 65–66, 90, 212–14
FENOCIN, National Confederation of Peasant, Indigenous, and Black Organizations, 54, 65–66, 71–72, 117, 212–14

governmentality, 35–37, 171, 197

greetings:
  in other Indigenous languages, 155
  local Kichwa greetings, 33, 34–35, 37, 160
  theorizing about, 155–56, 157, 158, 160, 161, 164–65, 167–68, 171, 173, 179, 180, 181, 185, 188–89, 191, 192–93, 194, 197
  in Unified Kichwa, 19–20, 22, 28, 32, 33–35, 36, 39, 40, 155–56, 157–59, 160, 161, 164–65, 167–68, 170, 171, 172, 173, 174, 175, 177, 178

Hale, Charles, 8–9, 10, 21, 197–98, 199, 200–1

Imbabura, 31–32, 70*f*, 83, 86, 110, 111, 113, 117
Imbabura Kichwa, 82–83, 84, 87, 89–90, 91, 94–95, 96, 115–16, 158, 159, 176–77
Indigenism:
  definition, 41, 86
  in Ecuador, 44, 49–51, 52, 63
  First Interamerican Indigenist Congress in Barbados, 55
  in Mexico, 29, 40–41, 42, 43, 44
  throughout the Americas, 44, 55, 86
Indigenous:
  Indigenous organizations and Correa, 30, 70–71, 165–66
  literature about Indigenous state agents, 10, 15, 198–200, 202, 207
  mobilizations, 47, 53–54, 65, 68–69, 212–14
  movements' directors, 59, 71, 120–21, 125–26, 135–36, 173, 199–200, 201
  movements in Ecuador, 12–13, 18–19, 53, 55, 58, 65, 120–21, 125–26, 173, 199–200 (*see also* organizations)
  movements literature, 9, 15, 16, 48, 201, 222n.1 (*see also* social movements)
  organizations in Ecuador, 15–16, 34–35, 37, 40, 47, 48–49, 51, 52–54, 56, 57–58, 61, 63, 64, 65–67, 69–70, 77, 90, 114, 115, 120–21, 122, 136, 138, 173, 199–200, 210–11, 212–14 (*see also* CONAIE; FEINE; FENOCIN; movements)
  population as a percentage of Ecuador, 5
  professionals (*see* professionalization)
  state agents, 4–5, 7–9, 10–11, 15–16, 22, 28, 31, 33, 35, 47–48, 53, 127–217
  as a term, 8

interculturality:
    as a concept, 22, 23, 26, 31, 40, 44
    genealogy of, 29, 31, 40, 44
intertextuality, 131, 133, 139, 142-48, 152-53
    See also cohesion
Iza, Leonidas, 212-15

Kichwa:
    alphabets, 88-91, 95-96, 105-6
    ideologies, 18-19, 110, 164-65, 205
    ideologies about Unified Kichwa, 39, 95-96, 102-3, 105-6, 138, 143-44, 153, 158, 173, 194
    Imbabura Kichwa (*see* Imbabura)
    Napo Kichwa, 93-94
    syntax, 86-87, 95-96, 105-6, 143-44, 146, 147-48
    teaching in classrooms, 18-19, 20, 174-95, 204-6
    Unified Kichwa (*see* ideologies about Unified Kichwa; language standardization; register; translation)
Kichwañol, 105, 132, 137-38
Kowii, Ariruma, 69, 69f, 70, 72, 73-74, 121, 125
Kuykayu textbooks, 134-36, 135f, 137-38, 139, 141, 143-44, 146, 147

language ideologies, 12-13, 14-15, 78-79, 132-33, 148, 164-65, 180, 194, 205
    additive, 194
    compartmentalization, 167, 194
    one nation, one language, 22, 34, 194
    purism, 102-3, 137-38, 164, 173, 194
    See also Kichwa ideologies
language reclamation:
    concept, 9-10, 11, 78
    for Kichwa, 11-12, 30, 35, 66, 78, 153-54, 156, 157, 158, 206
language revitalization:
    concept, 9-10, 14, 24, 203
    efforts, 92, 126, 181, 204-6
    romanticization of, 9-10
language shift:
    intralinguistic, 12-13, 23-24, 85
    lessons about, 11-13, 204-6
    as part of deeper changes, 123, 125, 126
    to Spanish from Kichwa, 9-10, 11-13, 27, 31, 44, 66, 92, 109, 117-18, 121, 123, 125, 126, 157-58, 181, 197, 204-6
    from standardization, 78
language standardization, 21, 85-87, 131-34, 202-3

in language revitalization, 24
normalization, 133-34, 147-48, 152-53, 154
theory about, 22, 26, 36-37, 78, 79-80, 81, 105-6
and translation, 129-30, 131-34
Unified Kichwa:
    definition, 11-12, 78-79, 80-85, 133, 202
    history of, 85-87
    talk about, 80, 81, 85
Lasso, Guillermo, 212-16, 213f
Law 150, 61, 63
literacy:
    and assimilation, 44, 53, 76, 88, 197
    as a demand of Indigenous organizations, 47, 53
    early Kichwa literacy efforts, 51, 52, 54, 55, 56, 88
    in state policy 26-27, 47-48, 49-58, 76

mashi, 37, 39, 81-84, 87, 92, 101, 106-7, 157, 158, 188-89, 191, 192
mestizaje, 3-4, 23
mestizo:
    definition 5
metalinguistic labor, 9, 35-36, 47, 77, 173, 180
Mexico, 5, 26, 29, 40-42, 43, 44, 197-98, 200, 205-6
missionaries. *See* Summer Institute of Linguistics
modernizing policies, 3-4, 26-27, 47, 48-49, 55, 59, 61, 68-69, 86, 152
modern linguistics, 22, 61, 161
Montaluisa, Luis, 51, 54, 59-60, 62, 63, 64, 65-66, 69-70, 72, 78, 82-83, 85, 87, 89, 92, 222n.14
Moreno, Lenín, 209-11
multilingualism:
    discussions of, 30, 83-84, 119, 123, 158, 177, 179-80, 192, 194, 208-9

nacionalidad:
    concept of, 8, 52-53, 171
National Directorate of Intercultural Bilingual Education (DINEIB), 14-16, 22, 30, 31-32, 38-39, 40, 48-49, 56, 58-68, 72, 74, 75, 76, 83, 90, 92-93, 95, 96-97, 109, 110, 115, 116-17, 119, 120-21, 125, 134, 138, 157, 163, 164, 181-82, 199-200, 222n.12
neologisms, 23, 25, 92, 93, 102-3, 134-35, 141

offsetting, 27, 79–80, 97–105, 106–7, 203
Organic Law of Intercultural Education
    (LOEI), 75, 76, 100, 129–30, 181–82,
    211, 215
Otavalo, 8–9, 33, 82–83, 86, 114, 117

Pachakutik (political movement),
    122, 135–36
Pachakutik (Indigenous cosmovision), 31–32
Peru, 5, 19, 22, 49, 56–57, 60, 80, 81, 86, 153,
    197, 202–3, 207–9
plurinationality, 40, 54, 71–72, 74–75, 215
Pontifical Catholic University of Quito
    (PUCE), 55, 56, 57, 59, 66–67,
    86, 88–89
professionalization:
    in Bolivia, 57
    concept, 108–9
    Indigenous professionals, 17, 27, 58, 83,
        108–9, 110, 114–15, 118, 120, 121,
        122, 123, 124, 125, 126, 182–83, 196,
        199–200, 201
    and Kichwa use, 17–18, 39, 81–82, 108,
        111, 118–19, 121, 122, 123, 125, 126,
        154, 158
    teachers as, 108–9, 120, 124, 125
Project of Intercultural Bilingual Education
    (Project EBI), 56–58, 61–62, 66–67

Quechua:
    explanation about different varieties, 3,
        11–12, 81, 86–87
    emerging initiatives, 207–8
    examples, 25, 26, 83, 145–46, 148–49
    and language planning, 88–89, 153,
        202–3, 207
    as a name for Kichwa, 80, 81, 84, 85–86
    in Puno, Peru schools, 56–57

raciolinguistics, 33, 47, 79, 97, 178, 219n.7
recognition:
    of bilingual education, 7–8, 21, 23, 48, 54,
        60, 63, 76, 85, 104–5, 110, 197–98,
        200, 207–8, 211–12
    concept of, 9–10, 21, 29–30, 34, 130, 155–
        56, 158, 161, 173, 179, 200, 220n.35
    demands by Indigenous peoples, 4–5, 8,
        21, 26–27, 29–30, 47, 48, 64, 70, 76,
        108, 170, 196
    and equivalence, 23

of Indigenous languages in Constitution,
    3–5, 7–8, 21, 22, 23, 25, 29, 40, 44, 52,
    54, 60, 61, 69–70, 76, 85, 105–6, 123,
    131–32, 147–48, 152, 163, 164, 170,
    173, 197–98, 202–3, 205, 206
and interculturality, 20, 21, 22, 38, 40,
    44, 63, 73–74, 165, 168, 180, 196,
    200, 205
of Kichwa, 9, 10–12, 18–19, 20, 22, 23–24,
    26, 28, 34, 37, 38, 50–51, 54, 63,
    71–72, 85–86, 119, 123, 129, 132,
    153–54, 157–58, 161–62, 173, 177,
    196, 205
politics of, 22, 200
refusal, of the state, 21, 200–2, 203, 205–
    6, 225n.2
register,
    in classroom instruction, 21, 177,
        204, 205
    concept, 3–28, 36, 79, 87, 93–94, 106–7,
        119, 132
    as linked to standardization, 24, 25, 36–37,
        78, 79, 85–86, 87–88, 132, 197
    of localized forms of Kichwa, 14, 19–20,
        27–28, 36–37, 50–51, 58, 79–80,
        82–84, 85, 86–87, 88, 89–90, 92,
        95–96, 97, 102, 103, 105, 106,
        131–32, 133–34, 137–38, 141, 143,
        148–49, 153–54, 188, 194, 202–3,
        204–5, 208
    overlay register, 23
    Unified Kichwa as a, 3–28, 33, 39, 79–80,
        82–84, 86, 87, 96, 97, 102, 106–7,
        132–33, 137, 145, 153, 154, 155–56,
        173, 176, 192–93
rejection, of the state. *See* refusal
Rivera Cusicanqui, Silvia, 7–8, 31–32,
    198, 203
Roldós Aguilera, Jaime, 48–49, 50–51, 50*f*,
    52–53, 59, 70, 113

scale:
    concept, 37
    and language planning, 25, 36, 37, 52,
        53, 130, 177, 201, 202–3, 206, 208–
        9, 217
    national as linked to organizing, 8, 37, 52,
        61, 77, 212–14
    small scale, 31, 37, 53, 205, 206
    for texts, 52, 53, 130, 201, 202–3, 206, 217

Shuar, 3–4, 50–51, 71, 223n.27
Social movements. *See also* Indigenous movements
   and national politics, 153–54, 209
   and the state, 5–7, 17–18, 21, 47, 59, 108, 157–58, 199
   theory about, 3–4, 5–7, 21, 47, 117, 161, 198
Spivak, Gayatri Chakravorty, 31, 34–35, 219n.13
strike of 2022, 212–16, 213*f*, 214*f*
sumak kawsay, 70–71, 161–62
Summer Institute of Linguistics (SIL), 44, 55, 81–82, 88–89

translation, 129–54
   colonialism and directionality in, 23–24, 25, 36, 40, 132, 160, 197, 209–10, 221n.40
   legal translation, 27–28, 129, 130, 131, 132–34, 138–40, 152, 153–54
   in Nasa, 131–32
   in Unified Kichwa from Spanish, 5–7, 25, 30, 36–37, 83, 92, 93–94, 103–4, 132, 133–34, 141, 143–45, 147, 148–49, 156, 157, 158, 176, 182*f*, 197, 209–10 (*see also* calques)
   translation theory, 131–34
   in Warao, 132

translanguaging, 181, 204–5, 221n.42

uprising, 1990, 64, 65, 122

Vallejo, Raúl, 68–70, 72, 74–75
variety. *See* register

wawa, 25, 26, 90–91
worldview, Andean, 26, 30, 31–32, 33, 93–94, 152

Yánez Cossío, Consuelo, 51, 52, 57–58, 86

Zapatistas, 206